Parenting by the Book

Parenting by the Book

Finding Answers That Work

Dr. David Walls

VISION HOUSE
PUBLISHING, INC.

PARENTING BY THE BOOK
© 1995 by David R. Walls

Published by Vision House Publishing Inc.
1217 NE Burnside Rd.
Suite 403
Gresham, Oregon 97030

Printed in the United States of America

Unless otherwise indicated, Scripture references are from the New American
Standard Bible, © the Lockman Foundation 1960, 1962, 1963, 1968, 1971, 1972,
1973, 1975, 1977

ISBN: 1-885305-30-3

95 96 97 98 99 00 01—08 07 06 05 04 03 02 01

ACKNOWLEDGMENTS

A book of any kind, subject, size, or shape does not just drop out of the sky. In the path of its formation, God has placed some key people who work together to make it happen. That certainly is the case with this book.

With that in mind, I would like to thank my editing team, Karl Schaller of the David C. Cook Publishers, and Rick Knox, of Advent Communications, who stayed with me and polished and refined this project. Without their commitment, I was dead in the water.

I would also like to thank Dr. John McArthur who, with time he did not have, supported this effort with his foreword. "Thank you" doesn't begin to cover my gratitude.

But most of all, I need to acknowledge and thank my faithful and loyal secretary, Mrs. Laura Burton. For five years, she has worked beside me, organized my schedule, office and life. She has weathered building programs, office changes, urgent requests, and never-ending deadlines. This is my fourth book, and Laura has taken each one and put them in order so the publishers could, and would, continue. Countless hours and as many smiles, seemed to come naturally from her, even as the work load and pressure increased. Thank you, Laura—I shall miss you deeply! Even as I write these words, I realize that this will likely be our last project together, since you are "retiring" this year to be a full-time mom. From everything I have seen and know, you will be great at that, too. God bless you, my friend, and thanks again!

Parenting is a slippery kind of thing. Just when you think you have it in your grasp, another bump on the road of life makes you lose your grip. But if parenting is that way, then writing about parenting seems even more impossible. That is why it is with great love and admiration— and I admit, a large lump in my throat—that I dedicate this book to those who have helped strengthen my grip on being a parent:

To my wife, Patricia, my best friend and parenting partner, whose wisdom in raising kids (and me) permeates the pages of this book. I have no greater joy than when I am in your presence, because it is there that I learn and grow. Patricia, you are a marvelous parent, graced with amazing tenderness and firmness. I notice your love for me and our sons daily, and I'll never forget it. Thanks for picking me.

To my two sons, Jeremy and Kent, both teenagers; without your encouragement I would not have written this book. I still remember your affirming words to me after I turned the project down for the second time: "Why won't you write it, Dad? You can do it!" Coming from a friend or editor, those words mean one thing. Coming from the products of my limited parenting skills, they send an entirely different message. Thanks, guys! Your consistency and character, your love for the Lord and others, made this book possible. Never forget that I am out of my mind with pride to be called your dad.

To my own parents, Robert and Doris Walls, who—like most parents—have probably been too hard on themselves in terms of critical thinking about their mistakes. They have certainly not been lavish enough in their complimentary thinking about all the things they did right. I hope you both realize that, as far as I'm concerned, the good things outweigh, outdistance and outlast the not so good. Many of the lessons I learned at home have survived and settled into the paragraphs of this book. Thank you for what you mean to me!

Dr. David R. Walls
Amherst, Ohio

For too many parents, raising children is a confusing and frustrating task. Modern society offers little help. In fact, too much in our culture works directly to undermine the foundations of the family. Add that to a plethora of books and programs that offer the most outlandish and appalling advice on child-rearing. Parents—even Christian parents—feel they have been set adrift on a sea of chaos and contradiction.

Since parenting is such a crucial task to get right, isn't it a little frightening that so many parents feel utterly clueless? Why is it that after centuries of human history, even the most basic issues in parenting are still under intense debate? Why do even the best-known "experts" hold views that are flatly contrary to one another? Can anyone shed some clear light on these matters?

Can anyone speak with confidence about right principles of parenting?

If those are questions you have asked, hold onto this book. What you are about to read will sweep away the cobwebs, dispel the shadows, and rekindle your enthusiasm for your task as a parent.

Dr. David Walls writes with common sense, biblical wisdom, wit, passion and good humor. He understands that the parent's task is not meant to be a drudgery or a hardship, and he shows how intensely practical and immediately relevant are the parenting guidelines we find in God's Word.

Scripture is full of advice for parents. Most of it is not the kind of parenting advice you're likely to read in many of the popular parenting handbooks that vie for your attention on your local bookstore's shelves. Such books usually focus on the child's emotional and material "needs." They offer bogus explanations for unruly conduct, or suggest unusual methods for training and correcting children. They usually advise parents that self-esteem is the greatest lesson they must instill in their children.

Scripture, on the other hand, stresses parents' responsibility to teach their children right spiritual values. Self-control, not mere self-esteem, is crucial to the biblical approach. Teaching our children to love and obey God, instilling in them a love for the Word of God, and modeling real godliness in the family context—those are the areas where Scripture directs parents to focus their energies (see, for example, Deut. 6:6–7). If we get those things right, all other parenting issues tend to fall into place.

This book will ignite your eagerness to practice that kind of spiritual parenting. In a lively—often humorous—fashion, Dr. Walls goes straight to the heart of biblical truth, and applies it with discernment and clarity. He draws from Scripture so many plain and helpful principles that you may be surprised to find how much clear guidance the Bible actually offers for parents.

I think you'll find *Parenting by the Book* refreshing, stimulating, illuminating, and above all, encouraging. Whether you're a new parent just starting out, a struggling parent frustrated by the challenge of getting your family's act together, or a confident parent seeking some ways to improve your effectiveness, this book offers the kind of biblical insight you need. I am pleased to see it in print, and my prayer is that it will have a long and widespread ministry.

Dr. John MacArthur
Author and Pastor

CONTENTS

The Goals of Parenting

Proverbs 1:1–8

IT HAS BEEN NEARLY FIFTEEN YEARS since I first stumbled into them. They were arresting, "take-your-breath-away" words. The moment I read them, I knew I'd never forget them. And ever since that day, several times a year, I religiously pull them out and cautiously lift the lid on their contents once more:

> Someday when the kids are grown, things are going to be a lot different. The garage won't be full of bikes, electric train tracks on plywood, sawhorses surrounded by chunks of 2" x 4"s, nails, a hammer and saw . . . and the rabbit cage. . . .
>
> Someday when the kids are grown, the kitchen will be neat. The sink will stay free of sticky dishes; the garbage disposal won't get choked on rubber bands or paper cups; the refrigerator won't be clogged with nine bottles of milk. . . .

Someday when the kids are grown, the telephone will actually be available. To adults. It won't be hot from being held an hour. It won't look like it's growing from a teenager's ear. It will simply hang there . . . silently and amazingly available! It will be free of lipstick, mayonnaise, Frito crumbs, and toothpicks in those little holes.

Someday when the kids are grown, I'll be able to see through the car windows. Fingerprints, licks, sneaker footprints and dog tracks (don't ask) will be conspicuously absent. . . . the tank will not always be somewhere between empty and fumes . . . .

Someday when the kids are grown we won't run out of bathroom tissue. I won't . . . have to answer to "Daddy, is it a sin that you're driving 47 in a 30-mile-an-hour zone?". . . .

Yes, someday when the kids are grown, things are going to be a lot different. One by one they'll leave our nest, and the place will begin to resemble order and maybe even a touch of elegance. . . .The house will be quiet . . . and calm . . . and empty . . . and filled with memories . . . and lonely. . . . And we won't like that at all. We'll spend our time not looking forward to Someday but looking back to Yesterday and thinking, "Maybe we can baby-sit the grandkids and get some life back in this place for a change!"[1]

Regardless of where we find ourselves on the family life "Richter scale," I think most of us understand those words only too well. They cause us to stop for a second or two at least—and think about our family (whether that may be past, present, or future tense).

Dreaming of better days

Some of us wish we could go back to the days before "Someday." Others, in the midst of real-life turmoil wonder if we will even make it to "Someday." Still others of us don't even care anymore—we've bowed our heads and given up. Maybe we have adopted, without knowing it, the advice of Mark Twain. He suggested when our children turn thirteen that we should put them in a barrel and feed them through the cork hole. When they turn sixteen, we should plug the cork hole.

The difficulty with parenting is that with very little formal preparation or ongoing study and effort, we wade quickly and confidently into the swirling waters of family life. Then we find ourselves in over our heads, or at the very least, treading water madly. Panicked, we grab for any life vest that floats our way. Invariably, we grab the wrong ones. And the results speak for themselves.

The decade that we have recently slithered through has been rough on families. You may be only too aware of that in terms of your own family, or what is left of it. But you may not understand the dimensions of the problem.

Society on the brink

Are you aware that today, one of four households with children under eighteen is a single-parent home? That translates into ten million children living in single-parent homes. Another million-plus witness their parents' divorce each year. Worse yet, 28 percent of all alcoholics in this country are under eighteen. In the eighties, cocaine use by teenagers rose 400 percent, and the number of teenagers in runaway centers has increased 2,000 percent! Today, a child runs away from home every twenty-six seconds. Furthermore, in the United States, the average teen spends only five minutes alone with dad and only forty minutes with mom each week.

In 1990, 1.1 million teenaged girls became pregnant and 400,000 of them aborted their babies. In fact, a teenager has a baby every sixty-seven seconds in our country, and a minor is arrested on a drug charge every seven minutes. More than five hundred thousand teenagers will attempt suicide this year.[2]

Between 1980 and 1987, the number of Americans between the ages of ten and nineteen who were discharged from psychiatric units ballooned 43 percent to 180,000. The *Wall Street Journal* gave these reasons for the alarming statistics:

Family turmoil—divorce, remarriage, frequent migration, and two-career households—have left many parents either too busy or too distracted to deal with adolescents. Psychiatric treatment . . . has become more widespread as churches, schools and other institutions that helped guide earlier generations through adolescence have lost influence.[3]

In his television documentary, "The Vanishing Family," Bill Moyers' despairing conclusion is that the family has all but disappeared from America's inner cities, and that disappearance, like the oil spill off the coast of Alaska, is leaking into suburban life quickly, with devastating environmental consequences. According to Dr. Arman Nicholi, professor of psychiatry at Harvard University, scientific research has established a clear link between the breakdown of the family structure and societal problems such as unwed mothers, criminal violence, drug abuse, suicide among children, eating disorders, and sexual identity disorders. Dr. Nicholi goes as far as to say that "without a change in attitudes toward the family that is drastic enough to turn the tide, all these problems are going to increase [dramatically] during the next twenty years." [4]

Understanding that, we embark through the doorway of this chapter on a journey into the lives of our families. My goal is not to paint a hopeless picture of the demise of the family, although we will look carefully and exactingly at the problems. My goal is to walk us through a section of the Bible that offers solutions.

You see, I am convinced that regardless of how you were raised, no matter what abuse or cruelty you witnessed or experienced, the potential for being a quality parent is within your grasp. Your past does not place a ceiling on the heights of parenting that you can reach. You are not destined to become what your parents were. Furthermore, regardless of how badly you think you have been doing as a parent so far, improvement is possible. Just don't quit on me.

Finding answers that work

You have the potential to stretch far beyond the adequate to raise a family the likes of which you never knew. The key lies in where you turn for help. In light of what is going on all around us, perhaps it is time to seriously consider the wisdom from the Old Testament book of Proverbs. Let me assure you that as we work our way through this book, I am learning just as you are. My kids are still in the radioactive years (sixteen and thirteen years old). I don't come to you as an expert on parenting, but as one who is in the jungle with you, trying to clear a path to solid ground and avoid as many of the swamps and alligators as possible.

So, journey with me, even as we consider the opening statement of the book of Proverbs:

The proverbs of Solomon the son of David, king of Israel. . . .

You may be thinking, "Why the book of Proverbs? Why study something written more than 2,700 years ago? Why not something current?" The answers to those questions lie partly in the detailed and disastrous statistics we considered at the outset of this chapter, and partly in the nature of the book of Proverbs itself.

Solomon, at one time king of the nation of Israel, was personally involved in the collection and authorship of a large part of this book. He didn't write it all, but had a hand in much of it. And if he was known for one thing, it was his wisdom.

But you might still be asking, "What did he want to accomplish as he put these proverbs together? And how does that help me to be a better parent?"

What's in a proverb?

First, we need to understand that the proverbs are laser-like truths about conduct and character. They work themselves out in the spiritual, moral, and social arenas of our lives.

A proverb is a short, wise, easy-to-learn saying that calls a person to character and then to conduct. By the way, don't try to distance character from conduct. That may work philosophically, but in the real world of parenting, the two stand together. When someone tries to convince me otherwise, it usually means they are worried that their character doesn't compare favorably to their conduct, or vice versa.

As you read the book of Proverbs you'll discover that it includes descriptions of all types of people. There is no mumbo-jumbo, no Rubik's cube theology to unscramble or decipher, no weird, new-age theories to unravel. It's just straight talk for all of us who live imperfect lives in imperfect homes.

But it's important to bear in mind that proverbs are by nature generalizations. They state what is generally true, but no invariably true. Many of the proverbs should be recognized as guidelines, not absolute guarantees, nor iron-clad promises. What is stated is generally and usually true, but exceptions do occur. Nevertheless, they are invaluable. Parents of Old Testament times understood this, as did Solomon.

Wisdom: knowledge put to work

He said, "Hear, my son, your father's instruction, and do not forsake your mother's teaching" (Proverbs 1:8).

From the day they were written, biblical proverbs were used by parents and teachers to communicate and instruct. And they were used in such a way as to make learning an adventure, a challenge. In fact, the wisdom of Proverbs was designed to be learned, even memorized, by young people. The tone of a father instructing his son concerning the basic truths of life oozes from the pages of this book. And while daughters are not mentioned specifically, they can be included (especially today), because they have as much freedom to make decisions as do sons.

But notice something else in this verse. The father and the mother are placed on exactly the same footing as teachers of their children. In fact, the word "teaching" that is bumper-stickered to the mother's job description is the Hebrew word, *torah*. That word regularly refers to the law (Torah) of God, and is also used to describe the first five books of the Old Testament.

So from the outset of this book we have a model in which the father and mother shared the responsibility for the education of their kids. Dads can't dump this on moms, nor can moms pass it off to the dads. It's a shared responsibility. And that makes sense, because children learn values, morals, and priorities by observing how both parents act and react every day, and by having the opportunity to hear a consistent message from both parents.

The need for consistent models

That is what makes the plight of the children of divorce so striking. One weekend they visit Mom and hear and see one message, one model. The next weekend they stick it out with Dad and usually hear and see a completely different message and model. No wonder that on Monday they are confused out of their minds.

Children of all ages look for that shared model in their parents. Believe it or not, a psychologist named Frank Farley asked 340 college students at the University of Wisconsin to rank their top five heroes and heroines. The overwhelming winners were the students' parents. In fact, moms got six times as many first-place votes as did any other heroine, and dads got twice as many as any other hero. When the good doctor asked elementary school children the same question, moms and dads again came out number one.[5]

It is safe to say that if any one factor influences the character development and emotional stability of an individual, it is the quality of the relationship he or she experiences as a child with both parents. Look at this excerpt from the book, *Real Men Enjoy their Kids*:

> Until recently, a father's part in raising and nurturing children was given little attention. "Real men" tended to leave the kids to mom—men's job was to work to support the family and when they came home, to mete out the punishment that mom had decreed. Happily for fathers and their children, that attitude is changing. Society now acknowledges that real men do enjoy their kids. There is a growing emphasis on the importance of the bond between fathers and children. They are central to the development of their children who need their love and support. Men are realizing that they, as well as women, need to learn to be parents.[6]

And what we have to learn first as parents as we cut our way through the jungle of society, is where we are going—what our overarching goal is as parents.

I know a lot of parents who are running fast and paddling hard, but they have no idea where they are going. They end up, for all their efforts, going in circles. They need to understand their primary goal or direction.

I think Solomon understood it as well as anyone. Here's how he called it:

> The proverbs of Solomon the son of David, king of Israel: To know wisdom and instruction . . . to receive instruction in wise behavior (Proverbs 1:1–2a, 3a).

The ultimate target for parents is to bring their children to the place where they exhibit "wisdom" or "wise behavior," as Solomon dubs it. In the mind of a Hebrew, wisdom was not simply theoretical or cognitive. It did not necessarily have anything to do with a college degree, high school freshman scores, or an IQ measurement. "Wisdom" to the Hebrews was not just the collection of information, it was collected information on which to act.

The skill of living life

Additionally, this wisdom was always practical and based on revealed principles of right and wrong that were fleshed out in daily life. To Solomon, wisdom was the skill of living life. It implied an ability to apply consistently that which we know to that which we have to do.

But keep in mind that wisdom in the book of Proverbs always focused on the application of moral and ethical principles of behavior. People of wisdom, regardless of their age, embraced a basic morality. They worked hard at living according to moral standards.

Now that is not easy. So perhaps that is why Solomon talked about "instruction" in these early verses also. Four times in this opening slice of chapter one, Solomon mentions "instruction." That word is an extension of wisdom. It includes the idea of correction and discipline, and expresses the painful process of appropriating wisdom. In other words, there is a price to be paid.

We've even implied that to our kids when we've mumbled, "Well, you're going to have to learn it the hard way." That's "instruction."

The learning process is not easy. It involves difficult and even painful, hard moments. It requires listening to counsel and heeding sound advice. Furthermore, it can mean enduring correction for behavior that violates a moral standard.

Parents must be willing to play a dominant role in the

process. They must be willing to confront and to correct when necessary. But they must first embrace their own beliefs and values, because they cannot model or teach what they do not own.

In order to have any impact on their children's behavior, a mother and father must have values. They need to believe in a set of right and wrong values and want to convey that set of values to their children.

When values are lost

You may have read several years ago of the fourteen-year-old boy in Mississippi who wondered what would it be like to kill someone. He took his younger friend out among the trees and beat him to death with a baseball bat. Then he left the body, joined in a snowball fight, and boasted to one friend that he'd just killed another friend. He even asked his buddy if he wanted to see the body. Finally, after an anonymous tip, the police discovered the body and the murderer.

The psychiatrist who examined that fourteen-year-old said: "Internally he does not know the difference between right and wrong—he knows the theory, but he doesn't know how to put it into action."[7]

That's where parents come in. The value system is received from the parents—or it is not received. Knowledge is good, but there is vast difference between knowledge (having the facts) and wisdom (applying those facts to life). We may think we know a lot, but without wisdom our knowledge is of limited value. We must learn how to live out what we know, and that learning begins at home.

Dr. T. Berry Brazelton is known as the "Dean of Pediatricians." He is the chief of the Child Development Unit at Boston Children's Hospital and a professor of pediatrics at Harvard University. He has helped to raise more than 25,000 babies in his forty years of practice.

Concerning the loss of values, he says: "We have a very

seriously stressed society in this country. We no longer have a set of values that people can really believe in . . . [but] what we need are real belief systems. We have diluted the ones we have so much that families don't know what they're raising their kids for any more."[8]

In case we are still not convinced of how vital this is, Solomon reinforces his point by hitching to the bumper of wisdom the trailer of "righteousness."

To receive instruction in wise behavior, righteousness, justice and equity (Proverbs 1:3).

The word "righteousness," as used here, is a relational word, and describes our relationships with people. Those relationships are to be "righteous," or "ethically right." In fact, the root of the word "righteousness" basically indicates conformity to an ethical or moral standard. In the Old Testament that standard is conduct that lines up with God's unchanging moral standards.

But here's the trick for you as a parent. On "Main Street USA," 67 percent of the American people believe there is no such thing as absolute truth.[9]

Righteousness without absolute truth?

George Gallup asked Americans whether they agreed with the statement, "There are few moral absolutes; what is right and wrong usually varies from situation to situation." Sixty-nine percent agreed.[10] Much of education today communicates to the student that there is no right or wrong in any particular situation; all value responses are equally valid. Under the banner of "values clarification," many educators insist that one can be right on a particular ethical or moral issue while one's best friend in the next row, who holds the opposite viewpoint, can also be right.

That's bad enough. But it gets worse. Even though you as a

parent have attempted to instill a particular value system or point of reference into your child, the school feels compelled to "clarify" that for your student. This usually means that you, the parent, come out looking like a Neanderthal—or a Victorian—who has lost his mind. That increases the difficulty of parenting, doesn't it? But difficulty in communicating moral standards does not mean abandoning the standard.

Richard Halverson, Chaplain to the U.S. Senate, expresses the importance of "righteousness" in this way:

> . . .[S]piritual and moral health is constructive and beneficial, [while] spiritual and moral sickness is destructive. This is without controversy. . . . This basic principle is working every day in the life of every person in the world. It is operative every day in home and family life . . . The degeneration, disintegration and demise of any and all people are inevitable if righteousness is abandoned. This is a simple fact of life, whether we accept it or not; whether we like it or not. This is the way things are.[11]

Now let me reaffirm something here. Nowhere is the need for example and modeling by parents more evident than in teaching morals and spirituality. If your words shout one thing while your behavior whispers something else, your words will be drowned out by the roar of your actions. If we make Johnny write ten reasons for using clean language every time he curses, but four-letter words are our favorite describers, what are we really saying? That it's okay to swear when you're grown up.

I have coached Little League baseball for seven or eight years. One of the unwritten, and sometimes even written, rules is that no profanity is allowed by the players or coaches during the games under any circumstances.

Great rule. But then I go to the coaches meetings and can't cut through the blue smoke. And these same coaches (who wouldn't dare swear during the game), curse like experts during practice. So what do the kids learn? If Suzie knows that she will be drawn and quartered if we ever find out she cheated at school, yet she listens to us lie about her age to get her into a movie for half price (or to get reduced airfare), what will she think?

What about morality, sexuality? Do we cross our fingers and hope our kids will stay morally pure? Some of us even suck up enough courage to talk about abstinence with them. But all the time we're talking, Dad and Mom may be stepping out on each other, or regularly enjoying sexually dominated videos and magazines.

I have sometimes wondered if our society's reluctance to herald abstinence is because in our heart of hearts we see the moral hypocrisy in our own lives—and so do our kids. If we think the kids aren't picking up on our mixed messages, we are fooling ourselves. Teenagers especially need a clearly defined value system against which to test other values and discover their own. But when the important adults in their lives do not know what their own values are, and are not sure what is right and what is wrong—or are unwilling to confront inappropriate actions and values—then the teenagers' task is even more difficult and more time-consuming.

How do parents begin to instill this hunger and desire for righteousness? My friend Howard Hendricks has a great insight:

We tend to teach what our values are, but we don't teach how we got them. In other words, we teach the product without the process. The kid obviously knows what we believe, but he doesn't know why we believe it because he's never gone through the process himself to make it his own personal property.

How do we teach that process? It starts with presenting a child with real-life situations. They come up in families every day, at school, in the home, in the community, at the office. They are the real problems of life, the issues for which people have to make value decisions. When a child is brought up in a home where he's confronted with these issues and encouraged to discuss them, to question them, to go through some good Bible study to come up with his own convictions, then he doesn't end up with a secondhand experience or set of values. But they become his own property.[12]

The condensed version of the above suggests a couple of basic principles:

1. Don't deny reality with your kids. It does no good to pretend that they are not being bombarded with thorny issues every day. Don't stick your head in the sand and hope that when you pull it out everything will be great.

2. Do discuss the realities with your kid. Don't allow your personal embarrassment with a subject, or horror of it, to deter you from discussion. Related to that, don't throw an embolism when your child of any age drops an off-the-wall question into the dinner menu. Your reaction will determine whether she keeps asking you or seeks other sources of information. And she will, if you go ballistic on her. The process of sorting things out requires discussion.

Solomon weaves another related concept throughout these early verses that lines up with the goal of parenting.

... To discern the sayings of understanding, to receive instruction in wise behavior, righteousness, justice and equity, to give prudence to the naive, to the youth knowledge and discretion (Proverbs 1:2b–4).

In verse 2, for example he uses the word *discern*. It means "to distinguish between things, to compare concepts, to make an evaluation." Then in verse 3 he talks about *justice*, a word that brings to mind a judge hearing a case, weighing the evidence, and reaching a verdict.

In verse 4, Solomon mentions the word *prudence*, which means "the ability to foresee evil and prepare for it." He is talking about the ability to make discerning decisions or judgments. All of us want our kids to be able to do that, because then their lives will begin to have a positive direction.

In verse 5, Solomon says, "A wise man will hear and increase in learning, and a man of understanding will acquire wise counsel."

Solomon calls that positive direction "wise counsel." That's an ancient word that pictures sailors guiding a ship to port, or navigating through a dangerous section of water. And wise counsel will guide our kids. They won't escape making mistakes.

They will have times when a shipwreck looks impossible to avoid, and we may wonder if they are ever going to get to the right harbor. But if we can instill into them the ability to be discerning, over the long haul their direction will be correct.

Wise behavior then requires the ability to reach sound decisions and to make the right choices. It involves the ability to discern the difference between right and wrong, what is wholesome and what is damaging, that which is important and that which is unimportant. This trait is vital for young people. Solomon knew that, and said as much in verse 4: "To give prudence to the naive, to the youth knowledge. . . ."

The term "naive" is not meant to be sarcastic. It refers to young people who are very open-minded. They're open to instruction, positive or negative. A naive person is gullible, easily won over, easily influenced, easily fooled (or in some cases, willing to be fooled). That is especially true in the teenage years.

Teen survival techniques

As a child moves into that phase of her life, she feels an increasing need to be popular, to be accepted. To do so, the teenager in our culture develops an "other-directed" personality. That is, she develops a kind of sixth sense, a sophisticated radar system, which enables her to pick up from others what they expect from her. Once she has a reading on that, she is able to conform to what she believes will gain her group approval or popularity, even if that behavior is negative.

During those tumultuous years, parental guidance and direction is so important. And we must not be afraid to speak up. We parents must be willing to endure a temporary disdain from our kids because we hold them to the line. That's far better than fooling ourselves into thinking we have won their love by never bringing them back on course morally and ethically. As a parent holding your kids to a standard, you may hear them scream, "I hate you, I've always hated you. You don't love me, you don't have any idea what my world is like. I wish I'd never been a part of this family!" You may have to listen to that kind of toxic waste for the short term in order to help salvage them over the long term.

We are deluding ourselves if we think that by caving in now and having them smile at us, we have won them over.

Young people want established limits. Oh sure, they'll fight you tooth and nail. They'll go fourteen rounds with you. They'll try to pin you to the mat and spill blood if they can. But they still want parents who will draw the line. If you don't, what you will hear from them at some time, in some way, is: "Why didn't my parents enforce the rules? Why didn't they care enough to see that I obeyed them?" The kids I talk to sometimes look at me and say, "You know, my folks don't care what I do, where I go, who I hang with." And when they say that, they're not bragging; they are crying for help. Give them that help.

You see, what Solomon is saying in all of this is that we can not leave our kids on their own when it comes to learning wise behavior that's anchored to a moral standard. He is calling for our involvement in their lives as moms and dads—involvement that is consistent, not only in words, but in actions.

Finally, as he wraps up his introductory remarks, Solomon emphasizes what he says in verse 7:

The fear (or reverence) of the Lord is the beginning of knowledge.

Beginning with God

If wisdom, wise behavior, is to be learned, the starting point must be the reverence or fear of God. To fear the Lord means to respect God for who He is, and to respond to Him in trust, worship, obedience and service.

In fact, the fear of the Lord is best understood as "reverent obedience." If God is not honored in a family, and His Word not followed, then wisdom that leads to wise behavior can never be attained. By and large, the people of Solomon's day were more God-conscious than we are, because no dimension of their family life was outside His domain. They did not leave Him in the temple as we leave Him in church, nor was He relegated to one day of the week or certain times of the day.

For families whose target is wise behavior, the cultivation of reverence fuels all that they do. So when the kids are driven to church or Sunday School, Mom and Dad come with them instead of ditching them to head for breakfast or the golf course. Furthermore, wise parents know that if the kids are attending Sunday classes, Mom and Dad should be at similar adult classes at the same time. They may even be involved in teaching those classes.

When it comes to worship, wise parents are very careful not to allow many loopholes. Soccer games, basketball practices, skating lessons, or whatever else we can add to the list should never replace or be given a higher priority than worship and the cultivation of reverence in the life of a young person.

Yet how many parents do you know who have erected the altar of sports over the cultivation of worship and reverence?

Certainly, worship and reverence can be learned outside the context of the church. But too many times during the week, everything else squeezes that out too. The one day of the week when you have a tremendous opportunity to model spiritual values is Sunday. But it won't work if you're off to soccer or baseball games. Your kids hear loud and clear: Sports are more important than church.

Face it, what are the odds of your kids making it to the NBA or major league baseball? Somewhere between zero and squat! But we protest, "They don't want to come to church, and I don't want to force them to." That makes as much sense as saying, "My son doesn't want to stop sleeping with his fourteen-year-old girlfriend, and I don't want to force him to stop."

Much of our life involves being forced not to do some things. When I am pulled over by a state trooper (hypothetically speaking), he is usually doing that to force me not to speed. Part of growing up, of maturing, of acquiring wisdom, is realizing that being forced not to do certain potentially harmful things is a normal part of life.

Solomon says that reverent obedience and worship are the foundation of everything we consider wise behavior. And without a commitment to wise behavior, we are heading the wrong direction on a one-way street.

Successful families

Dr. Ray Guarendi is a clinical psychologist working out of the Children's Hospital in Akron, Ohio. He has written a marvelous book entitled *Back to the Family*. The basis for the book was interviews he conducted with many positive and successful families across the country.

Some of these parents had come from very dysfunctional backgrounds. Others emerged from almost pristine environments. But each family had made it through the jungle in a marvelous manner.

Dr. Guarendi isolates some of the reasons for their successful journey. Significantly, "nearly all the parents place a high premium on imparting to the children a set of spiritual and moral values."[13]

Solomon could not have agreed more; neither could I. One of my favorite theologians puts it this way:

I call it the chalkboard hearth. It's that large wall of chalkboard that dominates every classroom, illuminating daily lessons in mathematics, history and grammar—right alongside moral values, sex education and patriotism.

This unemotional wall was never meant to take the place of a family gathered around a fire at home discussing feelings and attitudes. Yet every day, millions of children in this country gather in front of it in search of warmth from subjects that should be taught at home. . . .

The sad part about all of this is that most parents don't realize how much they have given away to the schools. Teachers have the children only six hours a day. Parents have them eighteen.

The chalkboard hearth is limited.

It can instruct them in sex. It falls short teaching them about the love and responsibility that comes with it. It can teach them how to drive, but not about accountability. It can help them select a career, but it can't provide the support and self-esteem it takes to pursue it.

It can spot child abuse, champion integration, expand the world with field trips and identify the gift, but it can't begin to teach manners, pride, nationalism, respect, stability, values or a feeling of belonging.

Isn't it time to rekindle the home hearth?[14]

Remember Chuck Swindoll's "Someday" scenario?

"Someday when the kids are grown, things are going to be a lot different around here."

Don't wait until Someday to make things different. Someday may be too late.

CHAPTER TWO

Tackling Temptation

Proverbs 1:8–19 and Selected

ROBERT FULGHUM HAS LIVED WITH HIS WIFE, among other places, on a houseboat in Seattle, and suggests that he is in training to be a grandfather. He's been a working cowboy, IBM salesman, professional artist, folksinger, parish minister, and amateur philosopher. I think (although I don't know him and can't say for sure) that what he does best is to write. In his recent book entitled, *Uh-oh*, he proves my point with this story:

> The most time-bound man I know lives in my neighbor-hood. He's always in a hurry—and always late. Always harassed. . . . I'm not exactly sure just what he does for a living, but it seems to involve buying and selling something downtown. . . .
>
> His choice of transportation . . . is a brand-new Range Rover, a vehicle built . . . for high adventure. This particular veldtmobile is equipped with a winch, a gun

rack, and a CB radio, as well as an impressive stereo system, two cellular phones, a fax machine, and a coffee maker in the glove compartment. . . .

Daily I see my neighbor rushing out of his house, burdened . . . carrying golf bag, gym bag, lunch bag, raincoat, umbrella, coffee cup, a sack of garbage for the dumpster, and his briefcase. On the day I shall describe, he has two little pieces of bloody toilet paper stuck to his chin from a hasty encounter with his razor, and a knitted brow from a hasty encounter with his wife. So far, it has not been a good morning.

About the briefcase. It is made of the purest, unblemished . . . leather, a quarter of an inch thick. . . . Solid-brass hardware, combination lock . . . and his name embossed in gold. By itself, empty, the briefcase weighs maybe ten pounds. Twenty pounds full. A heavy item in every sense of the word.

So it's a Tuesday morning. . . . A neighbor lady and I hit the street headed for work about the same time. She's a social worker for the Episcopal Church and drives an eight-year-old Ford Just-Get-Me-There-and-Back-Please-God sedan. And I drive a 1952 GMC two-ton Go-Ahead-and-Hit-Me panel truck.

At the same time, the owner of the Range Rover rushes up. . . . Time is of the essence. He is in no mood to make small talk. He grunts at us as he . . . leaps into the front seat and cranks the mighty engine. . . .

Uh-oh—he has left his coffee cup and briefcase on the roof, and there they remain as he rolls away. To the rescue the nice lady social worker . . . in her old Ford. She chases after him, urgently honking her horn, which he ignores because he is already on his cellular phone . . . . [but] her unceasing honking [drives him to] throw the phone to the floor of the car, [he] then leans out the window, and [makes a very rude gesture] to the lady. But [she] is focused on her rescue mission and honks on while waving [at] him to stop.

I, in the meantime, driving close behind, likewise try to get his attention. My horn [is] salvaged out of an old Model A. The combination . . . is too much. He jams on his brakes, flings open the door, and tries to get out—without first unlatching his seat belt.

At the same moment, his morning cup of coffee slides off the roof, bounces across the hood, and smashes into the street. Followed by his brass-bound briefcase, which crashes on the hood, scrapes across the paint with a fingernails-on-blackboard screech, and flops into the street on top of the broken coffee cup.

The dear lady, mission accomplished, coasts slowly around the scene of the accident, smiles, waves, sings out "Have a nice day!" to her neighbor dangling from the car in the clutches of his seat belt.

And no, she did not, as you might anticipate, run over his briefcase. No, she did not. I did.

The owner of the veldtmobile is a little distant these days. . . . I hear it cost him four hundred dollars to have his hood and fender repaired and repainted. I see that he has a new briefcase. In time, the dust will settle and he will sort this out. He's not a bad guy. Like me, he gets confused about what's important. In the meantime, he's unhappy with us. . . . he thinks we ruined his day . . . and cost him money and time. I think he may not know as much as he needs to know about the most basic business concern of all: profit and loss. Here's a very old profit-and-loss statement to put on the wall of his business and on the wall of mine: "What does it profit a man if he gain the whole world and lose his own soul?"[1]

Now as good as that story is—and as true as the concluding Bible verse is—for many of us, it's just another good story and just another verse from the Bible. Besides, there are other voices calling us.

In an article labeled "The Money Society" in *Fortune* magazine, the former chief of the Visa Bank Card operation made the following statement:

Now we live in a world where all values are relative, equal, and therefore without authority. It's not that people value money more but that they value everything else so much less . . . [and] they have no other values to keep greed in check.[2]

Or, as a University of Pennsylvania sociologist put it: "When there are no values, money counts.[3]

Trying to have it all

Researchers at the University of Southern California recently studied 133 people (primarily middle class, ranging in age from eighteen to eighty-nine) and found that about a third of them regularly experienced what they called an irresistible compulsion to buy. Perhaps that explains why today, one in twelve Americans is overwhelmed by debt.[4]

The problem is intensified now because the pattern and direction of adults filters down more quickly to our children than we might imagine. For example, an overwhelming 93 percent of recently surveyed teenage girls rated shopping their favorite pastime.

Back in 1967, around 40 percent of U.S. college freshmen told pollsters that it was important to them to be very well off financially. At the same time, nearly 80 percent of the same group listed developing a meaningful life as an important objective.

By the late eighties these numbers had reversed. Eighty percent aspired for the big bucks. But only 40 percent were concerned about the meaning and purpose of their life.[5]

That's not the worst of it, however. Many adults, teenagers, and children believe that being successful means "being able to have whatever you want whenever you want it."

And why not, when Madonna, the glitzy, immoral icon of many of our youth, sells herself as the "material girl"—have what you want when you want it. And our kids have caught on.

Each year, for more than the past thirty-five years, the Rand Youth Poll has conducted a nationwide survey of teens' attitudes and buying habits. A recent survey revealed among other things:

1. Teenagers are quick to label themselves and their peers "wasteful" in describing their shopping, spending, and saving habits.

2. The saving ethic, once considered crucial to money management, now appears to be largely ignored, a victim of parental neglect, materialism . . . and the lack of adequate role models.

In point of fact, only 24 percent of the young adults surveyed believe that their parents are thrifty and conservative in their buying, resulting in an example to be followed.[6]

How are we supposed to live?

The message that seems to be impregnating the foundations of our homes is that it *does* profit to lose your soul— as long as you grab the world.

And that is where parents must come to bat. Solomon suggests this in the opening chapter of the book of Proverbs. You'll recall his words in verses 8 and 9.

Hear, my son, your father's instruction, and do not forsake your mother's teaching; indeed, they are a graceful wreath to your head, and ornaments about your neck.

In Proverbs, the Hebrew verb translated as "hear" outlines a young person's response to parental counsel. But the word doesn't mean that kids patronize their parents by listening with a smug grin on their face that says, "Get your speech over with so that I can go on with my life."

The word "hear" means "listening with the attitude of actually doing what is said." Clearly Solomon regards what he says as directives that should be obeyed. And he makes the same point for moms in Proverbs 1:8:

Hear, my son, your father's instruction, and do not forsake your mother's teaching. . . .

The word for "teaching" is *torah*. It is related to a verb that means "to point or direct." So the idea of Mom's teaching is that it points in the right direction.

Directing our children God's way

What am I suggesting? Simply this. There is a place in your home for directives to be obeyed, not simply suggestions to be considered or voted upon. Now, that is not the only or primary method of communicating, but it is still appropriate and valid. Some of us back away from it. Most of us want our children's love more than anything else. We feel it represents proof that we are doing a good job of being parents.

In previous generations, the majority of parents wanted mainly respect from their children. That made things considerably easier, because those parents were not afraid to be momentarily disliked during the act of enforcing the rules.

But today, things are different. Parents feel weighed down with a sense of guilty responsibility. They have been made acutely aware of the complex emotional relationship between parent and child, and are thinking in terms of psychological cause and effect. We parents are led to believe that everything we say or do to our children will have an eternal effect on them either for good or evil. As a result, many of us have become uneasy, embarrassed and frightened. We're the first generation of immobilized parents who are letting their children practically take over their homes.

That is not Solomon's counsel. His advice is that we should point our kids in the right direction and expect them to go that way. Now in saying that, I realize you may zig when you're supposed to zag in your advice. But don't be paralyzed by that possibility.

According to Dr. Ray Guarendi of Children's Hospital in Akron, Ohio, "Honest mistakes made by loving parents do not damage children psychologically, not now or at some unknown point years down the road." He adds that "[Our mistakes] may make life a little tougher for a while, for all involved, but they don't ruin 'psyches.' Kids were built to withstand being raised by human beings, with all of our shortcomings and inconsistencies."[7]

So don't be afraid to provide directives that require obedience. Look at verse 9 again:

Indeed, they are a graceful wreath to your head, and ornaments about your neck.

As far as Solomon was concerned, obedience is rewarding. It is an attractive trait in today's society. Obedience is like wearing a gold chain or necklace, or finding a fitted University of North Carolina basketball hat, or a Chicago Bulls Starter hat. In other words, heeding parental instruction enhances our kids' quality of life.

Golden guidance

So don't hesitate on directives, especially when it concerns the use or misuse of money. In the next section of Proverbs 1, Solomon provides directives on finances in your home. It is no accident that the first subject he tackles after his opening remarks on wisdom is the subject of money and its magnetic pull.

Following as it does on the heels of his encouragement to parents to provide directives, it is clear that the parents are responsible to provide financial guidance. But bear in mind that directives on any subject need to be backed up by your own consistent actions or modeling. So what you say about money is proven by what you do with it. As models for your kids, you teach them how to handle money by the way you handle it yourself.

Perhaps then, before we look at the rest of chapter 1, it might be good to remind ourselves about some valuable instructions about money offered in chapter 23:4, 5.

> Do not weary yourself to gain wealth, cease from your consideration of it. When you set your eyes on it, it is gone. For wealth certainly makes itself wings, like an eagle that flies toward the heavens.

The expression, "do not weary yourself," sounds a lot like your life, doesn't it? It literally means "to overwork, to work so long and so hard that you are to the point of collapse—even pain."

Today we would substitute the word "burnout." Solomon says that we parents should not present that kind of a model to our kids.

We should not push ourselves simply to accumulate more money to buy more stuff. We ought rather to demonstrate restraint in our pursuit of money. Now this verse is not suggesting that you not work hard, or that making money is inappropriate. It is talking about being consumed in our life by finances.

The Golden Cow syndrome

Translated into daily life, the wiser course is to not take the second job just to get more money. Nor should we add the overtime and double shifts just to buy that super-wide TV set.

Let's not allow our addiction to things to drive us to the shark-infested waters of killer debt so that we are driven to do what I just suggested we shouldn't, in order to pay off our bills.

And yet, what do we repeatedly do? Just what Solomon said we should not. Market researchers say that as many as half of the seventy-six million baby boomers in our country consume products of a price and quality far beyond what might be expected for their incomes.

The Northern Trust Bank in Chicago ran an ad a couple years ago saying, "Anyone who lives within his means suffers from a lack of imagination."[8]

But here's the crazy thing about our mad pursuits; they never stop. Why? Verse 5 tells us: "When you set your eyes on it, it is gone. For wealth certainly makes itself wings, like an eagle that flies toward the heavens."

Our money disappears, sometimes almost without explanation. In the ancient world, the figure of a bird flying off pictured the short-lived nature of wealth. That in itself intensifies our stress and anxiety when money and stuff are our primary goals. An old Italian proverb says, "The last coat a man wears has no pockets in it."

And when we get caught on that treadmill, it is an unwinnable race. One astute observer of our time speaks to the heart of us all when he writes:

> As time passes we often become the slave of our things.
> We are fearful of taking a holiday because we're con-
> cerned about our belongings being left alone. A friend
> has a new [car] which he never parks in a parking lot or
> on a crowded street for fear of someone scratching it.
> But he is equally worried about leaving it on a side street
> for fear that it will be stolen. It's interesting to ponder
> whether he owns the car or the car owns him. But we are
> all in some way as guilty as he. . . .The more we have,

the more we seem to want and need, and the more we have to be concerned about."[9]

Now if you ask the average person what is more important to him or her, making money or being devoted to his or her family, most will say "family" without thinking. But watch how average people live. See where they really invest their time and energy. Invariably they do not really live what they say they believe.

We have let ourselves be persuaded that if we leave for work earlier in the morning and come home more tired at night, we are proving how devoted we are to our family by expending ourselves to provide them with all the things they have seen advertised.

At some point, we need to stop that merry-go-round kind of thinking. Some of us do, often between the ages of thiry-five and forty-five.

At that intersection in our life, we slow down long enough to realize that we've been pushing pretty hard. In fact, ever since we ejected safely out of school, at whatever level that was, we have been busy "doing," as opposed to "being." Somewhere down the pipe we realize that for all our doing, we are no better off personally. We may have more stuff, but we still lack contentment and satisfaction. And those insidious gray hairs keep popping up. So we begin to think.

Some of us think, "I've got to do more. I've got to push harder." And we do, and have the ulcers and heart medication to prove it. Others think, "I've got to feel young again." And we find that youthful fountain in an extramarital affair. But after the medication and the spice, we still have no more contentment or satisfaction.

Stop the world, I want to get off!

That's why some of us choose neither of the two options mentioned, but as we slow down we start thinking about being the right kind of person, not simply doing so much. We begin to think about character as opposed to accumulation. That doesn't mean we step off the edge of the world and rent a cave in the Rockies. But it does mean we reconsider who we are as opposed to concentrating solely on what we do. As that occurs, we begin to check out our value system, in terms of money and how we view it and use it. That normally causes us to readjust —to our family's eternal gratitude.

Solomon would applaud that move, because it is his observation that the other route is simply a wearisome routine.

Now you may be thinking, "Great, how do I get off the merry-go-round?"

The first step in the process of keeping our children away from constantly "wanting" is for us to make some value decisions. Then we need to discipline ourselves against our own desires. For as we give in to ourselves, we give in to our children. But as we discipline ourselves, our children also will learn restraint. If we're going to train our children, we have to make some decisions ourselves.

So many "needs," so little money

As a general rule, expenses rise to meet your income. Be careful—unless monitored closely, expenses often push to *exceed* your income. So after determining your family priorities and values, ask yourself how you can meet them realistically without falling behind financially.

Additionally, we need to instill in our kids a pattern related to finances. Certainly they can earn money as they grow older, and perhaps enjoy an allowance of some nature. But while acquiring money they must learn certain principles.

Let me tell you what we have done recently. We use the envelope system. Our two sons have on their desks four envelopes. Each has its own label and purpose, and that purpose relates to a principle regarding money.

The first envelope is labeled "giving." For our family, that translates into 10 percent of earned income, and that comes off the top.

The second envelope is labeled "savings." For our kids, we think in terms of 20 percent of their earned income. To help them visualize this concept, we established bank accounts for them when they began school. The amount they save is tucked into the second envelope, then banked each month. That amount is for personal use in the future. They can save up for something special for themselves, or for someone else.

The third envelope is labeled "long-term savings." This is different from regular savings. It is money put aside for the long haul, for things like car insurance, or a contribution to their college education, or a down payment for a car. They need help to understand long-term saving or investment. Again, in our makeshift system, this represents 20 percent of earnings.

That leaves 50 percent for the fourth envelope. That is "discretionary" money—they can use it as they wish. That means they will buy some very stupid things, and may even make some poor decisions financially. But isn't that part of the learning process? Trust them *implicitly* with this category. Don't interfere, unless of course, over the long haul they don't seem to be getting any wiser with their discretionary money.

But however you do it, be sure to develop a system and hold them to it.

Walking our talk

Now you can't do anything like this if you are not modeling something similar. I know the percentages may differ. Most financial counselors recommend a "10-20-70" plan. Ten percent is giving, 20 percent is savings (short and long-term) and 70 percent is discretionary. Whatever the percentages, you must have a model. In fact, American parents are very weak here. Nationally, our level of savings is around 2.3 percent, and our charitable giving contributions hover only as high as 3 percent.

In the bulk of churches that I know about, the majority of givers average less than twelve dollars a week in offerings, which represents a tithe on a annual income of around $6,000. Hardly a model to teach. Here's a challenge—a "double-dog-dare-you" challenge. Take your most recent income tax documents and show them to your family. Specifically, show them two entries: Highlight the declared income category before deductions, and then highlight the charitable giving deduction line item. Then, ask them to figure out what percentage of income your giving represents.

Now, regardless of the percentage it turns out to be, is it an amount worthy of modeling?

Beyond that, several other guidelines may be helpful as you wade your way through the swamp of materialism.

1. Never buy something unless you can pay cash. Or if you pay on credit because of a great savings, then be sure when the bill comes due you pay it off—certainly within two months.

2. Consider borrowing things rather than buying them. Friends are often glad to lend things (but they expect them returned).

3. Buy it only when you need it. A bargain is not a bargain if you buy it and don't need it.

4. Be patient for it. There is always a better price. Watch for sales. Ask people. Compare.

Several years ago, I needed to buy a new pair of dress shoes. I knew exactly the kind I wanted: Burgundy, wing-tips, no laces, slip-ons. And I also knew the price range I could afford. So, I recruited my then fourteen-year-old son, Jeremy, to go with me on my shopping tour.

Over the course of six weeks, we visited about ten shoe stores. At each one, he went in to find the shoe and check out the price. Upon completing his expedition, he would report to me and we would make a decision to move on in our search. Finally, after venturing into yet another store, he came bounding out with a grin a mile wide and yelled, "They've got them!"

Sure enough, the exact shoes in the acceptable price range were found and purchased.

But we gained more than shoes. We also purchased a lesson in financial policy. The lesson, however, goes beyond this one illustration. Believe it or not, I have never paid more than $12 for a dress shirt, no more than $16 for a silk tie and no more than $170 for a suit—and my last two suits are "Hartz, Shafner, and Marx" (no relation to Larry, Curly, and Moe). The stuff is out there in affordable doses, if you look around. Graft that lesson into the lives of your kids, and model it for them.

Now you may be thinking, "Why go to all that trouble?" Because as strong as the parental directives of the book of Proverbs may be, the voices of a mother and father are not the only ones crying for attention.

In Proverbs 1, we find the other major pressure your children face in terms of money and things in their lives. Verse 10 says: "My son, if sinners entice you, do not consent."

Peer pressure and your child

The verb "entice" means "to persuade or seduce." It is connected in history to the word "naive" in verse 4, which emphasizes the fact that young people are open minded, and easily pushed, persuaded, or fooled.

In verse 10, Solomon warns his son against peers who want to do just that: persuade him, fool him, convince him—and it adds up to tremendous peer pressure.

After all, we each travel in groups—whether with our social friends, our service club, our basketball team, our tennis set, our business colleagues, our bowling league, or our street gang. What we become is determined in a significant way by who we run with.

And yet, a recent poll showed that the majority of parents think peer pressure is not a significant influence in the lives of their kids. Yet 75 percent of the teenagers said that their peers influence them more than parents or anyone else.[10]

Today, every teenager knows the questions: "Where are you going?" "How will you get there?" "What time will you be home?"

But the most important question is, "Who else will be there?"

Wise parents give closest attention to unfamiliar names and families, and inquire carefully. Why? Because the wrong kind of pressure may be lurking in the unknown shadows.

That is what Solomon is describing in these verses. And notice how that pressure bubbles to the surface. It begins by offering acceptance or a sense of belonging. Eight times in verses 11–14, you'll read the personal pronouns "us" or "we." Those are powerful and magnetic words to our kids. They want to belong. Furthermore, they want to belong to a group that has money. Verse 14 says they can: "Throw in your lot with us, we shall all have one purse."

The enticement begins with being offered a place to belong—even if it is the wrong place.

Dr. Dan Kiley, in his intriguing book, *The Peter Pan Syndrome*, explains it this way:

Affluence without restraints creates a falling domino effect in the children. The value of work is the first to tumble as children take pleasure as a right rather than an earned privilege. Then, with too much time on their hands and too little security in the home, they search for group identity. They desperately want to find a place where they belong. In a state of near panic, the children are seduced by the profit-seekers who use dazzling media displays to promise kids that the key to belonging is to do what "everybody" else is doing. Consequently peer pressure invades every aspect of their lives, compelling them to belong, no matter what the price.[11]

But what makes this seduction, this enticement so strong, is the promise made: they will have what they want when they want it. In as many words, that is the pressurized message that verses 13 and 14 shout.

We shall find all kinds of precious wealth, we shall fill our houses with spoil; Throw in your lot with us, we shall all have one purse. . . .

Not only can they belong to the group, they can land some easy money, too. And the odds of getting their hands on this are a lot better than with the lottery tickets their parents buy so religiously.

The enticement feeds their basic instinct—get rich and get stuff. And if you as a parent haven't helped them see past that, they'll go for it. You see, once they've cracked a certain "in" group, the pressure to go along with that group (to wear the same pump-up running shoes bought at the same store) is immense. It will push your kids to do things that are wrong in order to stay with the group and enjoy their stuff.

In its most extreme form, it will push them to break the law. In its least extreme form, it will push them to break their principles. Look at verses 11 and 12 again:

If they say, "Come with us, let us lie in wait for blood, let us ambush the innocent without cause; let us swallow them alive like Sheol, even whole, as those who go down to the pit. . . ."

Solomon paints a worst-case scenario: kids ready to kill to get what they want. But here's the kicker.

In Old Testament thought, Sheol was the abode of the dead. It was also pictured as a devouring monster, with gaping jaws and a hearty and insatiable appetite for victims. And that is the point of comparison here.

Young people motivated by greed have an appetite that cannot be satisfied. But they are prepared to do anything they can to satisfy it, even if it means consuming themselves.

Self-destructive lifestyles

It's the same pressure you face to overprice merchandise, to sell shoddy or inferior products at superior prices, or to underpay your taxes. It's the same pressure you feel to keep climbing the ladder even though you know you've stepped on people on the way—and probably left your family in your dust.

It's the pressure to have just a little more, so you can really enjoy life. That pressure invariably comes from those we run with or from those we desperately *want* to run with, but don't think we can—yet.

That daily peer pressure on both children and adults is almost unbearable. How are we to know if our neighbors can really afford that vacation, second car, new television, remodeled kitchen, new suit or dress? Many adults rationalize both major and minor purchases by saying, "Because we live in the same neighborhood, if he can afford it, I must be able to afford it, too. Not only must I be able to afford it, I've got to have it."

Children experience the same pressure, and because they, too, want what their friends have, they put the pressure on you to cough it up.

The crazy thing is that there are few peer groups on the face of the earth that care whether your children live or die. That's a hard lesson for them to learn, but anyone who has ever gotten into a tight spot and had to turn to their peer group for real help, or real loyalty, has rarely found it. The fact is, few peer groups on the face of the earth care as much about any young person as his or her family.

Let me try to put it all together in two brief principles that you can bank on. The first emerges out of verses 17 to 19 primarily: *In our mad dash for "more," all we pursue is emptiness.* Solomon paints a bleak picture:

Indeed it is useless to spread the net in the eyes of any bird; but they lie in wait for their own blood; they ambush their own lives. So are the ways of everyone who gains by violence; it takes away the life of its possessors.

Verse 17 suggests that even a bird, when it sees a trap being laid for it, is sharp enough to avoid it. But the group Solomon has in mind figures they will beat the odds; they will be the exception to the rule.

They aren't.

Someone has suggested that "unhappiness is not knowing what we want, and killing ourselves to get it." That's the group Solomon has in mind in verses 18 and 19. Their pursuits are self-destructive and they are the real victims.

To join their mad dash is to share in their fate.

In our own mad dash for more, all we have gained is a joyless existence.

Suicide city

Consider the data from the most affluent suburbs of Chicago, the ten-mile stretch of communities along the city's northside lakefront that is one of the richest areas in the country.

The median income a decade ago was about $60,000. Children in these areas attend excellent schools, travel about the world on vacations, are admitted to the best and most prestigious private colleges, and often drive their own cars (Mercedes included). These are children of affluence who would seem to have it made.

And yet this cluster of suburbs has the highest number of

teenage suicides per year in the state, and almost in the nation. In one decade there was a 250 percent increase in suicides. This, despite serious efforts at suicide prevention. A nineteen-year-old from Glencoe, Illinois, says:

> Growing up here you are handed everything on a platter, but something else is missing. The one thing parents don't give is love, understanding, and acceptance of you as a person.[12]

What is alarming is that this area is not an isolated blip on the suicide radar screen. The same phenomenon is seen in similar counties around the country. Each of these areas has experienced a number of adolescent suicides disproportionate to the national rate.

Maybe that is what is behind these words from an unknown writer:

> This is the age of the half-read page
> and the quick hash and the mad dash,
> the bright night with the nerves tight,
> the plane hop with the brief stop,
> the lamp tan in a short span,
> the big shot in a good spot,
> and the brain strain and the heart pain
> and the cat naps until the spring snaps
> and the fun's done.[13]

That's the first principle: *Our search pursues emptiness.* The second principle surfaces in Proverbs 15:16.

> Better is a little with the fear of the Lord, than great treasure and turmoil with it. Better is a dish of vegetables where love is, than a fattened ox and hatred with it.

Here's the second principle: *We parents must do everything we can to instill a sense of proportion into our kids—a sense of perspective about what is really important in this life and the next.*

The real danger of unchecked wealth is that it can distort our sense of values and priorities, and make us blind or indifferent to spiritual realities. It can bring us to the point where a verse like "What does it profit a man if he gain the whole world and lose his own soul?" seems almost laughable.

What is really important

There is not a lot of laughter, however, in a home where we may have everything money can buy, but beneath the veneer, resentments, anger, and hatred smoulder away. It's much better to eat warmed-up pizza and donuts—where the family stands together—than to have it all and be driven apart. Chuck Swindoll says it well:

> The rich and poor must hear this. Those who want (and have) much and those who feel they need more are equally in need of this counsel. Discontentment rarely has anything to do with one's financial status. Greed is cancer of the attitude, not caused by insufficient funds but by inappropriate objectives. Some will never be satisfied, no matter how much they have. Discontentment is a sneaky thief who continues to disrupt our peace and to steal our happiness. Ever so subtly it whispers more. . . more. . . more. . . ."[14]

Our problem is that we want more . . . more . . . more . . . of this or that, and less . . . less . . . less of God.

Ron Blue, a fine Christian financial planner and C.P.A. puts it all on the bottom shelf for us:

> The way you handle your money cannot be faked. Your checkbook reveals the spending decisions you have made. It tells how you chose to use God's resources. Your checkbook reveals the priorities in your life. . . .

Most other areas of your life, except the financial one, can be faked if you really want to. But your checkbook reveals the actual commitment to the use of God's resources to accomplish God's purposes. I sometimes wonder if, when we get to heaven, all our check registers will have preceded us so that we can spend time in eternity reviewing how we used or abused [God's] resources.[15]

Checkbook checklist

Ask yourselves these questions today about your relationship to money and things. They'll help—if you answer them honestly.

1. Am I using my possessions and not just accumulating them?
2. Can I enjoy them, and honestly thank God for them?
3. Am I able to share them with others?
4. Am I able to give generously?

"The owner of the veldtmobile is a little distant these days . . . I hear it cost him four hundred dollars to have his hood and fender repaired and repainted. I see that he has a new briefcase. In time the dust will settle and he will sort this out. He's not a bad guy. Like me, he gets confused about what's important. . . ."

What is important to you?

CHAPTER THREE

Tackling More Temptation

Proverbs 5–7

Y OU MAY REMEMBER—as I recall it was in November, 1990—one of the great basketball stars of the Los Angeles Lakers, James Worthy, was arrested the night before a game and was accused of soliciting a prostitute. He was briefly detained in jail while his bond was being arranged. He arrived late to the next Lakers game. As a result, he literally entered the arena just as they were getting ready to play.

Seventeen thousand fans gave him a standing ovation. For what? Apparently without any consideration given to the humiliation, the betrayal, and hurt to his wife or to his child, they stood and clapped the lights out. What were they applauding for?

In the same vein, Irving Kristol, in a *Wall Street Journal* editorial, asked these penetrating questions:

Why is Magic Johnson regarded by our media as some kind of moral hero, even a role model for the young?

Mr. Johnson, a basketball player of extraordinary talent, has tested HIV positive, as a result— he tells us—of having been sexually promiscuous with more than 200 women. One or some of these women were infected with the HIV virus. As a result, a brilliant career has been cut short, as has a life. It is a sad story, to which compassion and pity are appropriate responses. But it is also a sordid story of a man defeated by his unruly sexual appetite. So why are we being asked to see him as an innocent victim, courageously coping with adversity?[1]

Karen S. Peterson continues the argument about moral values in a *USA Today* article. She refers to the release of the recent movie, *Indecent Proposal*. The question posed in the movie is, "Would you—a happily married woman—commit adultery just once for a million dollars? No strings, no lies. (The movie is a box office smash.)

According to Peterson, the issue is not simple; it is very complex. "What if you really needed the money?" she asks. Or "What if it would put the kids through college?"[2]

Oprah Winfrey, the first week after the film's release, polled her studio and television audience and discovered that 55 percent of the women polled would go to bed with another man for the money. A Seattle-based radio talk show found the percentage hiked to 62 percent.

So we continue to see a model of sex outside of marriage applauded. "What and who are we applauding?" is still the question.

Our deteriorating society

On the night Murphy Brown became an unwed mother, thirty-four million Americans tuned in, and CBS posted a 35 percent share of the audience. The show did not stir significant protest at the grass roots, and lost none of its advertisers. The actress, Candice Bergen, subsequently appeared on the cover of nearly every women's and news magazine in the country, and received an honorary degree at the University of Pennsylvania, as well as an Emmy award.[3]

The model continues, with the supporting cast of groups such as Planned Parenthood pitching their line—and I quote:

"Our goal is to be ready as educators and parents to help young people obtain sex satisfaction before marriage." The organization plans to put a birth control clinic in every high school in the United States during the 1990s.[4]

Can you hear the modeling—and thunderous applause? But where has this "enlightened" mentality brought us?

First, consider that the number of unmarried teenagers getting pregnant has nearly doubled in the past two decades. Teenage sexual activity will result in nearly one million pregnancies annually, leading to 406,000 abortions. (Twenty-five percent of all the abortions performed in America are on pregnant teenagers between the ages of fifteen and nineteen).

But the one million teenage pregnancies lead also to 134,000 miscarriages, and 490,000 live births. By 1990, 28 percent of all births in our country were illegitimate.[5]

Furthermore, at least six million teenagers are sexually active by the age of fifteen, which explains why more American girls under sixteen are getting pregnant these days. Some of these kids get married, but the marriages are short-lived. The divorce rate for parents younger than eighteen is three times greater than that for parents who have their first child after age twenty. And 44 percent of young women who give birth between the ages of fourteen and seventeen are divorced before they are thirty.[6]

There is more. This year about three million teenagers will contract a sexually transmitted disease (STD). In fact, STDs now rank as the number one reported communicable disease in the United States, with the most serious rate found in the sixteen to twenty age group—it is *triple* the level of the general population.[7]

The number of juvenile sex offenders is on the increase in our country also. More than 4,600 youths under age eighteen were arrested on charges of forcible rape in 1990. One out of three of them was under fifteen.[8]

The high price of low values

In the summer of 1990, a special commission of prominent political, medical, education, and business leaders issued a report, titled "Code Blue," on the health of America's teenagers. They wrote that "... never before has one generation of American teenagers been less healthy, less cared for, or less prepared for life than their parents were at the same age."

According to the Commission, the explanation for teenagers' deteriorating condition lies with their behavior, and not (as was the case in the past) with physical illness.

Pollster Daniel Yankelovich reports that our society now places less value than before on what we owe others as a matter of moral obligation; less value on sacrifice as a moral good; less value on observing the rules; and less value on correctness and restraint in matters of physical pleasure and sexuality. Higher value is now placed on things like self-expression, individualism and personal choice.[9]

So much is so that the case, that in one particular high school in Southern California, the senior boys have sex with the incoming freshman girls. Several years ago, one hundred forty-nine of the girls dropped out of high school with unwanted pregnancies—a few were in upper classes, but most of them were freshmen.

The principal of that school became concerned. He traced it back to junior high, from which both the boys and the girls had come into high school with this expectation—"We must be accepted! And whatever it takes to be accepted, that's what we'll do."

They longed to be accepted in high school. From the first day, they did whatever was demanded.[10]

A prophet ahead of his time, A.W. Tozer wrote more than thirty years ago:

The period in which we now live may well go down in history as the Erotic Age. Sex love has been elevated into a cult. Eros has more worshippers among civilized men today than any other god. For millions the erotic has completely displaced the spiritual. . . .

Now if this god would let us Christians alone, I for one would let his cult alone. . . . But the cult of eros is seriously affecting the church. The pure religion of Christ that flows like a crystal river from the heart of God is being polluted by the unclean waters trickling from behind the altars of abomination that appear on every high hill and under every green tree from New York to Los Angeles.[11]

Don't worry, be happy

If A.W. Tozer was correct thirty or more years ago, what would he conclude today?

Some of us thought that Magic Johnson's case would wake people up. At least that is what we prayed would happen. It didn't. The crisis of sexual immorality and AIDS hardly slowed for its second wind. Perhaps Magic's stellar play at the Barcelona Olympics only served to send another message— Don't worry about it; everything will be okay.

We want to believe that, even though we know it's a lie. And our track record as a nation shouts that lie to us.

The bottom line is that the social regression in our country in the last thirty years is due in large part to our failure to carry out a critical and time-honored task: the moral education of our families.[12]

We must return to that if the word "survival" means anything to us. The wisdom of Solomon may be covered with time and dust (and I am confident, even with gales of patronizing laughter). Nevertheless, in regard to our moral purity, it must permeate our thoughts and our lifestyles.

And that wisdom calls boldly from Solomon's opening words in chapter 5:1–3:

> My son, give attention to my wisdom, incline your ear to my understanding; That you may observe discretion, and your lips may reserve knowledge. For the lips of an adulteress drip honey, and smoother than oil is her speech.

In this chapter we have a man-to-man (or if you prefer, a person-to-person) warning about moral impurity. The chapter opens with a dad urging his son to cultivate purity. In fact, chapters 5–7 are an extended warning against sex outside of marriage.

There is a note of urgency to what he writes. His emphasis in verse 1 is on "wisdom and understanding."

Remember, "wisdom" in the book of Proverbs always focused on the *application* of moral principles to living. A person of wisdom, regardless of age, embraced a basic morality. Even the word "understanding" lines up with that idea, because it refers to the ability to discern intelligently the difference between truth and error, the difference between the con job and the real thing, the difference between the attraction of the moment and the long-range values that count.

Living in the real world

It is that loss of moral sense, of knowing the difference between right and wrong, that is haunting our families today—

especially when we come to the subject of sexuality. Solomon, however, faced a similar dilemma. His was no pristine, inviolate environment. In fact, I think Solomon took the time to include the painstaking details of these three chapters for several very up-to-date reasons.

First, illicit sex must have been easily available in his day or such a lengthy discussion of the subject would not have been necessary.

Second, I am sure Solomon was quite aware of the devastating effects this sin could have on individuals, and that pushed him to give it such heavy treatment.

But perhaps there is an even more basic reason behind the counsel we are about to examine. As a father, Solomon wanted to leave trustworthy advice for his son to read, and then live out. Maybe he wrote these words with an extra degree of emotion because his own father, David, had suffered the awful consequences of yielding to sexual temptations many years before.

Although David's adultery happened before Solomon was born, it still marked him. If you're in David's shoes, don't think that your own adultery will not leave its mark on your kids. You may tell yourself that they are mature and able to handle these kinds of things, and that they will get over it. They will not.

They may get through it, but they will never forget it. It leaves an impression that will follow them to their graves. And when you waltz back into their lives with the new "Ms. Right" or "Mr. Wonderful," don't be surprised when the welcome mat is jerked out from under your feet.

Solomon was raised in an environment that never let him forget his father's moral failure.

We wrote a lot about it, because he understood that the battle for moral purity never ends, and failure here will mark us for life. One man puts it in these terms:

Nothing in life so clouds our judgment and makes stupid fools out of the wisest of us as succumbing to illicit sex.

All our useful energies are drained off to defend or conceal that behavior. The colossal compromise of [immorality] colors all our other value judgments.[12]

It is from that perspective that we parents must offer our counsel. Look at how Solomon phrases it in Proverbs 6:20 and following:

My son, observe the commandment of your father, and do not forsake the teaching of your mother; bind them continually on your heart; tie them around your neck. When you walk about, they will guide you; When you sleep, they will watch over you; and when you awake, they will talk to you. For the commandment is a lamp, and the teaching is light; and reproofs for discipline are the way of life, to keep you from the evil woman, from the smooth tongue of the adulteress. Do not desire her beauty in your heart.

Now, link chapter 7:1–5 to what you've just read:

My son, keep my words, and treasure my commandments within you. Keep my commandments and live, and my teaching as the apple of your eye. Bind them on your fingers; write them on the tablet of your heart. Say to wisdom, "You are my sister," and call understanding your intimate friend; that they may keep you from an adulteress. . . .

Once again the theme of sexual seduction surfaces in the instructions from a father. Solomon begs sons and daughters to cling to the teachings of their parents. Implicit in these verses is the basic understanding that a good home life will go a long way to prevent a young person from tripping into sexual misconduct.

That is a more serious responsibility than we may realize.

In the April 1993 issue of the *Atlantic Monthly*, a thirty-seven page article on the absolutely incredible importance of the family concludes like this:

> More than a century and a half ago, Alexis de Tocqueville (a French historian and sociologist) made the striking observation that an individualistic society depends on an . . . institution like the family for its continued existence. . . . [because] the family is responsible for teaching lessons of . . . self-restraint, responsibility, and right conduct, which are essential to a free, democratic society. If that family fails in these tasks, then the entire experiment in [democracy] is jeopardized.[14]

That is why Solomon, when he talks about the instructions of parents in chapters 5 and 7, says to young people, ". . . bind them to your heart, tie them around your neck, stick them on your finger."

Meaning what? Meaning young people need to make their parents' teaching a permanent and indelible truth. You must be able to hang on to it, and make it so much a part of your life that you carry it with you, deep inside, in your heart of hearts. But, Solomon is no fool. He knows as well as you that the best advice is useless against strong temptation—unless it is owned personally and practiced courageously. That is why he paints the word picture he does in 7:2:

> Keep my commandments and live, and my teaching as the apple of your eye.

In the Hebrew language, the expression, "the apple of your eye," literally means, "the little man in the eye." It means that if you are close enough to someone, you will see yourself reflected in his or her eyes.

So Solomon's advice is for the son to keep his eye so close-ly fixed on his parents' teachings that he constantly sees them in his own mind's eye. We do this all the time. Somebody asks you a question and you pause for a moment and kind of look up into the corner of the room as you think. And as you think, you picture your answer in your mind. That's what Solomon is driving at here.

But in addition, the keeping of the "apple of the eye" reminds us that this teaching is vital. It, like your eyes, must be guarded closely, or protected.

In the NBA it is now fashionable to wear eye goggles. What was started years ago because of an eye injury by Kareem Abdul Jabbar, the retired center of the Los Angeles Lakers, is now being modeled by others, who may or may not have had trouble with their eyes. It's even become a fashion statement.

Do you know who wears eye goggles religiously for every game? None other than the "applause man," the same James Worthy who was arrested for soliciting a prostitute. He wears his goggles every game. Perhaps protecting his eyes is more crucial to him than protecting his purity.

But that is not Solomon's counsel. He tells young people to hang on to the advice of their folks about sexual purity.

The true worth of parental counsel

Now I realize there is always a tendency, when children get to a certain age, to figure the advice of their parents is out of touch with reality. All of us have thought that way from time to time. When kids reach the age of twelve or thirteen, their par-ents' I.Q. plummets suddenly without explanation to some-where around the level of a plant. And I know that fathers espe-cially embarrass their kids by their mere presence at times. (I embarrass the socks off my sons plenty.)

But do you know something? Around the age of thirty, their parents' I.Q. skyrockets back to the level of brilliance. About the time they find themselves married, with 2.6 kids, a dog, a mortgage, a car payment, and lots of headaches, suddenly they want to call dad and say, "I was wondering, could you help me out with something? I need your advice."

Well, I hope they don't wait until they're thirty to listen. In fact, if they die at twenty-five of AIDS, they'll never make that call.

So encourage them to fight off the urge to ignore your advice in the area of morality. Solomon insists that if your godly counsel is taken to heart and kept in clear view, it will prove more dependable than any peer group they run with. At the risk of overkill, let me say again to parents that it is your responsibility to teach your children moral values related to sexuality. Silence and lack of modeling in this area is a killer.

I recognize that you may be scared to death at the prospect of discussing sex with your kids. Well, the fear that silences you sends a shrieking message to your sons and daughters—a message that tantalizes them and pushes them to find answers where they shouldn't.

So take a deep breath and deal with it. But not just once. Please understand that your children begin learning about sex a long time before you realize it. So allow your children to ask questions and discuss the subject—over and over again.

In fact, by the time your child is ten, you should have talked to him or her openly about sexual facts and your own moral values. The most important thing is that your children know that you care passionately about their character and lifestyle.

Time to deliver "The Talk"

I was reminded of this in our family just about a year ago. Our two sons and I were tooling around town for something. My oldest son, Jeremy (now sixteen), was in the front seat. His younger brother, Kent, was in the back seat. (Kent was nine at the time.)

During our conversation, Kent spoke up from the back seat and asked an innocent question related to sexuality. I attempted to answer it properly without driving off the road. After I had finished, my oldest son looked at me and said, "Dad, I think you need to have 'the talk' with Kent!"

That was a good reminder. We had "the talk" a little later—and again several times since.

Moms and dads should talk to their kids about sexuality and AIDS because, as Solomon indicates, parents are responsible for teaching moral values. You know better than anyone else, how much and what kind of information your child can handle.

You don't need to go out and buy *Gray's Anatomy*, or a medical handbook fully illustrated with charts and color photos for them. Simply start with the facts and gear the information to what your child already understands. Just talk about what he or she needs to know.

How much is enough?

Small children only need basic information to satisfy their innate curiosity. Older kids can understand more about contagious diseases, drug abuse, and sex. Teenagers need detailed factual information in order to deal with what they are facing.

Be sure you approach it as a conversation and not as a lecture. And do it without blushing or embarrassment. Both lecturing and shame send the wrong message. Solomon's opinion is that your proper instruction in this area is vital.

Dr. Robert Coles is an eminent child psychiatrist, Harvard professor, and what some might describe as a member of the liberal intellectual left. Recently, he directed a vast survey across our country. Surveyors fanned out, visiting public, private, and parochial schools, in cities and suburbs. During several weeks, they posed more than ninety probing questions to more than five thousand children in grades four through twelve.

One of the most important question they asked was: "How

do you decide what is right and wrong? What system of values informs your moral decisions?"

An article I read in the March 1990 issue of *Teacher* magazine offered this conclusion to the research:

> The answers reveal a nation of children who do, in fact, have fairly complicated belief systems. But far more often than not, those beliefs run counter to traditional values. What's more, there is an unmistakable erosion of children's faith in, and support for, traditional sources of authority. . . . Increasingly they turn to their peers for guidance on matters of right and wrong.[15]

Today's "in your face" temptation

Dr. Coles himself wrote that "some of the parents who will gasp in horror at the corruption of children's values are, in reality, the inadvertent role models for their children's slippery beliefs. . . . and what it means . . . is that a majority of children have no firm religious or moral code to guide them."[16]

Here's the problem: With no moral code, those kids—our kids—are sitting ducks for the temptations that lurk insidiously in their daily paths. If you don't think the dangers exit, you need a reality check. Solomon was very aware of the temptations out there; he'd seen them a thousand times. Look at what he says in chapter 7:4 and following:

> Say to wisdom, "You are my sister," and call understanding your intimate friend; that they may keep you from an adulteress, from the foreigner who flatters with her words. For at the window of my house I looked out through my lattice, and I saw among the naive, I discerned among the youths, a young man lacking sense, passing through the street near her corner; and he takes the way to her house, in the twilight, in the evening, in

the middle of the night and in the darkness. And behold, a woman comes to meet him dressed as a harlot and cunning of heart. She is boisterous and rebellious; her feet do not remain at home. . . .

Solomon proceeds to discuss the easy availability of sex. He uses the descriptions of a prostitute or, as in this chapter, a married woman who's playing around. But don't pat yourself on the back if you think your kids are insulated from that. Think more along the lines of your television set when you think of temptation.

Inviting disaster via television input

During the day, the most sexual material is found in the soaps. Nearly all the "love in the afternoon" is between partners who are not married—at least, not to each other. During prime time, adult sitcoms score high in sexual content. Unprecedented levels of suggestiveness and kinky sexual behavior are found in prime-time sitcoms such as *Cheers*, *The Golden Girls* and *Night Court*.

Dan, on *Night Court*, for example, is consistently portrayed as sex-crazed and promiscuous. His relentless search for partners leads to sado-masochism in one episode and risky sex in countless others.

In fact, for every eighty-five instances of sexual content in television programming, Louis Harris and Associates estimated there was only one counter-balancing reference to the serious aspect of sex and responsibility.[17]

The presence of *HBO*, *MTV*, *Showtime*, and the other "paid for" cable channels are open invitations for your children and yourselves to be exposed to the raw edge of sexuality. It will only serve to magnify the temptation in all of your lives. Yet I am continually amazed at the number of Christian parents who willingly pay anywhere from ten to forty dollars a month to bring these stations into their family rooms.

Again, I hear the protesting, "But we have self-control in our family!" Really? If you are alone at home, with nobody else around, and you've got R-rated (and worse) material available with the tap of your remote controller, then you don't have self-control. You're setting yourself up for an immense struggle, regardless of how "spiritual" you think you are. *I'd* struggle with that kind of open invitation.

We need to be aware of the temptations present even in our homes. Face those temptations and deal with them—for yourselves and for your kids. Be sure to explain your reasons to them. Whatever you do, though, don't tell them they can't watch that stuff—but you can. That's the height of parental hypocrisy. The message your kids hear is, "My folks think I'm an idiot. I know what's going on here. So, I'll blow it off. Their advice stinks."

No, we parents must set the tone. We must be the model at home.

Keep an eye on the schools, too

Beyond the temptations at home, don't forget to carefully monitor what's going on at their schools. Why? Let me tell you some of the things your children may be reading, even by the age of ten.

One book, *Learning About Sex*, was called "a must for all young people" by Patricia Shiller, founder of the American Association of Sex Educators, Counselors, and Therapists. In it you will find glowing reports of the harmlessness of activities like sex with animals. On the subject of free-love, the book says:

> Some people are now saying that partnerships—married or unmarried—should be exclusive . . . [but] the freedom for both partners to love and share sex with others

should always be present.

The 1984 "health" textbook recommended as "must reading" for grade ten students at Norwin School District in Pittsburgh, described abstinence and self-discipline as "an improper value choice."[18]

These are just samplings of what is out there. So be aware, and be cautious, because the pressures are immense. When fueled by television, inconsistent role modeling by parents, and false education, the next step down is predictable. Look at chapter 5:3 and then 7:5.

For the lips of an adulteress drip honey, and smoother than oil is her speech . . .

. . . that they may keep you from an adulteress, from the foreigner who flatters with her words.

The word "adulteress" literally means "a wayward wife." The context makes it abundantly clear that this woman is married. So we are not talking just about unmarried teenagers having sex in the back seat of the car. This is a married woman fooling around. Her target, it would appear, is a minor, or at the very least, a young single man.

Her approach begins with flattery. She tells him what he wants to hear. "To flatter" means "to praise too much, untruthfully or insincerely, in order to win something." Her words feed on his loneliness, boredom, insecurity and ego. That is usually how it works. Our daughters need to know that a guy will tell them anything they want to hear if he can get them to bed by saying it. And our sons need to know that some gals who will do the same to them.

"You're so beautiful . . . I love you . . . I'll never love anybody like you . . . Your parents are a pain, they don't love you, but I do . . . I'll never leave you, even when I go away to college; you can count on me . . . I need you to help me perform better for the game . . . If you loved me, you would, Suzie . . . "

Or she will say, "You're so handsome . . . what a jock! Oh Stan, you're so studly . . . You must lift weights to have all those muscles."

Turn it up a generation and the line is the same: "You make me feel young again; I feel like a real man . . . my wife/husband doesn't understand me like you do . . . I don't know how I can live without you . . . I can't imagine what would have happened to me if you hadn't come into my life."

You get the idea. And the naive person falls for it, hook, line, and sinker. Verse 7 says: "And I saw among the naive, I discerned among the youths, a young man lacking sense."

A naive person, of whatever age, is simply gullible, easily enticed, and falls for the trap.

The temptation then moves from flattery to false piety. Did you catch her line in verses 13 and 14?

So she seizes him and kisses him, and with a brazen face she says to him: "I was due to offer peace offerings; today I have paid my vows."

What's going on here? Classic rationalization. She's just been to church and taken her "peace offerings." That could mean a couple of things. Primarily it refers to the fact that she made a religious sacrifice at the temple that afternoon and so that covers her for the rest of the day and night. She is also saying that she is ceremonially and religiously clean from her visit to the temple and the time she spent there in confession.

Dragging God into the conspiracy

She is pulling a terrific fast one here. She's got God involved in her immorality. But today people do the same thing. Right after church, a Bible study, or a Sunday school class, we pat ourselves on the back while we mess around morally. We may even double our offering just to be sure we cover our guilt a little better. Still, our behavior doesn't change. Then, just to be real sure, we use God-talk to convince ourselves. We say things like:

"This marriage was never God's will in the first place," or "God's will is for me to be happy; certainly He would not deny me anything that is needed for my happiness." Some say, "How can something that feels so good be wrong?," or "Hey, God made me this way, I have desires that He put inside of me—what can I say?"

Others will wrap their faith around the sin: "God brought us together," or "We're both Christians, we go to church. I'm in the youth group—and besides, we loooooo the each other." Still others use the time-honored ploy of displacing the blame: "Those Christians and their holier-than-thou attitudes! God is my judge, not them."

Rationalization—the name of this game

What do all of these lines have in common? First, we are saying, "I wish that God would allow me to do something." Now we are not completely brain dead, so we know that He won't. But we allow ourselves to do it anyway. Then we claim divine approval. And finally we convince ourselves that God actually recommended and smiled on the action in the first place.

No matter how you slice it, it's rationalization—the mental and verbal technique that lets you to do what you want to do and not feel so bad about it.

That's what Tai Collins, the former Miss Virginia (who was allegedly involved in a relationship with a United States senator and then posed nude for *Playboy*), seems to be doing as she gurgles about the Presbyterian church she recently joined. Her volunteer work there, she says, is "very fulfilling." When asked if her church membership would affect her nude modeling, she replied, "I don't think so. I mean there's a lot of people in my church that have been in *Playboy*."[19]

False piety works as part of the temptation process—as does the promise of full pleasure.

It is likely that the woman Solomon speaks about already knew this guy. Perhaps he was a friend of her husband, a business associate, or even an employee.

She hints at this in verse 15: "Therefore I have come out to meet you. To seek your presence earnestly, and I have found you."

The emphasis of the text is: "I've come to meet you—you and nobody else." Ladies and gentlemen, people are on the prowl, and you are the target.

Nobody's exempt from temptation

I have had women from the church proposition me over the phone. I recall one woman who wrote a detailed and explicit letter to me, recounting her sexual exploits while she was away from the Lord. But thanks to me, she said, that was changing. Then she gave me her phone number, address, and when she would be home alone—and very much available for me.

Look what was on her mind, and on the mind of the woman in Solomon's neighborhood (verse 16):

I have spread my couch with coverings, with colored linens of Egypt. I have sprinkled my bed with myrrh, aloes and cinnamon. Come, let us drink our fill of love until morning; let us delight ourselves with caresses.

She has prepared her bed in an exotic and attractive way. No flannel sheets, hair curlers, or cotton, floral-print nightgowns here. The linens were imported at great expense from Egypt. And spices were also mail-ordered, from India I believe.

Everything points in one direction. Her invitation speaks of complete sexual gratification. This is to be an all-nighter.

And don't think she wouldn't make good on the promise. Don't think this wouldn't be a night to remember. Don't think his pulse wouldn't race and that he wouldn't enjoy himself. He would. This is no half-hearted offer. It has it all.

By the way, when you talk to your kids about sex, don't tell them it's not exciting, or that it is not fun. Don't tell them it's something you endure, or that it's somehow dirty (even if that's your experience, or how you look at it).

That's not the biblical perspective. One of the legitimate purposes for sexual intimacy within the bonds of marriage is pleasure. (We will talk more about that in the next chapter.) So don't give your kids the wrong version. Besides, that is not what is being offered here. And it's not what's offered in your world either.

Take, for example, the case of another embarrassing letter. According to the newspaper, it was only two pages long, but it was full of sexually explicit references. The author was a four-teen-year-old girl. The recipient was a boy one year her senior. His older sister, his guardian, was not amused.

"I'm embarrassed to say what the girl wrote," the sister, a university professor, said. The letter, "talked about all of his attributes. . . . When I discussed it with my brother, he told me that the girls at his school write letters like this to boys all the time."

The article went on to say:

Blame it on rap music, MTV, the disintegration of the family, a lack of parental supervision. Whatever the reasons, experts agree that the incidence of sexually aggressive behavior among teenage girls is increasing. This behavior includes:
  • Phoning boys at all hours with propositions of sex, and leaving suggestive messages on

answering machines.
- Sending explicit letters.
- Trailing boys at malls and sneaking out at
  night to meet them.

A recent Ann Landers column on the subject prompted more than twenty thousand letters. The column included a letter from a mother whose seventeen-year-old son "was disgusted with super-aggressive, sex-crazy girls." Another mother said that she had changed the family's phone number three times "to get rid of the girls who pester the daylights" out of her fifteen- and sixteen-year-old sons.

The saddest part of the column, however, were the conclusions:

> ... The letter writing, phone calling and other types of aggressive behavior result from a lack of affection and attention from many parents who are too busy working and have little time to devote to their children, and because many teens have no adult supervision or no parents laying down the rules.[20]

Aggressive offers of sexual pleasure are out there and they usually come with safeguards, just as in Solomon's case study. According to verse 19, this woman's husband is out of town on business. He won't be back in town for two weeks. There is no way anybody will know—and we won't get caught. Sound familiar?

The bottom line, however, is that the Bible teaches that all sex before marriage or outside of marriage is wrong. Obviously, this woman is a two-timing wife who cheats on her husband without hesitation. In fact, she brings her lovers into the very bed she has shared with her husband. And the guy goes for it. Look at verse 22:

Suddenly he follows her, as an ox goes to the slaughter,
or as one in fetters to the discipline of a fool. . . .

Fools rush in . . .

Sex outside of a marriage relationship may thrill you, but it
will not satisfy over the long term. It may be fun, but it will not
fulfill. It promises intimacy, but delivers loneliness. It may give
momentary ecstasy, but it does not nurture a relationship.
Whether it is a one-night stand or a longer arrangement, it is a
dehumanizing twist that cannot bring joy. God intended sex as
part of a covenant relationship—as part of an exclusive, growing relationship between two partners committed to each other
for life.

Even the secular psychologist, Paul Pearsall, in commenting
on the offer presented in the movie *Indecent Proposal*, states
that "the act [of immorality] would haunt you for life. Intimacy
leaves a lasting imprint. Would it be worth it to have it on your
love map forever?"[21]

No, it would not.

Max Lucado reminds us of the Tempter's snares:

Don't think for one minute that just because you don't
want to fall that you won't. Satan has a special trick for
you, and he only pulls it out when you aren't looking.
He is the master of the trapdoor, and the author of weak
moments.

He waits until your back is turned. He waits until
your defense is down. He waits until the bell has rung
and you are walking back to your corner. Then he aims
his dart at your weakest point and. . .

Bullseye! You lust. You fall. You take a drag. You
buy a drink. You kiss the woman. You follow the crowd.
You rationalize. You say "yes." You sign your name. You

forget who you are. You walk into her room. You look in the window. You break your promise. You buy the magazine.

You deny your Master.

It's David disrobing Bathsheba. It's Adam accepting the fruit from Eve. It's Abraham lying about Sarah. It's Noah, drunk and naked in his tent. It's Lot, in bed with his own daughter. It's your worst nightmare. It's sudden.

It's sin.

Satan numbs our awareness and short-circuits our self-control. We know what we are doing and yet we can't believe that we are doing it. In the fog of weakness we want to stop, but haven't the will to do so. We want to turn around, but our feet won't move. We want to run and, pitifully, we want to stay.

It's the teenager in the backseat. It's the boss touching his secretary's hand. The husband walking into the porn shop. The Christian losing control.

And it's Satan gaining a foothold.

Confusion. Guilt. Rationalization. Despair. It all hits. It hits hard. We numbly pick ourselves up and stagger back into our world.

"Oh God, what have I done?" "Should I tell someone?" "I'll never do it again." "My God, can you forgive me?"

No one who is reading these words is free from the treachery of sudden sin. No one is immune to this trick of perdition. This demon of hell can scale the highest monastery wall, penetrate the deepest faith, and desecrate the purest home.

Some of you know exactly what I mean. You could write these words better than I, couldn't you?[22]

So who or what are we applauding for? Maybe it is about time we stood to our feet, but not for James Worthy and his like. Maybe we ought to remove our hats, bow our heads and thank our God for His wisdom and His plan for purity.

Maybe we ought to thank *Him* with our applause.

CHAPTER FOUR

Tackling Temptation —Again

Proverbs 5–7

IT SEEMS A COUPLE OF PROWLERS broke into a department store in a large city. They entered the store successfully, stayed long enough to do what they came to do, and escaped unnoticed. They took nothing. Absolutely nothing. No merchandise was stolen. No items were removed. But they created havoc, nonetheless.

They simply changed the cost of everything.

Price tags were swapped. Values were exchanged. These clever pranksters took the tag off a $395.00 camera and stuck it on a $5.00 box of stationery. The $5.95 sticker on a paperback book was removed and placed on an outboard motor. They re-priced everything in the store!

Crazy? You bet. But the craziest part of this story took place the next morning. The store opened as usual. Employees went to work. Customers began to shop. The place functioned as normal for four hours before anyone noticed what had happened. Four hours! Some people got some great bargains. Others got fleeced. But for four solid hours no one noticed that all the values had been swapped.[1]

The swapping of America's values

Hard to believe? It shouldn't be—we see the same thing happening every day. We are deluged by a distorted value system. We see the most valuable things in our lives peddled for pennies. And we see the cheapest smut go for millions.

Allan Bloom, in his best-selling treatise, *The Closing of the American Mind*, critically evaluates higher education in our country and makes this alarming statement:

> ... The most important and most astonishing phenomenon of our time, all the more astonishing in being almost unnoticed: there is now an entirely new language of good and evil, originating in an attempt to get beyond "good and evil" and preventing us from talking with any conviction about good and evil anymore.[2]

Christina Sommers is a professor at Clark University. She is co-editor of a book entitled *Virtue and Vice of Everyday Life*. She says that today we have a lack of common moral sense. The feedback she gets on examination papers is that students believe that there is no right or wrong—simply arguments, good and bad.[3]

That seems to be particularly the situation when we enter the arena of sexual behavior. A recent study, for example, reports that more single women are having sex today than ever before. In 1987, the percentage of single women having sex stood at 76 percent.[4] If I may borrow again from the pen of Allan Bloom, I think he explains as well as anyone why this is happening:

> The students of whom I am speaking are aware of all the

sexual alternatives, and have been from very early on in their lives, and they feel that all sexual acts which do not involve real harm to others are [permissible]. They do not think they should feel guilt or shame about sex. . . . They have lived in a world where the most explicit discussions and depictions of sex are all around them. They have had little fear of venereal disease. Birth-control devices and ready abortion have been available to them since puberty. For the great majority, sexual intercourse was a normal part of their lives prior to college, and there was no fear of social stigma or even much parental opposition. . . . There is no special value placed on virginity in oneself or in one's partners."[5]

A moral wasteland

A poll conducted by Louis Harris and Associates indicates that more than half of all American teenagers are sexually active by the age of seventeen. The poll, conducted for the Planned Parenthood Federation of America, also found that one-third of teenagers have never discussed sex with their parents. "Almost three out of every ten teens, aged 12 to 17, say they have had sexual intercourse," said Humphrey Taylor, president of the Harris polling organization. . . . The proportion increases with age, from 4 percent of twelve-year-olds and 10 percent of thirteen-year-olds, to 46 percent of sixteen-year-olds and 57 percent of seventeen-year-olds."[6]

According to experts at the University of California at Berkeley, young adults today have a sense that they alone call the shots on their sexual behavior. They say that social pressure is the primary reason they do not wait until they are older to engage in sexual activity. Both boys and girls say they are pressured by their peers. But more than that, in many homes, teenagers believe they have evidence of hypocrisy in the behavior of their adult role models. One girl said, "My mom has a date Friday night, and [then] he's in the kitchen eating breakfast Saturday morning. How can she preach about premarital sex?"[7]

The plot thickens

Pornography, a five-million-dollar-a-year enterprise twenty-five years ago, has boomed to a seven- to ten-billion-dollar-a-year industry today. And what is most disturbing is that young people are consuming pornography in greater numbers than ever before. A recent study in Ontario, Canada, demonstrated that young people between twelve and seventeen had the highest interest in pornographic materials, and were its prime purchasers.

Another study was conducted of one hundred males and one hundred females in each of three age categories: junior high, high school, and adult aged nineteen to thirty-nine. It found that 91 percent of males and 82 percent of females had seen a magazine that depicted couples or groups engaged in explicit sexual acts. The average age for first viewing such materials was thirteen-and-a-half. Furthermore, a larger percentage of high school students had seen X-rated films than any other age group, including adults. Forty-six percent of junior high students had seen one or more X-rated movies; and the average age for first seeing such a film for these students was fourteen years and eight months.[8]

I received a letter from a young man who had listened to one of my messages. His letter was a response to what I said and in part, this is what he wrote:

Being a senior and having been in public education all my life, I was able to directly relate to you on many of the topics you discussed. . . . I have watched abstinence shot down time and time again, coupled with the push of the "safe sex" façade. Oh, and let me tell you—safe sex education works great! Thanks to that [thinking], it is impossible (and I am not exaggerating) for me to walk down the hall and not see either a girl who's pregnant or a handful of unwed mothers. There are entire classes . . . for pregnant girls. I can think of two girls right now who are eighteen years or under and on their second child.

When you talked about freshman/sophomore girls who slept with senior guys to break into the "in" crowd, I could have given you a list of names that popped into my head at that moment.

Are Christians that different?

What is more distressing, is that despite the fact that the Bible is crystal clear in its teaching that God's gift of sexual intimacy is strictly reserved for a monogamous, heterosexual marriage relationship, the behavior of some Christians makes such standards laughable.

In case you are not aware of the biblical standard, consider these two New Testament verses:

But do not let immorality [the Greek word is *porneia*] or any impurity or greed even be named among you, as is proper among saints. (Ephesians 5:3)

For this is the will of God, your sanctification; that is, that you *abstain* [emphasis mine] from sexual immorality [the Greek word again is *porneia*]. (1 Thessalonians 4:3)

Now let me tell you what that word "porneia" means. It describes any non-marital sexual behavior, including homosexuality, pedophilia, prostitution and premarital sex. The Bible says very clearly that God's will for the believer in Jesus Christ is not to be involved in those kinds of sexual activities. That's God's absolute standard.

Yet a recent Roper poll conducted about illicit sex gathered some startling responses from Christians. Two percent of those surveyed said they were involved in such activities prior to coming to Christ. But 5 percent had been involved after embracing Christ. Furthermore, according to George Gallup, 70 percent of Americans believe it is important to do what the Bible teaches, but two-thirds of that same group reject moral absolutes. In fact, 53 percent of those who claim to be Bible-believing, conservative Christians say that there is no such thing as absolute truth.[9]

Our primary challenge as Christians, it seems to me, is not to raise the moral level of the non-Christian world. Rather, our first duty is to make the church better.

To do that, we must face courageously the subject of sexuality and temptation. God-given desires or urges are never wrong. But rejecting His source of satisfaction and pursuing a substitute is always sinful and self-destructive. As Rudyard Kipling has said, "The sins that they did two by two, they pay for one by one."

There are always consequences to sinful behavior. Consider Solomon's perspective on this in chapter 6, beginning at verse 27:

Can a man take fire in his bosom, and his clothes not be burned? Or can a man walk on hot coals and his feet not be scorched? So is the one who goes in to his neighbor's wife; whoever touches her will not go unpunished.

Solomon asks two rhetorical questions, using similar word pictures to underline the unavoidable pain that accompanies sex outside of marriage. His illustrations are obvious and to the point: If you play with fire you will get burned. Going to bed with someone outside of marriage is dangerous. The temporary satisfaction might soon destroy you with consuming fire. The standard rationale, "It's okay as long as it doesn't hurt anyone" sounds great. But it simply does not work very well when it comes to illicit sex. The fact of the matter is, someone is always hurt.[10]

One of the awful things about burn victims is that their scars are among the most obvious and painful. Even the most elaborate plastic surgery is no match for the searing results of flames. So it is with sexual sin—even though we may not realize it, because the searing starts inside, before it shows up on the outside.

You see, hidden sins—the sins others know nothing about—will mark you, because they lead to a deterioration of your character. For example, I may give assent to the doctrines of the church. I may even teach them. I may not be committing any outward sins—those others see easily. But if I am inwardly a sensualist and one practicing immorality in the closet, then my character will begin to shrink. And it is the hidden sins of God's people that destroy so many and bring defeat and discouragement to the church.

It is not an easy roller-coaster to get off. Max Lucado, in vivid terms, describes what happens to many:

> Should a man see only pleasure, he becomes a carnival thrill-seeker, alive only in bright lights, wild rides, and titillating entertainment. With lustful fever he races from ride to ride, satisfying his insatiable passion for sensations only long enough to look for another. Ferris wheels of romance. Haunted houses of eroticism. . . . Long after the crowd is gone he can still be found on the carnival grounds rummaging through empty boxes of popcorn and sticky cones that held the cotton candy. He is driven by passion, willing to sell his soul if need be for one more rush, one more race of the pulse. . . . [11]

The high costs of sin

It is that path of self-destruction that Solomon is worried about. Involvement in non-marital sexual intimacy has devastating consequences, both in the immediate and long-term calendars of our lives. Consider the financial ramifications for a moment. Proverbs 6:26 says that a prostitute reduces you to a loaf of bread, and the adulteress preys upon your very life. Proverbs 5:8–10 paints the warning in vivid colors:

> Keep your way far from her, and do not go near the door of her house, lest you give your vigor to others, and your years to the cruel one; lest strangers be filled with your strength and your hard-earned goods go to the house of an alien. . . .

Now remember, in these chapters, Solomon is warning about illicit sex. To bolster his arguments, he details some of the consequences. He does that primarily by using language that portrays the consequences to the man. But don't get snagged on that. The consequences affect both participants, male and female.

Solomon's point is that sexual sin, whether premarital sex or adultery, has a high financial price tag. Everything you have saved and worked for can go down the drain.

TIME magazine points out that teenage mothers are "many times as likely as other women with young children to live below the poverty line. Only half of those who give birth before age eighteen complete high school. On average, they earn half as much money and are far more likely to be dependent on welfare."[12]

It is reported that 94 percent of marriages that suffer adultery end in divorce. And a study in 1989 determined that during the first few years after a divorce, women who do not remarry experience a 30 percent decline in their standard of living. It takes years for them to recover financially.[13]

Alimony payments, child-support checks, tuition costs for two sets of kids—the list is endless. If the sexual behavior does not lead to divorce, there may be the incredible cost of feeding your sexual habit or paying a therapist $100-150 an hour to try to wrestle it to the ground.

When sexual activity occurs prior to marriage, the financial cost may appear minimal. But if a pregnancy results, there will be innumerable costs to deal with: costs of raising an unplanned-for child could shatter educational and career goals. At the very least, they'd go on hold. More often, they are completely lost as those involved settle for a solution that sabatoges their life goals. With a premarital pregnancy, the financial costs add up for a much longer period of time.

Beyond the financial consequences, there are deep personal and emotional results that stab at the heart and mind. One of the dominant emotions is never-ending guilt.

Look at 5:12: "And you say, 'How I have hated instruction! And my heart spurned reproof! And I have not listened to the voice of my teachers, nor inclined my ear to my instructors?' "

The moment the act of immorality has taken place, guilt steps to our side. Sometimes we can't believe that we did it, or that we didn't heed the warnings. But it's too late. The guilt has already checked in at the front desk and settled into the room of our heart.

Someone has suggested that "guilt is an uncomfortable feeling. It is a mixture of many emotions and thoughts that destroy inner peace."[14]

Guilt is also an expression of our disappointment in ourselves. We are anguished by our personal failure, realizing that we are not as good as we should be. According to a 1990 report in *TIME* magazine, 51 percent of women under the age of thirty-five regretted having a premarital sexual encounter.[15]

Dealing with the fallout

The vast majority of marital counseling that our church staff and I deal with has to do with the consequences of infidelity. In fact, eight out of our last nine cases focused on adultery.

But it is also significant that this guilt plagues common-law relationships. In fact, women in common-law relationships are 80 percent more likely to separate or divorce than women who had not lived with their spouses before marriage. In the first two years of marriage, women who had lived with their husbands before marriage split from them at a rate three times greater than women who had not lived with their mates before marriage.[16]

Why? They couldn't deal with the guilt, the regret.

The impact should be obvious on the coed who sleeps with her lover in the hope that sex would bind them together and lead them to marriage. A few months later, she wakes up disillusioned when he exits, stage right, for somebody else. Her dreams are shattered, and she suffers an emotional trauma from which it is most difficult to recover.

An article in *Psychology Today* speaks to this problem. Commenting on adultery, the author says:

> Romantic affairs lead to a great many divorces, suicides, homicides, heart attacks and strokes, but not to very many successful remarriages. No matter how many sacrifices you make to keep the love alive, no matter how many sacrifices your family and children make for this . . . relationship, it will gradually burn itself out when there is nothing more to sacrifice to it. Then you must face not only the wreckage of several lives, but the original depression from which the affair was an insane flight into escape.[17]

Is it any wonder that God has forbidden premarital or extramarital sex some thirty-eight times in His Word?

Connected to all of this is another emotional impact that results from immorality:

> For the lips of an adulteress drip honey, and smoother than oil is her speech; but in the end she is bitter as

wormwood, sharp as a double-edged sword (Proverbs 5:3, 4).

The lasting bitterness of immorality

Proverbs does not allow us to forget that there is an "afterward" to sexual immorality. Specifically, Solomon draws attention to "bitterness." To involve yourself in illicit sex is to be poisoned at some point with bitterness. The specific word that Solomon mentions, in other contexts, is descriptive of anger or temper. The two usually walk together. And although you may not spot it right away, one of the consequences of premarital sex is anger and resentment toward your partner.

That is certainly true if you break up, but it is also true even if you get married. Five years, ten years down the road, your marriage will often be rocked by conflict whose source you can't seem to identify. But you will often discover it goes right back to the premarital encounter.

I run across this often. Couples come to me who have been married five, ten, fifteen years and sometimes longer. They are struggling with a variety of problems, but one does not seem to be the major culprit. I have come to the point where one of my first questions is: "Did you sleep with one another before marriage?" The majority of those struggling couples answer in the affirmative.

The same is true of adultery. It raises tremendous levels of anger in the marriage. Sometimes the encounter leaves the offending partner with a rising resentment at his wife or husband, whom they often blame for their seeking illicit sex. On the flip side, the offended partner feels anger because he or she feels violated, used, deceived. And that anger remains for a long time. It is amazing how many men do not understand the anger their spouse experiences because of their betrayal.

Dr. Frank Pittmann, author and therapist, comments after thirty years of practice:

However utopian the theories, the reality is that infidelity . . . will blow . . . out a marriage. In 30-odd years of practice, I have encountered only a handful of established first marriages that ended in divorce without someone being unfaithful. I have cleaned up from more affairs than a squad of motel chambermaids. Infidelity is a very messy hobby. It is not an effective way to find a new mate or a new life. It is not a safe treatment for depression, boredom, or imperfect marriage. . . . And it certainly does not impress the rest of us. It does not work for women any better than it does for men.[18]

The last straw

And that brings me to the last and most obvious consequence of immorality: the physical results. Proverbs 5:11 is short and to the point:

And you groan at your latter end, when your flesh and your body are consumed.

The verb translated "groan" describes a person who is suffering. The word itself conveys an animal-like cry of anguish. Add that thought to the verb "consume," and the picture is complete. The word means literally "to waste away, to lose vital strength."

Solomon is talking now about the physical disease consequences of illicit sexual behavior. Sexually transmitted diseases (STDs) are a major health problem in our country. STDs strike an estimated twenty million people each year, or an average of one person every 1.5 seconds. They cause serious physical damage to more teenagers than do all other communicable diseases combined. An estimated 2.5 million teenagers are infected each year, and nearly half the total number of infected persons are under the age of twenty-five.[19]

A nationwide study showed one in five Americans are infected with a sexually transmitted viral disease. According to Cleveland's Health Department, the number of syphilis cases nearly doubled in 1992 in that area. And let's not forget AIDS. The number of people infected with AIDS has increased dramatically in Cleveland and throughout Ohio. Some fifteen hundred people in that state alone died of AIDS-related illness between 1989 and 1991. Dozens more died of syphilis and hepatitis B.[20]

Furthermore, 20 percent of those who contract an STD end up unable to have children due to infertility.[21]

Psychologist Susan Kegeles of the Center for AIDS Prevention Studies at the University of California, San Francisco, interviewed more than two hundred sexually active fourteen-to-nineteen-year-olds. She says the result are disquieting. Teenagers just don't believe that they could ever get a disease such as AIDS.

"They look around and say, 'Nobody my age has AIDS, so I must be okay."

But, Kegeles continues, "Adolescent heterosexuals need to know it's not just gay men who get AIDS, and nearly everybody who dies of AIDS in their twenties contracted it in their teens."[22]

What research indicates more and more is that AIDS is increasingly being spread by heterosexual activity. An article in *TIME* magazine warned: "Anyone engaging in sex with a new partner or with a long-term partner whose sexual history is unknown is *at risk* [italics mine]."[23]

Two principles to live by

What do we do as adults, as parents, and as young adults? Let me suggest two very basic principles.

Principle one is: *Be committed to a posture of courage that is able to say "no."*

Follow Solomon's counsel, beginning in Proverbs 5:7.

Now then, my sons, listen to me, and do not depart from the words of my mouth. Keep your way far from her, and do not go near the door of her house. . . .

Do not desire her beauty in your heart, nor let her catch you with her eyelids (6:25).

Now therefore, my sons, listen to me, and pay attention to the words of my mouth. Do not let your heart turn aside to her ways, do not stray into her paths. (7:24, 25)

The need for sexual discipline—the need to say "no" to offers of sexual intimacy outside of marriage—is the dominant theme of these chapters. Solomon is saying that if you suspect that you might be vulnerable to a particular sin, then take active steps to avoid it.

Most of us know what it is to be stirred sexually by someone of the opposite sex. If we are normal, it is inevitable that we shall be from time to time. There is nothing wrong with being tempted. Temptation becomes sin when we give way to it, when we nurture it, when we dwell on the thought and fantasize about it.

Solomon is not talking about avoiding all temptation. But he is talking about actively fighting it off, instead of encouraging it. Dr. Scott Peck, in his book, *People of the Lie*, puts it this way:

Evil is revolting because it is dangerous. It will contaminate or otherwise destroy a person who remains too long in its presence. Unless you know very well what you are doing, the best thing you can do when faced with evil is to run the other way.[24]

When it comes to temptation, we sometimes expect God to do something He has not promised to do. We must avoid walking into the jaws of a particular temptation and then shouting, "Lord, do something!" If we do that, we will find ourselves asking God to deliver us from a temptation that we have refused to walk away from ourselves.

In terms of applying Solomon's advice of "keeping our way far" from sexual temptation, that may mean changing your job, canceling a subscription, or breaking away from a particular group of friends.

In terms of your kids, you can do three things to help them courageously say "No!"

Discourage formal dating until they are at least sixteen. If they aren't allowed to drive until they are that age, why should you let them drive around with somebody else who is older?

Then, at age sixteen, allow only double-dates, or dates that involve a group of kids. Set a curfew—and insist on it.

You say, "Sounds like you don't trust them."

That's not true. Trust has nothing to do with this. I'm talking temptation. Put yourself in a car with someone other than your spouse who is coming on to you sexually, and how would *you* do?

Furthermore, talk to the parents of your teenager's date. See where their value system lies. If they don't have a strong set of moral values, their kids generally won't either.

The "key" to your child's purity

Dr. James Dobson suggests having a "key" talk with your kids. This is a personal, private time for a father and son (or mother and daughter) to talk again about how conception occurs, the biblical view of sex and marriage, and purity. Encourage questions and give frank answers.

An important part of this special occasion is for the parents to present a "key" ring to their teenager, who will wear it as a symbol of the key to his or her heart. It's a reminder of a covenant with God to remain pure.

Then on his or her wedding night, the ring is presented to their new spouse. This "key" talk should take place when a son or daughter begins to be interested in the opposite sex.[25]

In our ministry to sixth grade girls at our church we have recently done this. A letter is sent out to each mother of a girl, giving them the schedule of topics that will be discussed related to sexuality. For one evening, when the discussion deals with how to treat the opposite sex, we include this description:

"We will be encouraging the girls to discuss with you the topics we cover each evening. As we finish this unit, we will encourage each girl to make a pledge to the Lord of purity until marriage. We will present those who do with a special reminder of this pledge (a key necklace pendant) that they can wear to help them get through those tempting moments as they grow older."

Some programs of sex education in schools emphasize abstinence. You ought to encourage this kind of program in your school. One such program is called RSVP, or Responsible Social Values Program. Within the program is an Abstinence Contract your teenager has the opportunity to sign. It says this:

I _____, agree to remain abstinent in order to help achieve my goals and increase my chances of success. In order to remain abstinent, I realize I must resist peer pressure and practice positive means of solving my problems. I must remember to ask for help when I need it and to always think about how important my future is to me. Finally, I realize that I am the only person who can fulfill this contract. I must make the decision myself to remain abstinent. I will be the person, also, who profits most from this decision.

Signed _____   Date_____

Then at the bottom is a place for a witness to sign his/her

name to this statement:

> I _____, agree to help _____
> remain abstinent by offering my support and friendship.
> I will help by being available to talk, to remind of goals
> and to suggest seeking further help when needed.[26]

The witness is usually a friend. My oldest son, Jeremy, after being presented with this contract in school, brought it to my attention. I already knew about it since I had introduced the program to the school, but I listened. When he came to the place where a friend was to sign as witness, I suggested a couple of his buddies. But he didn't want them to sign it. Instead he turned to me and said words I hope I'll never forget.

"Dad, if you don't mind, I'd like you to sign and be my witness."

I did, with tears in my eyes. And that contract sits today in the top right-hand drawer of my office desk. Both Jeremy and I know exactly where it is.

Do you remember the senior whose letter I mentioned earlier? He added a couple more lines later in his letter that you would find encouraging:

"Contrary to what I've been taught in school, I know that abstinence is not unrealistic, and that abstinence until marriage, and then monogamy, is the only correct way. Anything else is wrong and self-destructive."

A checklist for caring parents

By the way, you can't expect sexual purity of your kids if you are not modeling it yourself. So let me ask you some questions:

1. Are you flirting with lust or fighting it off? Do you encourage sexual come-ons? Do you kind of get a thrill out of that?

2. Have you worked out a scheme that allows lust to maintain a foot in the door of your life?

3. Is there some secret sin you are hiding? Someone you're meeting with on the sly? Magazines? Video cassettes? Hotel pay-for-view movies?

If these are problem areas for you, deal with these issues now! Find someone you can trust who will help you, and don't wait until next week.

So that wraps up Principle one—Develop the courage to say "No!"

Principle two: *Nurture a high view of marriage and sexual intimacy within marriage.* Look at Proverbs 5:15–19:

Drink water from your own cistern, and fresh water from your own well. Should your springs be dispersed abroad, streams of water in the streets? Let them be yours alone, and not for strangers with you. Let your fountain be blessed, and rejoice with the wife of your youth. As a loving hind and a graceful doe, let her breasts satisfy you at all times; be exhilarated always with her love.

Make your marriage the best it can be

These verses describe the wholesome, pure alternative to sexual immorality. The emphasis is on faithfulness to your marriage partner. Cisterns and wells were prized possessions in a climate where rainfall was scarce. The techniques of drilling deep wells had not yet been invented. So the cistern collected valuable rain water, and could also store the overflow from a well.

Our marriage relationship is to have the same kind of value to us. There is probably no other person in the world we need to trust so much as the person we marry. And nothing creates trust like knowing that the other person is unconditionally committed to us. It takes a personal commitment to create trust, a commitment renewed every single day.

One man put it this way:

A lifetime commitment is about not having exit routes along the way, just in case things don't work out the way we had expected. For instance, a lifetime commitment would never sound like this: "I'll stay with you unless you get stomach cancer." Or, "I'll be with you as long as you remain thin." Or, "I'll stick with you until somebody better comes along." A lifetime commitment doesn't have escape clauses in the fine print. So lifetime commitments are simply commitments we intend to keep, no matter what.[27]

The high value of commitment

Your kids have got to know about that commitment. Talk to them about your marriage, your vows, your renewed love for your spouse. Let them know how important this marriage is to you. You see, one of the greatest fears children and young adults have is that their parents will split up just like everybody else's. Relieve that fear. Cement your commitment. I tell my sons over and over again that I will never leave their mother. Patricia and I are categorically opposed to divorce. We don't believe in divorce. (Murder we believe in, but not divorce.) Our kids know that.

A number of years ago, Cecil Fielder, the reigning home run king in professional baseball, was playing for the Toronto Blue Jays. But he wasn't performing well enough for them, so they let him go. He ended up playing baseball in Japan for a year until the Detroit Tigers picked him up. In his first year back, he promptly led the league in home runs. That was about four years ago.

Jeremy said to me one day: "Dad, how could Toronto let him go? I don't get it. What happened to Cecil? What made the difference? Did he get married or something?"

As far as my son was concerned, the only explanation for the home run turnaround by Cecil was the fact that he must have been recently married. My sons are getting the message that marriage is a great part of our lives, because Patricia and I are committed to it.

And part of the commitment will involve delighting in sexual intimacy within your marriage. Did the language of verse 19 catch you off guard? Did it make you blush? Why? It is incredibly important to see sexual delight in marriage as something God has given. The fact is that the Hebrew word for "love" at the end of verse 19 refers to love-making, or sexual intimacy.

Unfortunately, the Bible is often thought to take a rather dim view of sexual intimacy. In fact, some believe the Bible merely tolerates it as nothing more than a necessary evil or as a means of reproduction. But that is a distortion that tells us more about the sexual hang-ups of some of us than about what the Bible actually says on the subject.

God's blessing on sexual intimacy

Here we have a passage that speaks enthusiastically about the joys and delights of sexual relations between husband and wife. Enjoyment, not reproduction, is its theme. The verb "exhilarate" in verse 19 literally means "to swerve or meander." It was used to describe someone who was drunk, but in this case, he is intoxicated with love for his wife.

God does not intend faithfulness in marriage to be boring, lifeless, pleasureless, or dull. Sex is a gift God gives to married people for their mutual pleasure. Real happiness comes when we determine to find pleasure in the relationship God has given us, or will give us, in marriage—and then to commit ourselves to making it pleasurable for our spouse.

Translated into practical terms, that may mean trading in your flannel pajamas with the little bunny feet for something from Victoria's Secret. It could mean, men, that you shower and shave a little more, and quit spending your day off with that Neanderthal; bed-head look. It might mean being creative in your approach to intimacy, and not being satisfied with the same old let's-get-it-over-with approach.

Try talking about your sexual needs—and your partner's needs.

Talk about technique, approach, variety, frequency—and agree to grow in this area.

But don't start searching the Bible for the answers here. There aren't any. I know some people want a verse that says they can avoid sexual intimacy except for once a year, but you simply won't find specifics in Scripture. You'll need to address those on your own as a couple.

Many couples fail to establish a meaningful and open dialogue regarding each partner's sexual appetites. Instead of talking about problems as they occur (and they inevitably do in marriage), one or both partners ignore the difficulty. They use a variety of rationalizations like: "Sex is not the most important part of our relationship," or "Problems can be ignored without a lot of risk." Your favorite might be: "Maybe I am the only one who thinks there is a problem," or "When the kids get older, our sexual problems will work themselves out." Not wise.

Married Christians can cause pure sex to catch fire and build a wall of protection around their marriage. That is what Solomon is referring to. In terms of your kids, this also must be discussed as you help them prepare for marriage. Don't let them think that sex in marriage is dirty and boring and routine. If that's the way it is in your marriage, you need to see a counselor or pick up some of the many good Christian books on the subject. But don't ignore it or deny the problem.

By the way, as your kids hit their teen years, they have a

built-in radar screen. They will know how you view your sexuality even if you say nothing. In fact, by saying nothing you will communicate volumes. So model a positive view of marriage and sexuality before them.

Six guidelines for men

In specific terms of modeling for your kids, let me suggest to men that you follow these guidelines and talk to your teenagers about them and why you are doing them:

1. Whenever you need to meet or dine or travel with an unrelated woman, make it a threesome. Don't drive alone in a car with a woman other than your wife.

2. Be very careful about touching. While I may shake hands or squeeze an arm or shoulder in greeting, I embrace only dear friends or relatives—and only in front of others. Side hugs are the best. I would rather be considered cold and uncaring than have any other description attached.

3. If you compliment a woman, compliment her on her clothes or hairstyle, not on other physical characteristics. You will send the wrong message.

4. Avoid flirtation or suggestive conversation, even in jest.

5. Remind your wife, both verbally and in writing, of your commitment to her for your lifetime.

6. Spend as much time as you can with your family and your wife. Nurture romance. Date your wife. And tell your kids that's what you're up to. Let them know that you and Mom are going out on a date—and you don't have a curfew.

Adding romance to marriage

Three years ago, my wife and I celebrated our seventeenth wedding anniversary. We had dated off and on for five years before marriage, so we've been hanging around each other for nearly twenty-three years. As it turned out, I was scheduled to speak at a Bible conference in Ontario, Canada, and it wrapped up the day before our anniversary.

So, five months in advance, my boys and I got our heads together and planned a surprise anniversary weekend for Patricia.

I called up to Toronto and got the two best tickets I could find for the "Phantom of the Opera" at the Pantages Theater in downtown Toronto. (They were in the eighth row, left center section as I recall. The boys thought I could have done better, but. . . .) Then I booked a room with a view of Lake Ontario in the finest hotel I knew of. I even checked with an old friend who works in the city to be sure I was on the right track. I confess, I had a 50 percent discount coupon, but the thought was right. Then the guys and I arranged for them to be kept by grandparents and friends up at the Bible conference. And we kept it all a big secret. Patricia never knew. My boys loved the idea of keeping everything a surprise. And they did. Nobody let the cat out of the bag!

Patricia and I had a wonderful, romantic time, and our sons watched a model of committed marital love that they will never forget. I suspect they'll do the same someday, unless Cecil Fielder is still playing for the Tigers. Then maybe it will be tickets for the Blue Jays and Tigers, not the "Phantom." But that's okay. They'll get it right someday.

But then again, who wouldn't go for Blue Jays–Tigers tickets? . . . just kidding!

Principles of Priority

Proverbs 3:1–12

IN HIS WONDERFUL BOOK, *Bus 9 to Paradise*, Leo Buscaglia
goes out of his way to describe for us one of life's most
frustrating and emotionally painful experiences. It ranks up
there with trips to the orthodontist and screeching nails on
chalkboards. See if you agree:

> I must confess that there are certain occurrences in my
> house that defy any rational explanation. For instance,
> one of the great and perpetual mysteries is where my
> socks disappear. I can't seem to keep a matching pair. . . .
> After the first wash, some of them simply vanish.
> [But] they never go in pairs . . . .The annoying thing
> is that I am left with one green sock, one blue, and one
> black. I have accumulated a huge pile which I dare not
> throw out lest a matching sock reappear as mysteriously
> as it disappeared. So far this hasn't happened. . . .
> I have found that the sock problem has reached epi-

demic proportions all over the United States. . . Friends and family, men and women alike, from all over the country have offered comfort and helpful suggestions. There were the practical people who suggested that I simply pin, staple or use string to keep socks together . . . An artist suggested that being fearful of mixing colors is a cultural hangup. She encouraged me to wear mis-matched socks fearlessly. "The more outrageous the color combination the better," she said, "like flowers in a garden."

A less daring person solved the problem by purchasing all his socks in the same color. . . . A scientist assures me that it has been scientifically proven that socks disappear and coat hangers keep [multiplying] because socks are the larvae of coat hangers.

A believer in reincarnation offered that those of us who have a sock problem are paying for some heinous crime we committed in some previous life. . . . even . . . [a] cartoonist expressed his puzzlement about missing socks. In his cartoon, his pathetic figure gets down to his last pair of socks, when his washing machine sends him a message which reads "Quit trifling with the laws of nature and bring the machine more socks!"[1]

Family life and the laws of nature

There are many moments in our lives as parents when the same kinds of frustrations seem to mock us. We scratch our heads looking for the missing pieces of our family system. We wonder why it seems that if we have done everything right, there are still shrinking returns. You put everything into the family machinery in the correct order and still it seems to come out wrong.

And as our frustration grows you can almost hear the mocking laughter through the walls of your home: "Don't trifle with the laws of nature." In other words, there is nothing more we can do. We've tried everything we can think of, so what is the use. Give it up!

Some of us have. We've given up on the families we are already a part of. We may have decided to retreat into the protective walls of our own little world and let the rest of them do what they want. Or, we have bailed out on the whole deal, and in some measure attempted to start over with another family.

Still others of us have determined that, from what we know of family life, it is obviously not worth the hassle, any more than tracking down prodigal socks. So we are not into family at all.

Oh, we may go as far as to get married, but have no kids. We want the washer and dryer, if you will, but we don't want to have to deal with the problem of the socks. We don't want to endure any more injections of pain. I suppose that is one of the things that I wish I could communicate better.

Sometimes I don't think we realize the pain that children can bring to their parents, regardless of how old we children are. At the same time, I guess we parents have forgotten how much joy our kids bring with them. Do you think it's because the pain out-shouts the joy?

Not too long ago, the *Wall Street Journal* printed an article entitled, "The Shattered Middle Class." The author attempted to explain the frustrations of parenting in this era, and makes a revealing statement that helps, in part at least, to explain some of our dilemma:

> There is no longer one set of values that broadly fits the bulk of the middle class. . . .[In our] neighborhoods, there is a vanishing sense of community; among families, parents find fewer agreed-on guideposts for raising their children." [2]

As I survey the battlefield of what we call the family, and as

I attempt to walk past the mines along the way, I find the problem is not so much the lack of guideposts or values as it is our confusion over which ones should be a priority. In addition, some of us, having determined the guideposts, are still unwilling to hold to them when the frustrations mount.

Lou Holtz is a familiar name in college football, having coached at Notre Dame for some time. Several years ago he contributed a letter to *TIME* magazine that caught my eye. I'd like to share it with you. Listen to this rough, tough, football-coaching giant:

> The basis of any society is the strength of the family. This is true in 1989 and, for sure, it will hold true in the year 2089. As I write this, I am thinking that you will look back at our generation and refer to our times as the "dark ages," since the strength of a society is not found in the comforts of living but in its values, morals and concern for its fellow man. And I believe that these principles are predominantly developed in the family. The family is where our healthy values are formed and shaped. I know of no greater challenge or more important role in life than preparing our children to take their place in society as contributing citizens. I [also] believe that these qualities can best be nurtured in the church of your choice. . . . If trust, commitment and love lie within your generation, you will know that our family values were strong. [3]

Ageless truths

Centuries before Lou Holtz, Solomon talked and wrote about the family and the values that ought to be a priority. In fact, without knowing it, Coach Holtz mentioned some of the same values Solomon found essential to strong families. In mentioning them, the wisest King of Israel was not attempting to be exclusive or narrow. He was trying to remind us that certain priorities must be addressed in our homes if we wish to reduce the intensity of our frustrations.

Some of the things he talks about seem to have a rather tarnished image today. We have "moved beyond them." But in doing so, we've missed some things. That's why we need to go back and take another look and see what we missed.

Now remember the thread that runs through all that Solomon has to say: "Values are taught best at home." You will hear that again in the opening lines of chapter 3. Look at them with me.

"My son, do not forget my teaching, but let your heart keep my commandments; for length of days and years of life, and peace they will add to you."

With the words "teaching" and "commandments," Solomon is again emphasizing the role of parents to instruct and model at home. And what is crucial is that the word "teaching" refers almost exclusively to moral and spiritual instruction geared to the individual child.

Tailor-made values instruction

Stop for a moment and think that through. It is important to identify values that you as a "family team" will teach and model. But it is just as important to realize that teaching those values will need to be tailored to each individual in the family. In some families, even though the priority is the same, you will have to tailor your instruction to each child. Some children require little explanation. They get it right away with very little struggle. Other kids require detailed explanations before they buy in. Still others like to fight you on it, whether the explanation is general or detailed.

The point is, every child's learning process is different, and your approach will need to keep that in mind.

Our two sons are as different as night and day. Or, to hark back to the opening illustration, I think we have a blue sock and a white sock living in our washing machine. Our oldest, Jeremy, hears everything you say the first time. You don't need to go over it more than once. The only problem is that his memory is a little weak, so that about forty-five seconds later, or so it seems, we need to begin a refresher course.

Kent, our youngest, is on the opposite page. With him, details are next to godliness. So we go over and over and over each step. But once we've done that, he will remember it—and be able to give it back to you with even more details thirty-seven years from now. The way we teach values to these guys must keep in view that the same approach for both will not work.

That's the first thing to remember about your values teaching.

Teaching and "throwing"

But there is something else hidden in this word "teaching." Remember the Hebrew term *torah*? That's the word translated here as "teaching." It comes from a verb that means "to throw." That's important.

Think of it this way. I have been a Little League coach for eight years. And the ritual of springtime includes Little League tryouts. This year was no exception. On a windy, cool Saturday afternoon, all the coaches gathered at the assigned baseball diamond to watch seventy-five nervous ten-year-olds try out. Now a tryout is not designed to keep a kid out of Little League. Everybody who signs up plays.

It is designed to help the coaches assess their skill levels so that on the draft night, we can pick players with some idea of how they will do. At the tryouts, we basically look at three things: batting, catching, and throwing.

The first thing we look at is their catching. One of the coaches stands between the pitcher's mound and second base and throws the ball to a player at home plate. He throws the player some pop flys and some ground balls. The key is that his throwing has to be on target if the kid is going to have a chance at fielding the ball. If you throw that thing out past third base you have no way of determining the player's ability to catch. The same is true when the player is batting. You have to "throw" him a ball he can hit, near the strike zone.

The principle also works for you at home as a parent. For your children to field a value system, you have to be prepared to throw some values their way. They can't be off-the-wall kinds of things. They've got to be on target.

Show, don't tell

Furthermore, as a Little League coach, I've got to be able to model what I'm trying to coach. If I'm going to teach a young player how to throw the ball, I can talk to him all day about how important it is to throw accurately and with some speed. I can tell him how vital it is to have a good swing at the ball and to keep his eye on the ball as it comes his way.

But all the talking in the world will not do the job unless I show him how to throw and bat. That is the nature of "teaching."

One man puts it this way:

Want to hear what you sound like as a parent? Want to see what you look like? What you act like? Look in your personal mirror—your child. Kids are a near perfect reflection of our child rearing style and habits. Like sponges, they absorb our everyday actions—good and bad—and like mirrors, they reflect back at us what we are, sometimes when we most need to face it. . . . You tell your children the way to be, but they model their behavior on the way that you are.[4]

As parents, we can't get by with mouthing truths. We have to embody them. We can't kid our children. They know what we do, not just what we say. But don't be afraid to "throw the ball."

Writing in *In Defense of the Family*, Rita Kramer says:

The perniciousness of so much advice from experts that pervades the media is that it undermines the confidence of parents in their own abilities and their own values, overemphasizes the significance of child-rearing techniques, and grossly misrepresents the contribution the expert in psychiatry or education can make to the conduct of ordinary family life.[5]

The bottom line is that the central responsibility lies with the parents. So "throw the ball."

Well, you're thinking, "Sounds good, but what do I throw? What do I emphasize? What is crucial?" We've talked already about some of the essential items we direct toward our families.

Now let's try and isolate several more.

Practical "throwing" tips

The first of those comes under the label of kindness and truth. Solomon lays it out in Proverbs 3:3–4: "Do not let kindness and truth leave you; bind them around your neck, write them on the tablet of your heart so that you will find favor and good repute in the sight of God and man."

These two words, "kindness and truth," belong together. In fact, as you read the Bible you will discover that the word most frequently linked to the word "kindness" is the word "truth." When found together, they essentially speak of faithful love for others. Inherent in their meaning are the ideas of faithfulness, loyalty, reliability, and mercy. The words always imply personal involvement and commitment in a relationship, whether that be in your family or with your friends.

We need to pause here, because this concept of kindness, of faithful love, is sometimes difficult to grasp. While mothers and daughters sometimes struggle with problems of being too intertwined, what seems to characterize the father-son relationship is a difficulty bridging the gap between them.

Bridging the gap between fathers and sons

Fathers and sons speak the language of action, of sports, not the language of caring. Do you know many men who can say something like: "My father was around; he used to take me to ball games all the time."

But ask, "Well, what did you talk about?"

Invariably, they'll say, "We talked about baseball."

Or he may say, "My dad took me to the stock car races every Friday night." And you ask, "What did you talk about?" The response is usually, "Cars, engines, that kind of stuff."

You see the same thing in your own life. You head out golfing one Saturday morning with your golfing buddy and when you return four days later, your wife says, "Hon, what did you guys talk about all the time you were out chasing that little white ball?"

You look at her and say, "Talk? What do you mean talk? We played golf!"

I find it interesting around Father's Day to ask men: "How did you celebrate Father's day in your family?"

Some have pleasant enough memories, but many men say: "I bought my father something, but you could never really say, 'I love you,' or hug him and get that close affection, because it would make him feel uneasy."

Some sons are afraid to cry, because they've been told it's a sign of weakness. Sometimes they want to hug their dad and feel safe around him, but they are kept at arm's length because their dads want them to "be strong."

Other sons are afraid their fathers will break down and cry—and they don't know what they'll do if that happens.

Teaching children how to care

The language of caring is not one that fathers and sons major in. But it is a target we need to pay attention to.

The tragedy is that so much affection, or "faithful love," as Solomon describes it, between fathers and sons is repressed and pushed away. Then, when a son grows up, he sometimes has difficulty getting close, not only to his father, but to other significant people in his life.

If children do not grow to care for others and show this care in specific actions, they may develop into basically selfish persons. Even Dr. Benjamin Spock understands that when he writes: "Our only realistic hope...is to bring up our children with a feeling that they are in this world not for their own satisfaction but primarily to serve others."[6]

Kindness conquers selfishness because the two cannot live side by side for very long. Kindness feels what others feel; it shares their joys and sorrow. And, it is active and practical—it meets others' needs.

Now, remember that in Solomon's mind, "truth" stands beside kindness. In other words, compassion or faithful love for someone does not ignore their sin, or their actions that are morally and ethically wrong. True compassion is surrounded by truth, and lives in that environment. Loving your son or daughter does not mean you ignore disobedience. It does not mean that you bypass discipline and correction. That is not what Solomon is targeting. He gives a balanced message.

Still, if we have a weakness, it probably is in this area of cultivating a softness of heart, especially in our sons. You can begin to teach this very early. It is taught in small ways, such as helping a toddler share his precious toy. Or encouraging a brother to think of his sister when he buys a candy bar. Or thanking him for including her in his games when he has a friend over and she is alone.

As your kids get older, nurture within them the desire to reach out to others. Encourage them to include in their circle of friends those who might not naturally be included, who are sitting on the edges waiting to be invited in. Compassion can be demonstrated by having them gather the clothes that no longer fit them, but are still in good shape, then identifying someone they know who is in need. Packaging those clothes and delivering them with kindness can be a tenderizing lesson for their heart.

Encourage them to be involved in community agencies, such as volunteering at a local hospital, or homeless shelter. Maybe they need to find a senior citizen on their street who needs her lawn mowed each week. Encourage them to volunteer to do that for nothing. Then there is the opportunity of helping out at church camps without pay. All of these kinds of things will make a difference.

Simply helping them put a handle on their own emotions rather than shutting them off as signs of weakness will go a long way in addressing this priority. And then, when actions of kindness occur, notice them positively and compliment your child.

Real men can cry

Of course, even more important in this area is your modeling. Don't be afraid of expressing your emotions of tenderness and kindness. I wonder how many dads reading these words have ever cried in front of their family? Why is it something to be proud of, to be able to say, "My family has never seen me cry!" Modeling is the key. You set the pace. All it takes is an act of your will.

The nurse escorted a tired, anxious young man to the bedside of an elderly man. "Your son is here," she whispered to the patient. She had to repeat the words several times before the patient's eyes opened. He was heavily sedated because of the pain of his heart attack and he dimly saw the young man standing outside the oxygen tent.

He reached out his hand and the young man tightly wrapped his fingers around it, squeezing a message of encouragement. The nurse brought a chair next to the bedside. All through the night the young man sat holding the old man's hand and offering gentle words of hope. The dying man said nothing as he held tightly to his son.

As dawn approached, the patient died. The young man placed on the bed the lifeless hand he had been holding. then he went to notify the nurse. While the nurse did what was necessary, the young man waited. When she had finished her task, the nurse began to offer words of sympathy to the young man. But he interrupted her.

"Who was that man?" he asked.

The startled nurse replied, "I thought he was your father."

"No, he was not my father," he answered. "I never saw him before in my life."

"Then why didn't you say something when I took you to him?" asked the nurse.

He replied, "I also knew he needed his son, and his son just wasn't here. When I realized he was too sick to tell whether or not I was his son, I knew how much he needed me." [7]

Learning how to trust

Solomon talks of another priority you need to "throw out" to your children, beginning in verses 5–8.

Trust in the Lord with all your heart, and do not lean on your own understanding. In all your ways acknowledge

Him, and he will make your paths straight. Do not be wise in your own eyes; fear the Lord and turn away from evil. It will be healing to your body, and refreshment to your bones.

The verb "to trust" comes from another word that literally means "to throw yourself down on your face, to lie extended on the ground." It carries essentially the idea of relying on someone for security and being confident in that security.

Solomon is telling us that one of the key values we must concentrate on in our homes is developing in our own lives (and the lives of our kids) a confidence and security in our God.

Someone said, "To trust is to regard God as the source of wisdom and power, the guide in the moral life and in all other things, [and] to obey His law and have confidence in Him." [8]

Now that doesn't happen naturally, or overnight. It takes work to reach the place where we acknowledge Him in all our ways, or in all areas of our life. Translated, that means we are conscious of God in all aspects of our day-to-day existence. We don't exclude Him from certain areas of our life. We give Him a priority slot.

As parents we need to work very hard at weaving God into our own lives regularly, and communicating His involvement in our lives with our kids. We ought to be able to talk about His importance and His value to us, just as easily as we want to talk about the latest baseball stats or fashion statements.

Unfortunately, our commitment to developing a spiritual trust fund for our kids all too often comes after spending an average of forty-four hours of adult-television viewing per week. It comes after the half-hour in the newspaper on Sunday mornings. It comes after the three-mile run and the Jazzercize class, after vacations, after a sixty-hour work week. In short, our priorities say (and our activities shout) that we do not really believe that working at spiritual trust in our homes is worth it.

Karen Mains has written a wonderful article entitled

"Warrior of Light." It appeared a number of years ago in *Christian Parenting* magazine. She says:

> The situation will remain as it is until we become convinced that there is nothing greater that we can achieve, nothing more significant to which we can hold each other accountable, nothing more profound that we can give to one another, to our children, and ultimately to our society, than spiritual development.[9]

Building up your spiritual trust fund

We have found that one of the best places to cultivate a spiritual trust fund is in the car as we are taking everyone around to church, youth activities, soccer, basketball, baseball. You know the routine.

Use those times. Some of us have fooled ourselves into thinking that if we have a fifteen-minute devotional spot after dinner five nights a week, that will do the job. Not true. It needs a wider hearing than that.

Think of the time you spend in the car with your kids. And realize you have a captive audience. I mean, where are they going to go? I would guess that 85 to 90 percent of the times Patricia and I drive our kids somewhere, the conversation at some point turns to spiritual matters. It may be an extended conversation, it may last only a few minutes, but the pattern is established.

Just last week, Jeremy said to me in the car, "Dad, there is this kid at school who keeps punching me, coming after me, and trying to pick a fight. This weekend (they were away on a school choir trip) he punched me in the ear." He showed me the remnant of blood in his ear, and then asked, "What do I do, Dad?"

I then took a few minutes to explain what Jesus meant when He said to turn the other cheek. I suggested that meant not instigating a fight, and not trying to injure someone. But it did not stop him from protecting himself.

The next day the kid came against him again, and Jeremy hammered him. (No, just kidding.) But he did defend himself and, to make a long story short, his life is a lot easier now.

You develop spiritual trust funds any time you can.

Karen Mains does a great job putting this concept into practical terms:

> Spiritual leadership in our home...is the back side of a man in his study bending into the dim light over his study table. It's a wife's Bible so used that the pages are soft, the binding malleable. It is a mind so disciplined through the years by habitual considerations that its first questions now are, "What would Christ say?" "What does God think?" "How would the Lord act?"
>
> Spiritual leadership is a couple who loves worship, who call a family together on Saturday evening to ready their hearts for tomorrow's praise. It is the verbal reminder, "Come home early. Tomorrow is Sunday."
>
> Spiritual leadership is a one-to-one accountability Bible study on Amos with the oldest teenager. It's bedtime with the ten year old, and a heavy discussion about a playmate who has been influenced to change his reading material from pornographic magazines to Christian comics. . . . Spiritual leadership, it is as simple and as difficult as that. . . . We must place ourselves in a church that stimulates our growth and challenges our lethargy. We must read the Bible, pray and obey what we learn. We must exercise spirituality every day as much as possible and we must commit ourselves to it for the rest of our lives.[10]

That gift of cultivating a spiritual heart that beats with trust and confidence in God will never happen if, at the same time, we are not being careful to guard our kids and ourselves from our own self-importance.

You see, you don't learn to trust someone else if you're always right. Look at the last half of verse 5 and hitch that to the opening line of verse 7, and then verse 11.

And do not lean on your own understanding. . . . Do not be wise in your own eyes. . . . My son, do not reject the discipline of the Lord, or loathe His reproof. . . .

What is Solomon saying? Simply this: Don't forget to teach your kids to keep learning from others and from God—and not to rely only on their own insights.

That is one of the hardest lessons to get across.

We're not in this alone

Some time ago I read of an advertisement for *Fortune* magazine. It pictured a baby in diapers looking you straight in the eye with a childlike directness and curiosity. The line at the top of the picture was an attention-getter. It said: "We're all created equal. After that, baby, you're on your own."

Then beneath the picture was this line:

Nobody's going to hand you success on a silver platter. If you want to make it, you'll have to make it on your own—your own drive, your own guts, your own energy, your own ambition. [11]

That's what many of us believe. And when we do try to make it on our own, the idea of listening to the advice, the counsel, the correction of others—even God—is something we become very defensive about. Solomon goes as far as to say in verse 11 that we will even reject the discipline or correction that God brings our way. Why is that? Because we believe that we are right and that everybody else, including God, is wrong. We are unteachable.

By the way, those who are consistently unteachable often have very few, if any, friends. And that makes sense because they don't need them. They need only themselves because they are always right. When someone boasts that they have no friends, check out their teachability quotient. It will usually be very low.

I know as well as you do that it is never easy to be corrected. Our first response is to reject correction, to become defensive, to blame others or to attack them. Somehow we have got to fight that off, because a mark of wisdom, of maturity is to be able to listen to good counsel and then to change in that direction for the better.

The Bible repeatedly emphasizes the fact that growth cannot occur without a teachable heart. By teachable, I mean a progressively growing desire to learn, and then a willingness to change our behavior positively.

That requires the ability to admit fault and to ask forgiveness from others. Ultimately it means a willingness to do what is right. It is imperative within the family system to learn to say, "I have not arrived"; "I have more to learn"; "You may be right"; "Please help me develop in this area of my life." [12]

Unteachability ruins relationships

Watch out for your tendency to be unteachable. You'll spot it in statements in your own experience, and in the experience of your kids. It sounds like this:

"I didn't hear you say that."

"She made me angry. . . ."

"It wasn't me—it was him. I didn't do it—she did."

"It wasn't my fault—I couldn't understand what my teacher said."

"I never received the memo."

"A lot of people were sick; I got backlogged."

"If your mother would just do _____, I wouldn't be late so often."

Do you recognize any of those lines? They all have one thing in common—a heart that tends to be unteachable. It tends to see itself as always right.

I've heard arguments between family members escalate to ridiculous proportions simply because they refused to acknowledge the possibility of being wrong. Yet when we unburden ourselves of the responsibility of being right all the time, we are then free to learn from others. Just the simple admission that "I might be wrong," or "You might be right," can work wonders in a family.

You can model teachability in a number of ways. One is by reading books. Reading demonstrates a desire to learn, a desire to be taught. Watching TV does not. Watching TV demonstrates a desire to be entertained, not a desire to learn.

All of us enjoy entertainment, but don't forget learning. I've heard people say proudly, "I haven't read a book since I graduated from high school." So what's the big deal about that? That is really an admission of lack of teachability. I try to finish two books a week, if possible. I'm still reading, still trying to learn.

So model by reading.

Secondly, you can model teachability by reading the assembly instructions on all the new hardware toys we buy. Have you noticed men are real good at reading directions? You buy something at the hardware store, packaged with a label that says, "Some assembly required." Then you dump it all out on the antiseptically clean garage floor, and a million parts scatter to the mousetrap corners.

An hour later your wife or son comes out and says, "What are you doing?" The confident reply is, "I'm putting this 'whatch-ya-ma-call-it' together."

The next question is as natural as breathing: "Did you read the instructions?"

"Are you kidding, I could do this blindfolded. I don't need to read anything."

(This is the same guy who never gets lost on vacation trips because he doesn't need to look at a map, either.)

About four hours later, your wife or son revisits the scene of the crime and everything is put together. But there are about thirty-six small pieces still lying around. So they ask, "What are all those parts for?" And you say, "Oh, I don't need those. You have to understand how they pack these things up. They also include thirty-six spare parts for future use, but we don't need them now."

The cutting edge of re-education

Last weekend I learned this lesson again. My grass trimmer had gone to grass-trimmer heaven, so I purchased a new one. It was simple to put together and I had used it once or twice. Saturday afternoon I looked out in the back yard and my youngest son was out trimming the grass. I yelled out through the back screen, "Hey, Kent, do you know how to run that thing?"

"Sure dad," he said, and went on trimming. But he was struggling with the guard on the trimmer—it had slipped off. So, I shouted out again, "Hey, Kent, bring that here to me and I'll fix it. Bring it here!"

With that Kent put the trimmer down, turned to me and responded politely, but firmly, "Dad, I can do this—I read the instructions!"

Model teachability.

How often do you sincerely seek the advice of your wife? I don't mean just listening to pacify her, but listening for her wisdom?

When do you ask your kids for their input? I'm writing this book for a number of reasons, but one of the key reasons is that I had a lengthy discussion with my sons about the possibility and they pushed me to do it.

When do you admit to your family that you don't know what to do and that you and they must pray about the situation?

Do you catch where I am on this? Listen to one wise person's observations:

> . . .True freedom comes only when we assume full responsibility for who and what we are. As long as we feel comfortable putting blame on others, we will never be required to evaluate and change our own behaviors. We blame parents for lack of love, response, nurturing. We blame society for keeping us from total freedom. We blame friends, teachers, even life. As long as we can pass the blame, we feel no necessity to change our own lives. After all, we are victims. There are those who even blame God for their misfortune and unhappiness. I have heard people say "I'll never forgive God for doing that to me!" What egos! These individuals see themselves helpless and hopeless and a part of an existence in which they have no control. They comforably sit back in self-pity—waiting for lovers, family or God to "put it all right" for them. Sadly, many of them waste a valuable lifetime waiting![13]

Now let's move to the last priority Solomon has for us in this chapter. You might not like it, but it's here in verse 9. This probably represents one of the greatest priorities we can model for our family, and at the same time, help teach them about trust.

> Honor the Lord from your wealth, and from the first of all your produce. . . .

You don't have to be an Old Testament scholar to catch the drift here. Solomon reminds us of a goal we all have—to honor

God through our lives.

That much we can deal with. But then he throws a curve ball. He says that the way we honor the Lord is through our financial giving. Worse than that, Solomon makes giving such a priority that he tells us to give the Lord the *first* of our wealth.

That is, off the top, not the bottom.

Giving—the American way

Most of us give God our leftovers. If we can afford to donate something or give, we will, but only then. That's the wrong model, according to Solomon. He says we are to give God the first part of our income.

In Solomon's mind, giving to the Lord was a matter of freely giving Him the best. And God is after our best. It isn't when we have spent all our money on ourselves, and then socked some extra away in a mutual fund or savings account or real estate deal or college fund, that we trickle a little bit to God.

That's hardly the first of our wealth. But when we give Him the cream of what we have, then we are honoring Him.

I have said for years that you can tell more about an individual's dedication to God by looking at that person's checkbook than by looking at his or her Bible. What does your family learn about your spiritual commitment from your giving patterns? Who or what would they conclude is your security, or place of trust, after watching your giving pattern?

Do you talk to your kids about that pattern? Do they know how much you give? My kids do. We don't make a big deal about it, but they know. They see the offering envelope being prepared every week. I wonder what conclusions your family would reach if you were to show them the quarterly or yearly giving statement that your church sends out to you as a record of your giving? Would they learn anything about giving our best to God?

The fact is that 80 percent of the people in our country who give to churches give less than $500 a year. That represents a tithe on an annual income of $5,000. Another 10 percent give between $500-$1,000 a year, or a tithe on a maximum income of $12,000. That covers 90 percent of the givers in this country.[14]

Ron Blue, a fine Christian gentleman and financial counselor, frequently mentions in his seminars that "if all Christians were reduced to a welfare income and they tithed on that amount, the church would double its receipts."[15]

What saddens me most is that among those who contribute to religious groups in our country, the Mormons are the most generous.[16]

Amazing! They have no connection to Jesus Christ, but a greater degree of giving.

When it comes to giving, are you throwing a ball your kids can catch or hit? Or are you pitching way out of the strike zone?

Our use of finances, our giving patterns, tell our families where our security and confidence in life lie. What are we teaching our kids about that?

Ruth Harms Calkin put it this way:

> O God When I think of Your
> Tremendous goodness to us
> Your continual poured-out blessings
> Suddenly I am overwhelmed
> With a convicting thought:
> Everything You do
> For my husband and me
> All Your love and kindness
> So lavishly bestowed
> Become an indictment
> Unless we willingly
> Allow each blessing

To flow through us to others.
All Your abundance
Must constantly be on the move
Or we will stagnate
In a sea of plenty."[17]

So, what are the priorities Solomon attempts to "throw" our way? To what must we give ourselves in terms of "teaching values" in our families?

We need to be spiritual men and women whose spiritual commitment can be measured, known, and seen.

We need to commit ourselves to lives that model spiritual trust in our own homes. We need to be obsessed with the cultivation of tender hearts of compassion that revel in truth. We need to have a teachable heart that is prepared to admit when we are wrong, and when others are right.

We must also examine and change our patterns of giving, and do so in the full light of our families.

We must march, together with our families, to the beat of a different Drummer—whose name is Jesus Christ.

Sticks and Stones

Proverbs—Selected Verses

Y OU MAY BE FAMILIAR WITH THE STORY, but then again, it may be news to you.

Toni Dunn, at the time, was twenty years old. She was a beautiful girl. Toni had been married only sixty days. She had gone out on December 23, and was very late getting home. In fact, it was Christmas Eve before she got back.

She explained to her husband that something horrible had happened.

Two young men in a black car—which she described very specifically—had taken her and molested her and she was terrorized. In a rage of anger, her husband went out to the suburban shopping center in Atlanta with a shotgun. He looked for the black car and for someone about the age she described.

He found the car. The guy had just left work and was making plans with a friend for the weekend. Suddenly, confronting him through the window is this enraged husband with a shotgun.

"Get out of that car," he shouted, "or I'll blow your brains out." When the young man stepped out of the car, the husband shot him in the chest and he died instantly.

Toni, the twenty-year-old wife, reported the incident to the police and testified to the accuracy of her husband's account. Ten days later they called her back and asked her to give her statement again. That's when she disclosed that it was all a lie. On the night she had disappeared, she had not been attacked. There hadn't been any black car. She was, in fact, with her lawyer that night, discussing a divorce from her husband of two months. She spent the night with her lawyer because she was having an affair with him.

Her husband is in the penitentiary, serving life for first degree murder. Toni, the wife—still twenty, still beautiful, was sentenced to one year for lying.[1]

The power of words

An extreme example? Perhaps. But it illustrates what happens when we determine to twist the truth or invent a story line to cover our tails. And none of us is immune to the epidemic of a diseased tongue. Maybe our actions are not as dramatic as Toni's, but we do struggle with what we say, don't we?

One author brings this right to our front door when he writes:

"In the Solomon Islands, in the South Pacific, some villagers practice a unique form of logging. If a tree is too large to be felled with an ax, the natives cut it down by yelling at it. Woodsmen with special powers creep up on a tree just at dawn and suddenly scream at it at the top of their lungs. They continue this for thirty days. The tree [is supposed to] die and fall over. The theory is that hollering kills the spirit of the tree. According to the villagers, it always works.

Ah, those poor naive innocents. Such quaintly charming habits of the jungle. Screaming at trees, indeed. How primitive. Too bad they don't have the advantages of modern technology and the scientific mind.

Me? I yell at my wife. And yell at the telephone and the lawn mower. And yell at the TV and the newspaper and my children. I've even been known to shake my fist and yell at the sky at times. . . .

Don't know what good it does. Machines and things just sit there. Even kicking doesn't always help. As for people, well, the Solomon Islanders may have a point. Yelling at living things does tend to kill the spirit in them.

Sticks and stones may break our bones, but words will break our hearts.[2]

At home, what we say and how we say it can have incredible results in the lives of our family. Hit me with a stick and you may break my arm, but in six weeks I will have made a full recovery. Hit me in the head with a stone or a baseball, and you may open a bloody gash, but a few well-placed stitches will repair the wound.

But when you gouge my heart with a brutal verbal assault or an insensitive criticism, you will scar me for the rest of my life. If you aren't convinced of that, you aren't acknowledging the power of your words. Consider Solomon's experience, and look at what he says as a father in Proverbs 23:15, 16:

My son, if your heart is wise, my own heart also will be glad; and my inmost being will rejoice, when your lips speak what is right.

Children obviously bring joy to their parents by making wise decisions and careful choices. But more than that, our level of joy explodes when we hear our kids speaking "rightly."

That primarily refers to direct and honest speech. Solomon's point is that there is no difference between their speech and their intentions. What they say they do, they do. What they say they believe in, they believe in.

Why is that important? There are several reasons. The first is that many of these proverbs dealing with our tongue emerge from the belief that what a person says demonstrates who she really is—in her heart of hearts.

The things you say will be worth only what you are worth inside. You see, the way people use their tongue is a dead give-away as to their true identity. You and I realize that the root problem is not in the mouth, but in the heart—the person deep within us.

But there are other reasons to speak "rightly." Look at Proverbs 21:23:

He who guards his mouth and his tongue, guards his soul from troubles."

Now add 18:21 to that thought:

Death and life are in the power of the tongue and those who love it will eat its fruit.

If you take this seriously, it's heavy stuff.

I have personally never met anyone who has not at some time struggled with using his or her tongue in an inappropriate manner, or who has not borne the brunt of another's tongue.

A matter of death and life

Apparently, Solomon was in the same boat, because he says matter-of-factly that what people say can lead to life or death. And those of us who love "it" (that is, talking), had better come to grips with the fact that we must also live with the results of our talking. Some of those results aren't so hot.

Solomon uses the word "troubles" to characterize some of those results. He suggests that we who control what we say are more likely to avoid getting ourselves into trouble than those who regularly shoot their mouths off first and think later. Interestingly, the word "troubles" literally means "a place of distress."

It comes from a word that describes a narrow or tight spot. And that is exactly where we find ourselves because of what we say. We talk ourselves into a jam. We back ourselves into a corner. And what usually happens when you find yourself in a corner, in a tight spot?

Often you come out fighting verbally, don't you? You've been there. You know exactly what he is driving at. And so speaking "rightly" is not just a theoretical concept with you.

But let me suggest something else.

When Solomon says that "death and life are in the power of the tongue," the word he uses for "life" is a Hebrew word that can be described by the word "community." So he is saying that our tongues can provide a sense of community or fellowship. And most of us long for some kind of community.

Searching for life in community

While flying to Denver once, I took along a periodical called *Vital Speeches of the Day*. It's published twice a month and prints what some consider the most significant speeches given in the country during that time frame. This particular issue, for example, included the President's State of the Union address for this year. (That's not the speech that drew my eye.)

The one I noticed was given by the professor of history at South Dakota State University. It was entitled, "The Continuing Search for Community in Higher Education"—one of the primary challenges of our times.[3]

The search for community, Solomon says, begins with

speaking rightly. In fact, in the Old Testament, this word we are talking about—community, or life—described either a group of families or individuals within one family who were united by important ties.

Your family is tied together, and the speech that characterizes your family system ought to be that which provides for community. It involves speaking "rightly."

Now, before we move on, glance at Proverbs 12:18a. It reminds us again of the potential of our tongues: "There is one who speaks rashly like the thrusts of a sword."

You might have read about it. You probably watched the videotaped footage and were shocked, outraged perhaps. It was the recent stabbing of one of the tennis world's finest female players, Monica Seles. I listened to the horrified reaction of one of my sons as he watched the slow-motion replay on ESPN. Everyone took a step back.

But do we have the same reaction when we or someone else stabs at others with their words? It can cause the same pain, the same scarring, the same "always looking over your shoulder from now on" reaction, that Monica Seles will experience every time she sits down between tennis games.

Do we stand up and say, "That shouldn't happen! We need better security, better protection!"? We do need protection—from verbal knives.

Max Lucado, in his book, *No Wonder They Call Him the Savior*, speaks for many of us:

No doubt you've had your share of words that wound. You've felt the sting of a well-aimed gibe. Maybe you're still feeling it. Someone you love or respect slams you to the floor with a slur or slip of the tongue. And there you lie, wounded and bleeding. Perhaps the words were intended to hurt you, perhaps not; but that doesn't matter. The wound is deep. The injuries are internal. Broken heart, wounded pride, bruised feelings.

Or maybe your wound is old. Though the arrow was extracted long ago, the arrowhead is still lodged . . . hidden under your skin. The old pain flares unpredictably and decisively, reminding you of harsh words. . . . [4]

I remember it as if it were yesterday. It wasn't, though. In fact, it was back in 1978, and involved a couple who attended the small church I pastored. The husband was himself a former pastor. They became involved in ministry, but at the same time came to dislike me intensely. One day I heard a slight movement outside my office, but before I could get to the door a note had been slipped under it. The note was from this couple, and its message was to the point: "If the rapture were today, you would be left behind!"

An old wound, with lingering pain.

Not too long ago, the *U.S. News & World Report* included a letter to the editor that brings this idea home to parents. Janet Carson is the writer, and in part she says:

The biggest lie we tell our kids is that "sticks and stones may break our bones, but names will never hurt us." Words hurt and, when they do, it isn't funny. . . . Words have power . . . We have to control the abuse of the power of words ourselves. Parents have to say: "Not in my house."[5]

Weigh your words carefully

I don't know where I found the quote that follows, but it has been hanging around my files for more than a dozen years. Every time I move a shelf of books from one part of my library to another I consider these thoughts:

Words, unlike books, weigh little. Have you ever moved books? Heavy things. But try to weigh a word and you'll find it hard to catch, much less weigh.

Strange how words can crush us. Weightless things.
How very clever our critics who assail us with words
which rise into thin air and vanish.

[But] how just when eternity proves the Bible is true:
Every idle word will stand in review. Words, written or
spoken, heavy things.[6]

It is important in our family systems that this underlying
thesis permeate its way through the fabric of our home. To help
us see the prevalence of the problem, I'd like Solomon to
remind us of the two most popular verbal flame throwers. The
first one is lying.

Lies—abominations in God's eyes

The book of Proverbs continually refers to our weakness in
this area, but a slice of Proverbs 6:12 will say it all: "A worthless person, a wicked man, is the one who. . . . "

Who what? Commits murder? Steals? Has an affair? All are
serious offenses, but they're not mentioned here. The worthless
person is, as the rest of the verse says,

> . . . the one who walks with a false mouth, who winks
> with his eyes, who signals with his feet, who points with
> his fingers; who with perversity in his heart devises evil
> continually (Proverbs 6:12–14a).

Both terms, "false" and "perversity" are related to words
that mean "to twist something, or to be crooked." That's part of
the heart of lying, isn't it? You take something that is true, just
enough of it. And then you twist it, you wrench it out of shape
until it becomes crooked, and you pass it along. Your intent is
to deceive, to get out of one of those tight spots I talked about
earlier that our machine-gun speech gets us into.

Or maybe we just have enough anger in us to want to rip on somebody, spill a little blood because they have hurt or offended us. But every time you fire off a twisted message, you gouge at someone's heart or reputation.

Yet most of us, whether we admit it or not, are guilty as sin on this point. A recent book entitled, *The Day America Told the Truth*, is based on an extensive opinion survey that gave participants a guarantee of anonymity. It discovered that almost half of those responding regularly call in sick when they're not. Ninety-one percent admit to lying regularly, at work and at home.[7]

A somewhat more flattering result from a Louis Harris poll reported in *TIME* magazine revealed that six out of ten people in our country feel that lying is justified at times.[8]

You may say, "That's not true in my family!"

When our words betray us

Well, think about it. When was the last time the phone rang, and you were immersed in the NBA playoffs or your favorite Matlock or Columbo mystery and you told your daughter or son to say, "I can't come to the phone right now," or "My dad's not available right now?"

Or worse, your son or daughter asks, "Who is speaking?" and they pass the answer on to you. But you reply, "Tell them I'm not here, I'll call them back." But you *are* there and you don't have any intention of calling them back.

Perhaps you've made excuses for your kids not having an assignment or project done at school. "She was sick all weekend," or "We had a family emergency." In some families that could be translated, "We spent the weekend loafing around, we went to the lake (or whatever else they were actually doing)."

What about the time you called in sick for work and your kids overheard you—and then you grabbed your golf clubs and headed out the door—what about that?

What about the promises you keep making to your kids? And when you don't come through and they call you on it, you say, "I didn't say that. I didn't promise you that! Don't you tell your father what he did or didn't say! I know what I said!"

You get the point. We are easily tilted toward lying. And the God of the Bible is not impressed. Look what he says in Proverbs 6:16–17a: "There are six things which the Lord hates, yes, seven which are an abomination to Him: haughty eyes, a lying tongue . . ."

I think perhaps one of the reasons God reacts to lying so strongly is that lurking in the shadows of the word "lying" is the meaning "to betray." That's what people do to us when they lie about us, isn't it? And if the name Judas Iscariot rings any bells, then it would be safe to say that God the Father knows about lies that betray.

That's what our children do to us, and we to them, when we lie about what is going on in our lives. We betray a trust, we violate our love, and we decimate our family community.

Community cannot exist in a church, a marriage or a family when we allow consistent lying to occur. People stop trusting other people, and when trust evaporates, community flies out the window with it.

Gossip and slander

But the same thing could be said about gossip and slander, which are the second favorite verbal flame thrower Solomon talks about, starting at 10:18.

He who conceals hatred has lying lips, and he who spreads slander is a fool. When there are many words, transgression is unavoidable. . . . A worthless man digs up evil, while his words are as a scorching fire. A perverse man spreads strife, and a slanderer separates intimate friends (Proverbs 10:18–19a; 16:27–28).

The term "slanderer" literally means "a whisperer." It describes someone who is very smooth and able to slide something by. But understand what he is sliding by. Solomon does not mean a rumor about someone that gets started out of ignorance. He is talking about a *calculated* rumor invented for the purpose of hurting someone. He describes the guilty parties as those who "dig up evil," meaning they love to look for garbage in people's lives. If it is there, they will find it. If it isn't, they will invent it. Then, like an uncontrollable fire, they spread the news.

Solomon is unusually concerned with this subject because he talks about gossip and slander at least a half dozen times in Proverbs. Again, our inclination is to deny involvement with gossip or slander, especially those of us in the church. So let me define it in several ways that will help to crystallize not only what it means, but how we get tied into it as families.

Gossip is a false or exaggerated report that is maliciously discussed, and/or circulated, about another person. Even Webster's dictionary supports that. It defines slander: "The utterance in the presence of another person of a false statement or statements, damaging to a third person's character or reputation." [9]

An old parish priest, more than a hundred years ago, understood what this was all about. He undoubtedly reflected his own personal pain when he wrote:

> What is slander? A verdict of 'guilty' pronounced in the absence of the accused, with closed doors, without defense or appeal, by an interested and prejudiced judge. [10]

He was right, wasn't he?

But the Bible generally ratchets this definition up a notch.

In *Words that Hurt—Words that Heal*, Carole Mayhall writes: "Based on the Old and New Testaments, slander is the open, intentional sharing of damaging information, and is characterized by bad reports that blemish or defame a person's reputation whether they are true or not."[11]

That makes this problem of slander tougher to deal with because slander includes not only those things that are false, but even some that are true (but ought not to be shared in public). Even some things based on fact are not to be repeated.

But the gossips of our towns, churches and families love to tell "the truth" for truth's sake. They tell everything they know as soon as they hear it, tell it to anyone within earshot, regardless of what it is. They use truth like a machete. They slice their way through people and leave them bleeding in the overflow of sacred truth. Their bloodshed is rationalized by the truth they misused.

In *The Angry Book*, his book about angry people, Dr. Theodore Rubin offers this perceptive word that may describe you—or someone you know:

> Telling the truth . . . is a primary kind of poison used by some people. They invariably look for . . . truths that will hurt. They are not interested in truths that will . . . make for feeling good, that will be supporting or comforting. Somehow the truths they find will be linked to bad memories, skeletons in the closets, fears, and hurts. When they run out of these they will distort, exaggerate, and often lie. . . .
>
> Of course they will deny distorting, subtle lying, and especially blatant lying. How can they admit to lying? Such an admission would uncover and link them to their true intent—namely, to hurt, to cause pain, to tear down, to maim. . . . "Truth" is their big rationalization, their big cover-up for intense hostility. Under the guise of "truth" they are able to deny being angry. . . . [12]

You see, that's what you have to watch for in your family.

People who suffer from the affliction of gossip sometimes do it out of a need to express hidden anger. Maybe you need to explore your own hidden reef of hostility or that of your children. Try to talk about it. What has happened that has lit this slow, destructive fuse?

But most people gossip in order to be entertaining, to impress others with their importance so that they will be liked. Maybe that is true in your family. Your self worth has never been very high and you have done a pretty good job on your kids and wife in terms of shooting down their personal value. And you know it.

Then again, maybe you aren't conscious of how worthless your wife feels, how neglected she is, how much like an appendage she sees herself. Maybe, in your preoccupation with your job, your leisure time, your own pursuits, you have successfully ignored your kids to the point that they don't believe you view them as valuable. And maybe then, their propensity to gossip and slander others is their attempt to win approval and attention—the approval and attention you haven't bothered to give them. The sad thing in all of this is that it doesn't work for them. Gossip destroys confidence and respect, and people eventually figure it out.

Solomon anticipated that when he said "a slanderer separates intimate friends."

The painful impact of slander

The verb "to separate" has the idea of causing those who are close to us to begin to doubt and distrust us. Slander and gossip not only separate the gossiper from his friends, but they also drive a wedge between people who are close friends.

Saying bad things about others, questioning what they do with raised eyebrows, or making subtle accusations against them through innuendo all succeed in turning people away from each other.

In our family it is so important to talk about this, to remind each other and to hold each other accountable for the way we talk about others. This is essential to helping the members of your family cultivate relationships and friendships that are based on trust and mutual respect. If there is anything that will explode in your kids' faces, it will be the lack of positive friendships. And that will occur over and over again if they are unable to control their tongues.

Now you might ask at this point, "Well, how do we as a family move toward controlling our tongues?

How do we begin to teach our children how to speak rightly?" Let me suggest a couple of practical principles.

Turn back to Proverbs 12:19, 22.

Truthful lips will be established forever. . . . Lying lips are an abomination to the Lord, but those who deal faithfully are His delight.

Practical tips on healthy speech

Within our families we must be committed to honesty and truthfulness. You see, truth-telling is not just a practical option based on wonderful maxims like "cheaters never prosper," or "honesty is the best policy." Biblical families model honesty because lying is a violation of the character of God.

Truth then, must be our goal, no matter where it leads.

Teaching children honesty can be a real challenge, given the examples of dishonesty they encounter every day in the world around them. Your example and your constant feedback about your child's behavior can be a powerful influence on him or her.

But to make truthfulness part of your family bloodline, make every effort to be completely honest with your family. Answer their questions truthfully and candidly. If a question is off-limits, tell them simply and honestly that you won't answer it.

Never let them hear you tell convenient white lies on the phone and never ask them to tell one for you. Don't exaggerate in conversations about events or people.

In another section of Proverbs, Solomon says to his boy:

Give me your heart, my son, and let your eyes delight in my ways (Proverbs 23:26).

It is unlikely that you will give your heart to anyone whose model of speech is less than true, less than honest. You wonder about the inconsistency of it and you keep the guard on your heart lifted high.

In terms of gossip and slander, you set the tone. Monitor your own conversations around the dinner table, in the car. Who do you talk about? What do you say about absent people? (Remember, your kids are listening and learning.) One way to slow the tide of gossip when someone who is absent is being spoken of in a negative way is to gently stop the conversation. Then say something like, "You know, I'm getting very uncomfortable about this," or "It would really hurt her if she knew what we were saying, don't you think?"

Here's another approach that may be appropriate: When a member of your family begins to discuss an absent person, ask them: "Have you talked to _____ about this?"

If the answer is "No," suggest the conversation not be pursued. If the answer is "Yes," then suggest that you wait and include that person in the conversation the next time you see them. That will slow the slander process.

A positive approach

One couple suggested that you give praise and the chance to start over. What they mean is that we should not be anxious to catch our kids in a lie. Instead, catch them telling the truth, and praise them for that. If they do tell, or begin to tell, what you think is an untruth, interrupt and say, "Wait; think for a minute. Remember that it is important to tell the truth." Then let them start over.[13]

By the way, do not punish your kids for telling you the truth. Normally, punishment follows wrong behavior or sinful behavior. That's a given.

It is one thing to punish your children (whatever their age) when they foul up, when they break a well-established guideline in your home or sin against God's Word. And they get themselves in double trouble when they try to lie their way out of their behavior.

But here is where we parents sometimes blow it. We instruct our kids to always tell the truth. So, when they act in a manner that they know requires some form of punishment, they speak to us about it and come clean. And what do we sometimes do? We blow a gasket and double up the punishment.

Why? They told the truth. Certainly punishment is in order—but don't penalize them for being honest, or they will learn very quickly not to tell you the truth. They simply won't tell you anything. Be careful here.

Also, in the process of modeling truthfulness in your home, remember that parents set the pace in terms of "speaking rightly." If you are modeling gossip, slander, or lying, admit it. Apologize for it. Ask for forgiveness, and then set out on a path that models the opposite.

Four gates to shut out slander or gossip

Study the following principles related to passing information along. They ought to be embedded into the structure of your family. We will call them "conversation gates." If all four gates are open and give you approval, you may confidently share the information you have heard.

Gate 1: Is the information confidential?
If it is, never mention it. By the way, that applies to information that comes not only from outside your family, but also from inside. As family members we must respect each other's privacy. Many adults today are still filled with anger because of some parental invasion of their privacy during their teen years.

At some point, a parent intercepted a letter, read a diary, monitored a phone call, or searched a drawer. Twenty years later, the son or daughter is still upset about it. The family needs to be a place where we can make mistakes and be ourselves without the details getting outside the home.

Some of the problems children face as they grow up are sensitive. We parents easily forget how mortifying it was to have our problems brought to the attention of those outside the family. If parents remain insensitive in this area, trust breaks down in the family system. Children learn to be on guard and not share the important things of their lives.

So talk to your kids. If they ask you to keep something confidential, honor that request. Don't tell the story even if it will get a big laugh. Don't betray their trust even if they don't know you've told someone. If it is confidential information, keep it that way. Anytime I share anything about my family that may be misread, I ask for their approval in advance. If I don't get it, it is a closed book.

Gate 2: Is it true? This may take some time and energy to determine, but make sure you verify it before you pass it on.

Gate 3: Is it necessary? Sure, everybody will be impressed. People will be amazed at your inside scoop, but so much of what we pass on is simply unnecessary.

Gate 4: Is it kind?

Alan Redpath, at one time the pastor of the famed Moody Memorial Church in Chicago, had a similar idea under the acrostic THINK.

T —Is it *true?*

H—Is it *helpful?*

I —Is it *inspiring?*

N—Is it *necessary?*

K—Is it *kind?*[14]

It is that aspect of kindness that brings me to the last principle I'd like to share with you. Not only should we model honesty and truthfulness, but we must go out of our way to be verbal encouragers.

Follow Solomon's thought in Proverbs 10:11–21: "The mouth of the righteous is a fountain of life . . ." (10:11).

"The tongue of the righteous is as choice silver . . . the lips of the righteous feed many" (10:20, 21).

"But the tongue of the wise brings healing" (12:18b).

"Anxiety in the heart of a man weighs it down, but a good word makes it glad" (12:25).

Making people glad

One of the single most significant ministries we should cultivate in our homes is the ministry of mutual encouragement—honest expressions of appreciation, and words of gratitude for what another person means to us.

I realize that our children do not always make us proud, or give us joy to have them around. We yell at them. We tell them to get lost. We all have made mistakes with our children. We look back on them with embarrassment and guilt and wish to God we had not done or said what we did.

But sometimes there is a pattern.

A prevailing mood. Some parents hardly ever display pride, or feel joy, about their child. They seldom give the voice and touch of love, and their child gets a certain signal that, in at least some ways, she or he is not loved, is not important, is not owned.

And if she is not owned by her parents, it must be because she is not nice enough, good enough, beautiful enough to be worth owning. Not by them and, as a result, not by herself.[15]

Many children have been slain, and many others saved, by parental tongues. Kids long for encouragement and thrive on even the slightest compliment. No child, whatever his or her age, should go through even one day without at least one encouraging word. That is what children will remember, far more even than your reactive disciplines. Children may forget your advice, but they will never forget your applause.

Some parents resist this. They respond by saying:

"But I don't want to inflate my child's ego."

"I'm afraid if I praise them, they'll take advantage of me and won't finish their work."

"They know I love them without my having to say it."[16]

Parents, are you aware that it takes nine compliments to undo the pain of one criticism?

Our minds tend to fix on a negative comment when it's directed our way. The pastor who hears fifty compliments for his sermon can have his afternoon meal ruined by one burning phone call. Every person who is breathing has something about him worth encouraging. The genuine compliment is rare as silver, but it is also one that crystallizes the strength of a person in words, just as trophies inscribe it in silver.

A word to children of all ages

The same applies to children and young people in the home. I know parents who are dying for, longing for, waiting for, crying out for a word of appreciation and encouragement from their kids. They know they are not perfect, but they seem to never hear anything positive from their own kids. Do you know how hard that is to endure? It's a parental killer.

I don't care if you think your parents just fell off the turnip truck, look at them once in a while with eyes of kindness and verbally encourage them. Once in awhile, if all the doors in the house are locked, the blinds drawn and the lights are down, you might even go over and give your folks a hug. Nobody will see, nobody will tell, but you will add years to your parents' emotional life.

Some time ago, our day school on the church campus held a "Grandparents Day." I was asked to speak. Probably eight or nine hundred people attended—mainly grandkids and grandparents. I walked throughout the crowd and asked several dozen kids what they loved the most about their grandparents. I had to fight them off; everybody wanted to speak.

But as I listened, I watched the faces of the grandparents. There were only two responses: a smile that wouldn't stop, or tears of joy that kept flowing. Then, I flipped it around and asked the grandparents to tell me the one thing they loved the most about their grandkids. Guess what? The results on the kids faces were the same.

Leo Buscaglia, a great encourager, tells us that "Mark Twain once said he could go for two months on a good compliment. . . . Nearly every one of us is starving to be appreciated, to be the recipient of that most supreme compliment—that we are loved. We need others to recognize our strengths or sometimes just to prop us up in the places where we tend to lean a little. Honest compliments are simple and cost nothing to give, but we must not underestimate their worth."[17]

Jim Elliot, the martyred missionary to the Auca Indians of South America, put it this way in his journal:

I spoke . . . words fell aimlessly on ears. Later one said, "your word—it helped that day."
I turned . . . wondering—forgot I said that word.
Let me speak those words often. Helpful words that I forget.[18]

You know, the natives of the Solomon Islands were more right than we might have admitted. Yelling at living things does tend to kill the spirit in them, because it will always be true that:

"Sticks and stones may break our bones, but words—they'll just break our hearts."

Discipline that Delivers

Proverbs—Selected Verses

My old friend, Chuck Swindoll, in one of his first books, illustrates how difficult the training of our children can be:

Many years ago, Cynthia and I decided we all needed to work on our table manners. We were beginning to look and sound more like a pen of pigs than a home of humans.

Before supper began I whispered to Curtis (who was six) that he should serve Charissa (she was four) before he served himself. Naturally, he wondered why, since the platter of chicken sat directly in front of him...and he was hungry as a lion. I explained it is polite for fellas to serve girls before they serve themselves. The rule sounded weird, but he was willing . . . as long as she didn't take too long.

Well, you'd never believe what occurred. After

153

prayer, he picked up the huge platter, held it for his sister, and asked which piece of chicken she wanted. She relished all that attention. Being quite young, however, she had no idea which piece was which. So, very seriously, she replied, "I'd like the foot."

He glanced in my direction, frowned as the hunger pains shot through his stomach, then looked back at her and said, "Uh . . . Charissa, mother doesn't cook the foot."

To which she replied, "Where is it?"

With increased anxiety he answered (a bit louder), "I don't know! The foot is somewhere else, not on this platter. Look, choose a piece. Hurry up."

She studied the platter and said, "Okay, just give me the hand."

By now their mother and father were biting their lips to restrain from laughing out loud. We would have intervened, but decided instead to let them work it out alone. That's part of the training process.

"A chicken doesn't have a hand, it has a wing, Charissa."

"I hate the wing, Curtis. . . . Oh, go ahead and give me the head."

By then I was headed for the bathroom. I couldn't hold my laughter any longer. Curt was totally beside himself. His sister was totally frustrated, not being able to get the piece she wanted.

Realizing his irritation with her and the absence of a foot or hand or head, she finally said in an exasperated tone, "Oh, all right! I'll take the belly button."

That did it. He reached in, grabbed a piece and said, "That's the best I can do."[1]

As parents, we all find ourselves from time to time in those kinds of situations, where our desire to instruct, to teach our children, turns into a miniature circus and there is lots of laughter. At the other end of the playing field however, sometimes the game is a lot different. All our efforts to instruct, to teach, seem to have backfired and there is very little to even smile about.

Dealing with the "D" word

Because nobody is perfect, part of the package we call parenting involves failure, frustration, and pain. People get wounded, and scars form. Things get tense and relationships suffer.

Maybe that prompts some of us, when we hear the word "discipline," to almost recoil. We shy away from discipline for fear that it will drive our kids away from us.

In fact, if there is one word that raises the hair on people's necks, it is the word "discipline." It erects images of abuse and dictatorship. And yet, biblical discipline knows nothing of either.

Significantly, solid secular experts now drift toward the use of appropriate discipline. Dr. Ray Guarendi, of the Children's Hospital in Akron, Ohio, observes of successful parents:

> . . . love guided their discipline. Overall, these mothers and fathers can best be described as authoritative. Motivated by love, they possess the willingness to discipline quickly and firmly when a situation calls for it. . . . The essence of parenthood [is] unconditional love coupled with the will to discipline.[2]

With unusual fatherly insight, Solomon, the ancient king of Israel (who is still renowned for his wisdom), leads us to the subject of discipline in our homes with these thoughts from Proverbs, chapters 12 and 13. Glance at three verses with me.

> Whoever loves discipline loves knowledge, but he who hates reproof is stupid [or a fool] (12:1).

The way of a fool is right in his own eyes, but a wise man is he who listens to counsel (12:13).

A wise son accepts his father's discipline, but a scoffer does not listen to rebuke (13:1).

Changeless principles—handle with care

Now before we tackle these verses directly, allow me to make a couple of general observations related to parenting.

First of all, please remember that raising children has never been easy. At no time in history have the negative forces been dormant or overwhelmed by righteousness. Without minimizing the pressures of our generation, we must realize that each era of history has had its own peculiar hazards and anxieties. It has always been tough to raise unselfish, responsible, and godly children. It was tough for Solomon, as it is for you. But this also suggests that the principles he learned are also valuable to us today.

Second, be careful even as we wind our way through Proverbs. Many parents are looking for packaged solutions to raising kids. That is, if you always do this, and never do that, your children will always come out right. That's where many parents suffer a blind spot. What I am trying to communicate in this book are some principles of parenting that do not change. The specific application of those principles may vary from family to family, and even from child to child within the same family. So keep that in mind.

And third, as we talk about discipline now, realize that it is a long-range process. Often parents take an isolated example of misbehavior in their child or teenager, project it into the future, and convince themselves that their kid is going to become a delinquent or simply be a wasted person. Of course, that is not usually the case.

Focus once again with me on chapters 12 and 13. In the

verses we read, three words probably jumped out at you: discipline, reproof and rebuke. Before you decide too quickly what those refer to, let me explain them.

The word "discipline" that is used throughout Proverbs refers to correction which results in learning or education for a child or young person. It is, first and foremost, verbal instruction. It also includes punishment for wrong behavior, but that is not its dominant side.

Dr. Wes Willis, the senior vice president of Scripture Press, does a good job helping me understand the word "discipline." Listen to his explanation:

> Discipline and punishment are not the same thing. . . . Punishment is part of discipline, but discipline is the broader concept. Punishment is requiring payment for an infraction. It is the negative part of discipline—dealing with a problem after it has arisen.
>
> But discipline includes a positive dimension too. Discipline means helping a child know what is right and encouraging that child to do it. It is guiding and directing so that punishment will be needed only on rare occasions. Discipline involves building a strong, loving relationship of mutual respect and encouragement. And when positive discipline characterizes the parent-child relationship, punishment will be needed much less often. When punishment must be administered, the results will be positive and long-lasting.[3]

That's the first word. Now I know that you can verbally encourage right behavior from now to the end of time, yet there are times when your kids choose to go another route. At that point you move to the second and third words Solomon highlighted.

The word, "reproof," which also appears in verse one of chapter 12, is a little different than the word "discipline." It has some force to it, because it includes the ideas of rebuking or correcting behavior that is inappropriate and wrong. It involves confronting children with wrong behavior and pushing them with determination to acknowledge their wrong and to change.

The word, "reproof" tilts toward the punishment side of parenting.

Then there is the third word, translated as "rebuke" in Proverbs 13:1. It is another strong word that joins the ideas of verbal correction and parental actions that correct or punish wrong behavior.

So the process involves not only positive verbal instruction that encourages your children to do what is right, but also some sterner correction, or punishment, which we might think of as negative or harsh.

Now some people hear this and say to themselves, "So what? What's the point or value to discipline?"

The point is that children who are disciplined appropriately and who learn to respond positively to that process will be better equipped to function wisely or knowledgeably in their lives.

Solomon said it succinctly:

Whoever loves discipline loves knowledge. . . . A wise son accepts his father's discipline (12:1a; 13:1a).

Now remember, whenever the word "wisdom" crosses our path in the book of Proverbs, it refers to *the ability to make wise choices and to live successfully according to moral standards.*

That is the goal of parental discipline. Discipline is teaching a child the way he should go. Discipline includes everything you do to help your child learn. The purpose of discipline is positive—to produce a whole person.

The bottom line is that whether you do or don't discipline your children, you educate them to a specific set of values.

If you choose not to administer loving but fair discipline to your children, you can take it to the bank that society, sooner or later, will. And your kids need to catch on to that quickly.

They can pay now, or pay later

That is why Solomon's emphasis is on cultivating teachability in our children through discipline. Dr. William Glasser, in his book, *Reality Therapy*, puts it this way:

People who are not at some time in their lives, preferably early, exposed intimately to others who care enough about them both to love and discipline them will not learn to be responsible. For that failure they will suffer all their lives.[4]

That suffering is described by Solomon in Proverbs 13:1 with the word "scoffer."

"A scoffer does not listen to rebuke."

A scoffing child has no respect for authority. And because he thinks he knows what is best, he is not teachable. He does not respond well to any level of discipline. But Solomon indicates that if you cannot accept advice, counsel and correction from your own father, then you are well on the way to trouble. Children must understand early that if they wish to improve themselves so as to function as contributing individuals to society, then they must begin to accept correction and learn from it.

Discipline, then, is teaching a child how to live in this world. It is constant directing. And we parents must discipline them today, or someone else will tomorrow—a teacher, an employer, a landlord, a judge. But few will ever discipline them with even a fraction of the love and understanding of a parent.

Now if we choose not to discipline and punish our children for wrong behavior, what characteristics might we expect to see in their lives?

Let me briefly quote Solomon regarding several marks of an undisciplined life.

The first one may surprise you. It's found in Proverbs 15:32:

He who neglects discipline despises himself, but he who listens to reproof acquires understanding.

It may be difficult to understand, but children who are not taught to accept discipline or who have no parental discipline directed their way, will sooner or later develop a very poor self-image.

The verb, "despise" in this verse highlights that. It means "to reject yourself, to have poor self-esteem." In order to grow as a person, we must begin to understand our strengths and weaknesses. Building on strengths often helps us face weaknesses, and change them. It's a long process. Normally, we become aware of those weaknesses as we are corrected for inappropriate behavior by those who we know love us and are concerned about our growth.

A tale of two teachers

Back before Noah had completed the ark, and I was a junior high student, this principle was imbedded in my brain through the examples of two contrasting teachers. I still remember their name—Mr. Eiler and Mr. Sebo.

Mr. Eiler was my history teacher and a man who taught me to love the game of chess at the same time. He was an incredible encourager. He used to mark our exams and papers with large flowing letters, and if you received an A it was hard to miss.

Mr. Sebo was not so flamboyant, although he made his point in a different way.

Mr. Eiler, whenever I did poorly, would always kindly show

me where I had messed up and how I could improve. He was so good at it that I would have done anything for him. To this day, I love history and chess because of his encouragement. He helped me see that my weaknesses in study habits or grades were not terminal and that there was hope. I didn't mind when he pointed out my weaknesses because I knew he wanted me to grow.

Mr. Sebo—he's a different story. I remember working like crazy on a science project on the subject of birds. I did everything I could to make it perfect, even to the point of including some Latin terms. The great part is that I did it completely on my own. When it was returned to me it was marked with an A—but the A was crossed out and beside it was a large C, with the following words: "This project is too good for you to have done by yourself, so I have lowered your grade!"

Now although I ultimately went on to earn my Bachelor of Science degree, it was *in spite of* Mr. Sebo. I was convinced he was not interested in seeing me grow—just in tearing me down.

But here is the key: We need to be aware of our weaknesses, and when those who are concerned for us point them out to us, we have a great opportunity to grow and feel better about ourselves.

If we consistently fight off correction, however, our weaknesses will not magically disappear. They will grow to haunt us. And as they do, our self-esteem will take a beating. We will see ourselves with less positive value as time goes on.

On the other hand, if we parents do not confront weaknesses through correction, our sons or daughters will conclude that we really have no interest in their life and growth. That too will sabotage their self-image, and guarantee their rejection of themselves. And they don't need additional help with that.

"Everybody who hates Graham," the note read, "sign here."

By the time the teacher intercepted the note, which

was on its way to Graham, all the students in the class had signed it. Graham not only had no friends among his fourth-grade classmates, he was the object of intense hatred and rejection.

Psychologists estimate that up to 10 percent of the children in elementary school classes are without friends. Many of these children are, like Graham, actively disliked.[5]

Why Johnny hates himself

Children don't need parental assistance in submerging their self-worth, which already takes a beating at school. Yet the lack of parental discipline or the child's unwillingness to accept correction will do exactly that.

It will mark your kids in another way, though, that is just as negative.

A man who hardens his neck after much reproof will suddenly be broken beyond remedy (29:1).

The rod and reproof give wisdom, but a child who gets his own way brings shame to his mother (29:15).

Lack of discipline, or an unwillingness to respond well to it, will ultimately produce a "hardened" adult. Solomon is describing someone who stubbornly refuses to change. He is involved in continuous sin or behavior that is not helpful to them. Despite repeated counsel to change, and offers from others—presumably parents—to help in the process, he doesn't listen.

When we become immune to the counsel and help of others, we eventually develop a chip on our shoulder and the attitude that only we have the solutions. We do this to cover our sagging self-image and to make ourselves feel important. We stubbornly dig our heels in and fight for our way. Solomon says that approach might someday keep us from listening to a life-saving piece of advice.

You can often spot this in adults who have never grown up and who always demand their way. When they don't get it at work, they create a scene or simply quit in a huff. They move from one job to another as regularly as they change their shirt. And it is always the company's fault, or something like that. Their merry-go-round marital experiences reflect the same problem. They won't stay in a relationship very long if they can't get what they want when they want it.

You've met kids and adults like this, haven't you? You throw up your hands, scratch your head and walk away because they are incredibly self-destructive in their lifestyles, but they are not listening to anyone. They are hardened because they received no consistent discipline at home.

You may say, "Well, I know kids who are not disciplined and they aren't like that."

Perhaps that's true. If it is, then you will find their behavior described in the last part of 29:15. If they are not hardened, they will be spoiled rotten.

> . . . a child who gets his own way brings shame to his mother.

The phrase translated in our English Bibles as "who gets his own way" literally means "he is let loose, he is unrestrained." Airlifted into the nineties, it describes a child or a young adult who always gets his way, who never has to face the possibility of self-denial or self-discipline.

The tremendous value of "No!"

Positive, successful parents appreciate the value of the word "No." They depend on the word often, because they base their decisions on their child's well-being, and not on how much he nags, pleads, sulks, or threatens until he gets a "Yes."

Good parents love their kids enough to say "No" when necessary. One father writes:

> "No" is among the smallest of words, but it speaks one of life's biggest lessons: You can't always have what you want. And the younger a person is when she grasps that lesson, the smoother her life will be. That is why better parents aren't afraid to say "no," be it in response to a two-year-old's climbing onto the table, a four-year-old's sobbing for more ice cream, or a fifteen-year-old's, "Can I go to the quadruple drive-in feature with Rocky tonight? I promise I'll be back in time to study for exams tomorrow."

Bob from Cleveland asserts that the word "no" must become a comfortable part of a parent's vocabulary. The kids have to see that life is not a candy store with all the shelves open all the time.[6]

"A child who has everything is a deprived child." That is not the opinion of an amateur, but the observation of an expert. Dr. Joseph Noshpitz once headed up the children's division of the State Mental Institution for Kansas. Later, he was in charge of the Mental Health Institute in Washington, D.C. Today he teaches psychiatry in two universities. He's a consultant to mental institutions throughout the nation and has an extensive private practice. He is concerned about parents who are too permissive:

> When the child says: 'I want it,' he often gets it. He says, "I want this," and he often gets it. "I want that," and he gets that. Then he says, "I want the moon," and his parents patiently explain, "Dear, you can't have the moon." To which he now responds, "I want the moon, I want the moon, I want the moon."

Dr. Joseph Shroeder, for some years the director of the San Diego Zoo, has observed that in the animal kingdom no offspring is allowed to do as he pleases, and that there is no juvenile delinquency known within the animal kingdom.[7]

One of the less popular words

Now you realize that when you say "No," your kids won't roll over and play dead. Their first response will usually not be: "Well, thank you mother and father for demonstrating the courage to stand up to my selfish, egocentric, myopic desires. I realize now that I was being very shortsighted. I was not thinking of others. I was only interested in gratifying myself. I am truly sorry and I beg your forgiveness and indulgence."

What you are likely to hear or see instead is the slamming of a door, the rolling of the eyes, a long, painful sigh or a flat-out verbal shot fired right back at you.

Don't weaken. Your persistence will have long-term benefits, and will quite likely avoid the third mark of an undisciplined life.

Solomon describes the situation potently in Proverbs 19:26, 27:

He who assaults his father and drives his mother away is a shameful and disgraceful son.

Well, you may ask "How would he become that way?" Look at the next verse for the answer.

Cease listening, my son, to discipline and you will stray from the words of knowledge.

I want you to notice carefully the verb "assault" in verse 26. It's not a nice term. It means "to mistreat someone, to abuse someone, even to deal violently with someone."

In Solomon's day, he may have had in mind the son or daughter who worked overtime to take over the father's real estate or business prematurely. You know the kind. They either can't wait to grab their share of the inheritance, or they actively pursue pushing their parents aside so they can take over. People do that when they're spoiled—when they always get what they want because they are always right; correction and discipline have never been a part of their lives.

Godly discipline builds respect

Interestingly, the writer of the New Testament book of Hebrews offers an insight into this kind of behavior when he observes:

> . . . For what son is there whom his father does not discipline? . . . Furthermore, we had early fathers to discipline us, and we *respected them* [italics mine]. . . . " (Hebrews 12:7b, 9a).

You don't normally "assault" or "abuse" someone you respect, do you? The biblical author is careful to point out that parental discipline builds respect for that parent. But if there is no discipline, there will be no respect. And when there is no respect, you will discover abusive and assaulting mentalities.

The word "assault," when used today, has an even more sinister side. According to the FBI, police across the nation receive more calls for family conflicts than for murders, aggravated batteries, and all other serious crimes. The category of family conflicts includes not only quarrels between husband and wife but also between parent and child.

It is reported that more than 50 percent of all homicides are violent attacks by one member of a family against another member of the same family. In general, police don't like dealing with family quarrels, because they don't know what to expect. And frequently, the calls are very dangerous. Twenty-two percent of all police fatalities occur while investigating domestic disturbances.

The sad fact is that 30 percent of all American couples experience some form of domestic violence during their lifetime. More than two million people have used a lethal weapon on a spouse during their marriage.[8]

What pushes that kind of button? Solomon says it is the mark of an undisciplined life.

It doesn't have to go that way. I am convinced that entirely the opposite pattern is very possible—if we adopt some clear principles related to positive discipline of our children. Let me give you two very basic principles, along with some points of application.

Two principles of godly discipline

The first principle is that *discipline must always be given in the context of parental love and fairness.* Discipline is, in fact, a demonstration of that love.

Glance back to Proverbs 13:24—"He who spares his rod hates his son, but he who loves him disciplines him diligently."

(You may be wondering if I am going to address the issue of spanking. Yes, under principle two—so hang on.)

Significantly, the writer of the Hebrews passage I mentioned earlier picks up on this idea as he talks to us about God's relationship to us.

These are his exact words:

My son, do not regard lightly the discipline of the Lord,
nor faint when you are reproved by Him. . . .

Don't miss those two words—*discipline* and *reprove.* Those are two of the three that Solomon has focused on.

. . . For those whom the Lord loves, He disciplines (Hebrews 12:5-6).

One of the best indicators that people love you is their willingness to correct your misbehavior and their desire to help you grow in a positive way.

The emphasis then is that discipline must be reinforced with love and fairness.

Discipline must always have within it the element of love. "I care enough about you to force you to act in a better way, in a way you will learn through experience to know, and that I already know, is the right way."[9]

Balancing control and support

Two powerful factors influence our kids: parental control and parental support.

Parental control is the ability to manage a child's behavior. Parental support is the ability to make our children feel loved. When parental support is low and parental control is high, the parents become domineering and produce children who are fearful and do not see themselves with any value.

A report released in *The Harvard Medical School Mental Health Letter* concluded that unfair, harsh, and inconsistent discipline in children was strongly associated with adult depression and alcoholism. Forty-one percent of those studied with a history of depression, and 40 percent of those with a history of alcoholism reported that they had been beaten by their parents.[10]

That is discipline outside the context of love.

The reverse picture is also a problem. When parental support is high but parental control is low, you will breed a spoiled and manipulative child who knows how to exploit your "love" to his or her own advantage.

Solomon would not endorse either approach. What he

would endorse is that genuine parental love is displayed in disciplining children responsibly. Those parents who truly love their kids realize the importance of consistent discipline. A child senses that his parents care when they stand their ground and maintain the parameters that they have established.

When you have an understanding with your kids and have laid out the ground rules, then they know what is expected of them. If they don't do what is expected and agreed upon, they expect—even demand—a correction. Not to follow through is to weaken and negate the possibility of future effective follow-through in regard to other requirements. Believe it or not, when kids do something wrong and get away with it, they usually, until completely hardened, feel guilty about it. The only way to relieve the guilt and to reinforce your parental authority and love is to effectively deal with the problem.

As you do so, try to clearly separate dissatisfaction with behavior from love of your child. Assure and reassure your children of your unconditional love for them. With every occasion of discipline or correction, reemphasize that it is what the child did that you do not like, and that your love for your son or daughter cannot be altered by anything.

Mention this frequently to children of all ages and don't be embarrassed to back it up with a hug and physical affection. Say something like, "Son, I was very upset when you were two hours late getting home from school and didn't call us, and you deserve the penalty you're getting. But I want to remind you that it is what you did that upset me. I still love you as much as ever. I always do, and always will."

In their book, *Teaching Your Children Values*, the husband and wife author-team, Linda and Richard Eyre, add this good word:

"Love is better taught in settings where "repentance"or restitution is an alternative to punishment.

Teach children that when they make a mistake, or lose

their temper, or break a family law, they can often avoid a punishment if they apologize, make restitution, and promise not to "do it again". . . . When two children fight or argue, sit them on [a] bench and tell them that the only way to get off the bench is to say what they (not the other guy) did wrong, to apologize (including a hug), and to promise not to do it again. . . . Praise them and show pride for any "repenting" they do. The whole process can add to the love that is expressed and felt in your home.[11]

We have done that regularly in our home, with a slight variation. If our boys are at each other's throats and blood is abou to be spilled, I will step in and ask what's cooking. Usually I get two different stories. When that happens, it's off to their rooms until they can sort out the truth. You'll be amazed at h quickly they start negotiating with each other to come up wit the truth.

Instead of fighting against each other, they are now work with each other. The key is that their "story" must be the trut not simply a manufactured version that gets them both out ol hot water.

I think our youngest son expressed the context of love in discipline recently as he completed, without our input, an assignment from school dealing with what he thinks. Responding to a question about the future he wrote:

"I want to be strict with my kids," (that's parental control, right?), "but not too strict" (that's parental support).

What principle is he expressing? Discipline in the context of love and fairness.

Start early and apply consistently

The second principle is that *discipline must begin early and be consistent in its application.*

Look at Proverbs 19:18.

Discipline your son while there is hope . . .

Foolishness is bound up in the heart of a child; the rod of discipline will remove it far from him (22:15).

In chapter 19, Solomon talks about disciplining your children while there is hope. What does that mean?

It refers to the formative years of childhood, before patterns of behavior become ingrained and are difficult to change. It means that the process of discipline must begin right away. No parent can expect to suddenly tell a sixteen-year-old what he can or can't do if, for the past fifteen years, the child has never had rules enforced. The earlier you start, the easier it is.

As children get older, they get bigger, smarter, more independent, and overall, more determined to do things their own way. Regardless of how much time and energy it takes to teach limits to a two-year-old for the first time, it will take far more time, energy, and grief to teach them to a seven-year-old for the first time.

The ancient Greek philosopher Plato understood this principle when he wrote:

The beginning is the most important part of any work, especially in the case of a young and tender thing; for that is the time at which the character is being formed and the desired impression is more readily taken. Shall we just carelessly allow children to hear any casual tales which may be devised by casual persons, and to receive ideas into their minds the very opposite of those which we should wish them to have?[12]

Creating a "period of hope"

A parent has a crucial part to play in defining "the period of hope." You can shrink that window of hope by not being consistent and persistent with your discipline. You see, the lesson your children should learn early is that when you promise discipline, correction, and punishment, you deliver discipline, correction, and punishment. The biggest mistake many parents make is to just talk and use the same old bromides their kids have heard for centuries. Such as:

"You'd better shape up or else."

"If you do that again, you're going to get it. . . ."

What do "else" and "it" refer to? Usually not too much. Perhaps you prefer statements like:

"I don't know what I'm going to do with you. . . ." Those words are music to your kids ears, because they mean you don't have a plan of attack. They love that.

"I've had it with you," is another favorite and meaningless threat.

Consistent parental discipline never uses empty threats or empty words. You explain what the consequences will be if certain behavior is continued or if certain responsibilities aren't met. When the child fails to listen or follow through, no discussion is needed, unless you sense that the extenuating circumstances require some Columbo-like investigation. Otherwise there is simply a price to be paid.

Guidelines to help you discipline

Parents must make their own decisions about methods of discipline, but to be consistent, remember these guidelines:

1. Children should be disciplined in private rather than in public. I've witnessed some of the most virulent forms of discipline in grocery stores that I ever want to see. That's not a good thing to do. Take the child out of the cart and go to the car and deal with them. You see, they're figuring if they get you in a public spot, you won't do anything. And I give them credit for thinking that far. However, their logical error in thinking is to then conclude that you will not do anything at all. You should

do something. Either privately in the car, or when you get home, but not publicly.

2. Children will repeat the actions that attract the most attention. The key, then, is to give more attention for doing something right than for doing something wrong. Give lavish, open praise for the right, and quiet, automatic discipline for the wrong. In other words, don't be afraid to ignore their acting out. Some children grow up and have discovered that they can almost always get the attention they crave through negative behavior. I know adults like this. Somewhere along the line someone needed to ignore them. If your child wants to hold her breath until her lips turn blue, let her do it. She will breathe at some point, believe me. If Johnny decides to throw a fit in the kitchen, walk to the family room and do not respond to his negative behavior.

3. Children should know the reasons for the rules they are expected to keep. The old line, "Because I said so," is usually not very fair. Of course, in cases of behavior that are dangerous to your child and require immediate action, that response may be appropriate, but not as a normal rule.

4. Children find great security in consistent, predictable discipline.[13]

I cannot emphasize this last guideline enough. To be truly consistent, it is important to decide what our standards are and what boundaries are to be enforced. What is acceptable and unacceptable behavior to you as parents? Are the boundaries reasonable? Are we setting standards we can consistently uphold? Consistency requires commitment.

Setting realistic boundaries

We must decide the boundaries for our family and then stick to them time after time in any and all circumstances. And to do that, our boundaries must be realistic and enforceable without being arbitrary. We must stick to them whether we are on the phone or not, whether we have company or not, whether we are at home, at another's home, at the store, in a restaurant, or at church. Our standards should be the same, and our children should have a clear understanding of them. Knowing the boundaries and the penalties for crossing those boundaries gives a child great security.[14]

Let me offer several other suggestions at this point that may prove helpful. The first relates to mothers and fathers.

You must get together on the standards in your home. You must talk to each other and agree together, and then support each other in the follow through. The worst thing that happens is that Susie figures out which one of you is the soft guy and leverages you against the other parent.

So Mom spends all day wrestling with three adolescent delinquents and has punished them appropriately. Then old Dad rolls home and the three angels meet him with tear-stained eyes and big hugs and before you know it, Dad has vetoed Mom's discipline. In the long haul, that's disastrous. You must stand with each other. Now certainly, there will be occasions when you don't, but don't make it a habit if you value your life.

Second, if you are divorced, this presents an exceedingly difficult situation. Often your kids are shuttled to your former spouse's home one weekend, and back to yours for the next. In that cycle, one of the parents usually tries to sabotage the other's style of parenting. If they know your standards, they lower them at their house. Furthermore, they often let the kids do anything they want and have anything they want. Why? They are still mad at you and are now attempting to get back through the kids.

What does that do to the kids? Ultimately, after the initial "Oh, isn't Daddy wonderful and Mommy a jerk" response, it sows seeds of unbelievable confusion in their minds. If you are living as so many divorced people tell me they are—"Oh, we're still friends"—and if you have a relationship with Jesus Christ, then bury the bitterness hatchet for the sake of your children. Then talk about consistent application of standards and discipline, regardless of whose home they are in on any particular weekend.

Finally, let me say a word to grandparents. Don't try to do penance for your mistakes with your kids by spoiling the grandkids. (All right, you can spoil them a little, but be reasonable.)

Do you know it takes about two weeks to de-program kids who spend time with grandparents who feel guilty about the way they raised their own kids? The best thing a grandparent can do is to talk to Mom and Dad and find out what the standards are, then love your grandkids enough to back up Mom and Dad.

Consider these consequences

I mentioned some time earlier the consequences for wrong behavior. Some of the consequences you might want to consider in your disciplining process would include:

Time out—where your son or daughter spends a time of cooling off alone.

A period of grounding—no phone, no video games, no social activities. The level of incarceration should be contingent on the level of crime, but I would submit that the period of grounding should not exceed a week unless we are talking about some kind of felony. Beyond a week, in my opinion, you're bordering on abuse.

A reduction in privileges—less TV time, restriction of leisure activities.

Repayment of damages—in terms of money and confession to the offended person(s).

Extra chores, or reduced allowances.

In terms of grounding, I would also suggest that seldom should choir practices, school club functions, or even sports practices and games be used to discipline irresponsible behavior. That type of restriction punishes others in the groups needlessly, and should be avoided.

I tell the parents of my Little League team, "Don't punish the whole team by grounding your son on the day of the game." Find something parallel that does not punish a group for something they were not a part of. Now look again at Proverbs 13:24 and 22:15.

He who spares his rod hates his son. . . .

Foolishness is bound up in the heart of a child; the rod of discipline will remove it far from him.

When Solomon talks about "foolishness," he is describing a morally immature person. Foolishness is that "little devil" that makes its presence felt even in the sweetest angel. The trouble with little devils is that they have a habit of growing up into big ones if they don't learn any better.

Addressing the "will"

Part of the fabric of humanity is the matter of individual will. Kids come into this world, into the family, without any controls on their will.

One of the most significant aspects of maturity is learning to be self-disciplined, to control the "foolishness" that is bound up in our nature. Now a child or young adult who is characterized with the word "foolishness" is marked specifically by three traits: (1) stubbornness, (2) chronic quarreling or arguing with those in authority, and (3) a flippant and deviant attitude.

How do you deal with that? That's what Solomon addresses in these two verses.

Obviously, the Lord (through the pen of Solomon) has corporal or physical punishment in mind. One authority put it this way:

Discipline here is the idea of inflicting pain in order to associate pain with wrong. The child learns two simple yet essential facts: wrong brings pain, right brings pleasure.The spanking communicates a firm, painful message. I am not referring to a slap on the face. Neither the face nor the upper part of the body are designed to handle such a blow. God has provided a perfect place on the body for pain. He has even supplied that area with some extra padding! And when the rod of discipline is administered His way with the right motive, firmly and briefly, no permanent damage will remain. According to God's promise, it will drive foolishness from him. . . .You owe it to your neighborhood, the teacher at school, to society in general to drive foolishness from your child. If you do not, you will live to regret it."[15]

To spank or not to spank

With our sons, who are well past this stage, we used spanking, but infrequently. With our oldest, we resorted to it perhaps no more than ten times. And with our youngest, probably less than that. They were spanked with one to three swats, never any more. Beyond that tends to push the one administering discipline out of control, and it is simply not necessary for communicating the message.

Please understand that spanking is not child abuse. Spanking and abuse are not necessarily related phenomena. Nor is there any solid evidence that spanking, by itself, will lead a child to be aggressive or to approach life with his fists. So don't throw the baby out with the bath water. Spanking is an effective method of discipline when implemented properly.

Dr. James Dobson, perhaps better than anyone else I have read, explains that proper implementation in this way:

When and under what circumstances is it appropriate to

use this form of discipline? You will not damage your child emotionally if you follow this philosophy:

1. Establish the boundaries in advance. Tell the child before he breaks the rule just what the rule is . . . .
2. When he defiantly challenges your authority by disobeying your instructions, then he will expect you to act. Don't disappoint him. A spanking, therefore, is to be reserved for that moment of conflict when the child dares you to defend your right to lead. It should come in response to his sassiness, haughtiness, or outright disobedience. *No other form of discipline is as effective as a spanking when willful defiance is involved* [italics mine].
3. Do not spank the child for mistakes and accidents. Do not spank him for forgetting to feed the dog, or make his bed, or other acts of immaturity. . . . Do not spank him for something today which was ignored yesterday.
4. After the spanking [he] will probably want to be loved and reassured. By all means, open your arms and let him come! Hold him close and tell him of your love. . . .
5. Your spankings should be completed by the time a child is eight or nine years old. Never spank a teenager. Since the self-esteem of an adolescent is in serious doubt anyway, a spanking is the ultimate insult. . . .[16]

Let me add here that if you blow it—you spank your child while your emotions are out of control, or when really he or she should not have been spanked—then go to him or her and admit it.

Say, "You know, I blew it. I overreacted to what you did. What I did was wrong. Will you forgive me? I've asked God to forgive me. Now I'd like it if you would forgive me also."

Don't be too proud or stubborn to do something like that. It will pay rich dividends in the end.

Solomon summarizes those dividends in 29:17: "Correct your son, and he will give you comfort; He will also delight your soul."

That sounds a lot better to me than in-house fighting, open hatred toward one another, and trying to cover the wounds by denying the problems. That approach just does not work. The wound is always there. And the scar never seems to go away.

I don't know where I found the following words, but everytime I read them, they strike a responsive chord:

I searched—but there definitely was *not* [italics mine] a packet of instructions attached to my children when they arrived. And none has since landed in my mailbox. Lord, show me how to be a good parent! Teach me to correct without crushing, help without hanging on, listen without laughing, surround without smothering and love without limit—the way you love me.

A Little Blood, Sweat, and Tears

Proverbs 6:6–11 and Selected Verses

For many years, Admiral Hyman Rickover was the head of the United States nuclear Navy. His admirers and his critics held strongly opposing views about the stern and demanding admiral. For many years, every officer aboard a nuclear submarine was personally interviewed and approved by Rickover.

Those who went through his interviews usually came out shaking in fear, anger, or total intimidation. Among them was former President Jimmy Carter who, years ago, applied for service under Rickover. This is his account of a Rickover makeover, as it were:

I had applied for the nuclear submarine program, and Admiral Rickover was interviewing me for the job. It was the first time I met Admiral Rickover, and we sat in a large room by ourselves for more than two hours, and he let me choose any subjects I wished to discuss. Very carefully, I chose those about which I knew most at the time—current events, seamanship, music, literature, naval tactics, gunnery—and he began to ask me a series of questions of increasing difficulty. In each instance, he soon proved that I knew relatively little about the subject I had chosen.

He always looked right into my eyes, and he never smiled. I was saturated with cold sweat. Finally, he asked a question and I thought I could redeem myself. He said, "How did you stand in your class at the Naval Academy?" Since I had completed my sophomore year at Georgia Tech before entering Annapolis . . . I had done very well, and I swelled my chest with pride and answered, "Sir, I stood fifty-ninth in a class of 820!" I sat back to wait for the congratulations—which never came.

Instead, the question: "Did you do your best?" I started to say, "Yes, sir," but I remembered who this was and recalled several of the many times at the Academy when I could have learned more about our allies, our enemies, weapons, strategy, and so forth. I was just human. I finally gulped and said, "No, sir, I didn't always do my best."

He looked at me for a long time, and then turned his chair around to end the interview. He asked one final question, which I have never been able to forget—or to answer. He said, "Why not?" I sat there for a while, shaken, and then slowly left the room.[1]

We have each struggled with doing less than our best in our own lives and in the lives of our kids. In fact, sometimes, after pulling our hair out for the forty-fifth time, we wonder if our kids will ever give a hundred percent to anything around the house. That's why I appreciate the counsel of the eminent scholar and theologian, Erma Bombeck, as she reflects on her kids and their athletic prowess at school:

How could I ever forget those athletic banquets where I sat there hearing about sons I had never known before? Who were these enigmas who were comatose at home and came to life on a school campus?

I sat there stunned one night as the coach put his arm around our son's neck and announced to a crowd, "This boy is probably one of the best sprinters I've had in my entire career here at South High. Hang onto your hats, folks. He set a school record this year by running the 100 yard dash in 9.9!"

9.9! I figured it had to be nine days and nine hours. I once asked him to run the garbage out to the can and it sat by the sink until it turned into a bookend.

And in a testimonial to another son, a coach said, "I don't know what this baseball team would have done without this boy's hustle. We've had chatterers on the team before who get the boys whipped up, but this one is a world-class chatterer. There isn't a moment when he isn't saying something to spark the team when they're down."

Our son smiled boyishly and hung his head.

Chatterer? From a kid who spoke only six words to me a week: When you going to the store? . . .

I was numbed by the announcement that one of our children threw a ball weighing eight pounds a distance of 100 feet. He couldn't throw a six-ounce Saturday edition of the newspaper from his bike to a porch on his paper route.

"Have you forgotten how your son got an award for picking up wet towels and suits for an entire swim team and couldn't pick up his own feet at home?" I asked [my husband one day].

"You know how kids are," he said, "They're two personalities. One for home and one for show."[2]

If you're a parent, you understand what Erma Bombeck is talking about. Somewhere there seems to be a synaptic gap in the behavior of our kids. And while it is encouraging to hear others speak so glowingly about them, it frustrates us to death that they don't exhibit at home some of the exciting characteristics others seem to spot at school.

In fact, we are justified in our frustration.

If young people can behave with one level of intensity "out there," they ought to be able to muster the same level of enthusiasm at home. And not to face that issue with our kids is to teach them duplicity or hypocrisy. That lesson goes like this: "Learn to just play the part where you are; the part that will get what you want. If you're not pushed, don't sweat it. Don't worry about producing; it will be okay. Just do what you have to, and only when you must."

That's a lesson parents cannot afford to teach.

Doing our best with what we have

Consider Solomon's perspective for a second, from a couple of verses buried deep in the book of Proverbs. Chapters 6 and 10 will be our advisors for the moment. Look at Proverbs 6:6 first.

Go to the ant, O sluggard [or lazy person], Observe her ways and be wise.

He who gathers in summer is a son who acts wisely, but he who sleeps in harvest is a son who acts shamefully (Proverbs 10:5).

One of the primary truths that Solomon has attempted to drum into our minds is that the goal of parenting is to instill "wisdom" into our kids. But remember that in Solomon's frame of reference, this does not simply mean stuffing their heads with facts. It is not just making sure they get an education, as valuable as that is.

Wisdom is the skill of living life. In fact, wisdom has a moral aspect to it. It is to be a part of our character. In order for a person's character to grow, wisdom must somehow begin to be a part of his or her life. Solomon is driving at this: being willing to work hard and do one's best at any given job is part of wise living; it is part of character building.

Unless that lesson is grafted into our hearts and the hearts of our kids, we miss an opportunity at character development.

That process begins with Solomon's perspective in 14:23. Look at it for a moment:

"In all labor there is profit, but mere talk leads only to poverty."

From a biblical perspective, work, labor—in whatever form that takes,—gets high marks. And please observe that Solomon says "all labor." Not some, not just the glamorous, "everybody notices" kind of a job, but all labor. People often think, "Look, I'm just a _____. Compared to so and so, my job stinks."

Solomon is not into categorizing types of jobs. From his vantage point they are all profitable. The word "profit" comes from a word that means "superior, preeminent." In other words, it is valuable, it is significant.

You may work at home or on the assembly line at Ford; push a broom at Browning Ferris Industries, or run the press at the steel mill on the midnight shift; coordinate a team of medical personnel at the hospital, or commute to an office in the city. Whatever you do, your work is significant. There is profitability to it.

Part of the profit is that it builds character.

Character building: mission possible

Recently I read through the findings of a forty-year study conducted at Harvard Medical School. Started in an effort to understand juvenile delinquency, the study followed the lives of 456 teenage boys from inner-city Boston, many from impoverished or broken homes. When they were compared at middle age, one fact stood out: regardless of intelligence, family income, ethnic background or amount of education, those who had worked as boys, even at simple household chores, enjoyed happier and more productive lives than those who had not.

"It's not difficult to explain," declares Dr. George Valiant, the psychiatrist who made the discovery when he was at the Harvard Medical School. "Boys who worked in the home or community gained competence and came to feel they were worthwhile members of society. And because they felt good about themselves, others felt good about them."

What parents can do

As parents, our role is crucial in at least two ways. First, we must model the attitude that communicates to our kids that our job, our work, is valuable. Instead of complaining about everything at work and everyone associated with it; instead of concentrating on what we don't like about our jobs; instead of continually expressing dissatisfaction with what we do; instead of transposing to our kids the idea that the only reason we keep this "stupid" job is because of the paycheck, sooner or later we must begin to take personal pride in the career God has placed us in. Our attitude toward work will leak through to our kids.

Second, we must not be afraid to require effort of our children, both around the house and in the community. One thing is certain: if your kids do not learn to work as children, they will never do much when they grow up.

Before I was old enough to hold down a "real" job, I delivered papers. During high school I had a full-time job throughout the summer months, and often worked part-time during school. That was particularly the case during my last two years of high school, and all through college and seminary. I worked at a steel mill on the presses from 6:00 P.M. to 4:00 A.M. I delivered pizzas, did maintenance work on a golf course; stocked shelves at grocery stores, drove a truck on an inter-city delivery route; worked in the histology lab or a hospital, and assisted a pathologist during autopsies. I even was a senior grader for an Old Testament class during seminary.

I believe that, almost without exception, the people who get things done as adults are those who learned to work as children. We need to teach our children the dignity of labor and the pleasure of accomplishment.

One authority on children put it this way:

> Every child is born with tremendous potential. Excellent parents believe this. They also believe it is their duty to make a child explore his potential, sometimes initially against his will. Regardless of their unique talents, all children possess the ability to behave a cut above the crowd. Settling for average—in morals, manners or character—is not something these parents are comfortable doing . . . To teach children to reach for their best, parents must reach for their best. Put another way, great expectations for a child begin with great expectations for oneself. To be a successful parents, we must be willing to do more than the average. . . . Excellent parenting means striving continuously to improve, not to look better than others, but because that's the only kind of parenting we're content with."[3]

The value of extra effort

Attention to this aspect of parenting is crucial unless we want to produce kids who are basically apathetic and lazy. Solomon was well acquainted with people like that because he talks about them in some detail. In both chapters 6 and 24 you will find a characteristic of those who never learn to value work. Look at 6:10:

How long will you lie down, O sluggard? When will you arise from your sleep? A little sleep, a little slumber, a little folding of the hands to rest . . .

Now look at chapter 24:30 and following:

I passed by the field of the sluggard, and by the vineyard of the man lacking sense; and behold, it was completely overgrown with thistles, its surface was covered with nettles, and its stone wall was broken down. When I saw, I reflected upon it. I looked, and received instruction. A little sleep, a little slumber, a little folding of the hands to rest . . .

Laziness: the soil in which poverty flourishes

Young people or adults who are plagued by laziness have no sense of urgency about their work. Their laziness focuses on the obstacles that seemingly stand in the way of the task. Those who are lazy just can't seem to roll up their sleeves and plunge in full bore. When you ask them when something is going to be done, they don't have a clue, nor do they want to. They just need a little more time to rest up, to get ready. And people pick up on that.

According to chapter 24, Solomon spotted it right away as he walked by the person's property. By the way, there is a lesson here.

What do others see when they look at our property? A junky garage, peeling paint, and obvious needs for repair? Do our sloppy, lazy habits make us so careless that others easily spot our lack of urgency?

"Mediocre" is a word that covers a lot of us. It means "of a middle quality." We recently leased a new mini-van. A neighbor friend of mine owns a dealership, and it was easy to work with him. When we talked though, I did not say, "Look, Larry, I know exactly the vehicle we want. First and foremost, it has to be mediocre!" None of us approaches the buying of a new car that way.

The same is true when you eat out at a fine restaurant. When the hostess greets you, do you respond by saying, "We'd like a mediocre table, with mediocre service, and above all, make sure the food is mediocre?" Let's not kid ourselves. For what kind of service do we tip our waitress? Superior service. Interestingly, the word "mediocre" originates from the Latin word that means "halfway up a mountain." That's the way it is with some of us. We do something halfway, with no sense of urgency or pride.

A study during the last decade found that although the vast majority of Americans want to work hard and do the best they can on the job, the fact of the matter is that half of those same people said they worked just hard enough to avoid getting fired.[4]

I suppose it is that kind of attitude that led to the publication of the following announcement by one company:

> Due to increased competition and a keen desire to remain in business, we find it necessary to institute a new policy. Effective immediately we are asking that somewhere between starting and quitting time and without infringing too much on the time devoted to lunch period, coffee breaks, rest period, story telling, ticket selling, horse selection, vacation planning and rehashing of yesterday's TV programs, that each employee try to find some time that can be set aside and be known hereafter as "THE WORK BREAK." Signed, The Management.

Regardless of how intelligent or talented you may be, if you don't have this sense of urgency, now is the time to start developing it in your own life and the life of your kids. Our society is full of very competent people who honestly intend to do things tomorrow, or as soon as they can get around to it. Their accomplishments, however, seldom match those of less talented people who are blessed with a sense of the importance of getting started now.

Which links us to the second characteristic of a person who is given to laziness. They often live in a dream world—a world of "what-ifs" or "I hope so's"—not a world of reality. Look at Proverbs 12:11.

He who tills his land will have plenty of bread, but he who pursues vain things lacks sense.

Here's the strange thing. Although we have already seen that a young person or adult who is given to laziness has no sense of urgency about his/her work, don't get the idea that they have no energy. They do, but it is funneled in other directions. Solomon says that kind of person "pursues vain things."

The word "pursues" means that they go after something intently, almost frantically. So we've got energy, but it is misdirected. It is focused on what Solomon considers "vain things." He means things that are not worth a lot, things that have no significance."

Refusing to face the present

In other words, here is a person who spends a great deal of time and energy on useless projects. We're talking about a dreamer here. This person doesn't like to deal with reality, so he creates his own fantasy world. His ship is always about to come in. He's inches away from hitting it big, winning the lottery, getting the promotion, landing the scholarship, making a million. Someone described that kind of person as one who "fixes tomorrow as the due date for success but tomorrow becomes today and the magic moment is postponed."[5]

I know a lot of kids who are dreamers—not in the sense of planning for their future, but in the sense of not facing the present. And they are like that because one or both parents live in a fantasy world. According to mom or dad, their life and work is not what they thought it would be like. It has disappointed them, and so they create a fantasy world. Somehow, life seems more bearable when a dreamer creates a fairy tale life for himself.

But all it succeeds in doing is pushing him from the responsibilities and duties of the moment, and his family usually suffers as a result of his delusions.

Helping our children manage time

One of the vital principles we parents need to share with our children is how to recognize those things that cause us to waste precious seconds on useless and unrewarding activities and pursuits. One father helps put this on the first floor when he gives this advice to parents:

One very basic and understandable way to help children manage time is to discuss together the things they have or want to do that day. If they are pre-school age, this is a good opportunity to help them be creative . . . As they make the list in their own printed style, let them explore the realm of creating. . . . After the creating process is complete for the day, help them think through which item on the list is most important or the one they want to do first. Put a number "1" next to that task and proceed through the rest of the list. Then let them rethink the process to see if it is clear in their minds.

Now comes the most important part. . . . Help them to finish number "1" before they go on to number "2." If possible, give them a work area where they can have everything they need to do the job, and keep all other project materials out of the way. If they get sidetracked, and you know they will, when they come back to work, they will be able to start where they left off. If you can help them learn to do one thing at a time until it is finished, you will have made a most important imprint on their minds. . . . In addition, teach them the importance and the joy of accomplishment as they cross the finished project off the list . . . It is wise to keep the list of "to do's" to no more than three items. As they get older, they will naturally enlarge the list, but for starters it could be a bit overwhelming to see thirty-two things to be done.[6]

Excuses, excuses

Now you realize that even as you attempt to instill in your children the value of hard work, they will come up with a host of excuses for taking it easy. Even Solomon dealt with that, according to Proverbs 26:13.

The sluggard says, "There is a lion in the road! A lion is in the open square!" As the door turns on its hinges, so does the sluggard on his bed.

The sluggard is wiser in his own eyes than seven men who can give a discreet answer (26:16).

The lazy person comes up with one excuse after another. This guy can't leave home to go to work because he might be attacked by a lion. Today we would say, "My car might be carjacked, or I could get into an accident." So the best plan is to stay put and dream.

Children or adults who have a bent toward laziness have a remarkable ability to think up excuses.

They actually believe them, regardless of how ridiculous

those excuses sound. Here are some of the best ones I've heard:
"I'm not feeling well, dad; I think I've got the flu."
"I'll do it, just five more minutes of Nintendo, then I'll do it."
"Dad, I think I pulled a muscle in gym today—it really hurts. I don't think I should lift anything."

Or when they are rock-bottom desperate, they moan, "Dad, I'd love to help with the lawn work, but I've got lots of homework to do." When you hear that one, you know you're looking at a manufactured excuse.

But as Benjamin Franklin observed: "The man who is good for excuses is good for little else."

George Washington Carver concurred when he said: "Ninety-nine percent of failures come from people who have the habit of making excuses."[7]

The crazy thing about all of this is that when you suggest to this person that they are lazy or they're just coming up with excuses, they will argue with you. Solomon says in verse 16 that these types of people view themselves as pretty sharp, as if they have all the bases of their life already covered. How common.

And if you confront them on their lazy tendencies or their lack of performance, they will come right back at you and blame somebody else. It is never their responsibility. They are a better person than you have prematurely judged them to be. And they pass that smugness on to their kids.

A problem with reality

An international study of thirteen-year-olds found that Koreans ranked first in math and Americans ranked way down the list.

Yet surveys show thirteen-year-old Americans are three times as likely to think they are good at math as are Koreans of the same age.[8]

Unrealistic self-assessments like that have some pretty damaging results. Proverbs 18:9 says: "He also who is slack in his work is brother to him who destroys."

A lazy person doesn't simply hold an organization back; he destroys its motivation and drive. A lazy father doesn't just create economic distress for his family; he models a style of life that puts his kids to sleep. They never deal with reality. A lazy baseball player doesn't just weaken the team; he destroys its spirit and its desire to win. A lazy pastor doesn't merely limit a church; he destroys its excitement, its passion to see lives changed for Jesus Christ.

In each case—family, team, or church—everyone else must do more to make up for that one person's laziness.

Of course, our laziness is even more destructive..

The *U.S. News & World Report* cites one estimate that in a year American workers will "steal" $160 billion from their employers by arriving late, leaving early, and misusing time on the job.[9]

As I suggested earlier, the problem is widespread.

Public Agenda Forum undertook a major survey of the American nonmanagerial workforce not long ago, with the following disturbing results:

- Fewer than one out of every four jobholders say that they are currently working at full potential.
- One-half said they do not put effort into their job over and above what is required to hold onto it.
- The overwhelming majority, seventy-five percent, said they could be significantly more effective than they presently are.
- Close to six out of ten Americans on the job believe that they "do not work as hard as they used to." [10]

Your personal industry inventory

Just think about it in terms of your personal situation. Maybe these questions will help you evaluate your level of industry:

1. Are you usually late for appointments and meetings?
2. Do you put off doing your homework until late?
3. Are you a time waster, like on the phone or with TV?
4. Is your reading limited to only the basics rather than heavier material?
5. Are you prompt in paying bills and answering mail?
6. Is your attire attractive? Things match? Shoes shined?
7. Do you have many unfinished projects lying around?
8. Does your desk stay cluttered? How about the tops of tables and counters?
9. Can you put your hands on important documents right away?
10. Can you concentrate and think through decisions carefully and then begin to implement those decisions?

Can you see how it begins with us? See how we begin to model sloppiness or laziness to our kids?

Let me suggest an alternative model—one that Solomon recommends. He begins in Proverbs 6:6.

Go to the ant, O sluggard, Observe her ways and be wise, which, having no chief, officer or ruler, prepares her food in the summer and gathers her provision in the harvest.

What's the point? The point is that the ant—in needing no oversight, is self-motivated. It is not uncommon for lazy people to be extremely skilled, creative, and bright. They can talk and dream and even sketch out a game plan, but the discipline of self-motivation is not there.

Is it there for you?

The benefits of self-motivation

Look at the three words that pop out of verse 7: chief, officer, and ruler.

The word "chief" literally means "the one who makes the final decisions," like the president of the company.

The word "officer" goes down the ladder a step. This isn't the president, but it could refer to your immediate supervisor, the department head, or a branch manager. It literally means "the organizer." It is whoever helps organize your life, which could be your spouse or secretary.

The third word, "ruler" is different again, but would probably describe the plant foreman of today.

Solomon says that even without the president of the company, your immediate supervisor, your manager, your secretary, spouse, or foreman looking over your shoulder, you still do the job. You are self-motivated. You don't need to be pressured into doing the job; you will do it whether there is anybody there or not.

The apostle Paul picked up on this idea in the New Testament. This is how he saw it:

Whatever you do, do your work [from the soul], as for the Lord rather than for me; knowing that from the Lord you will receive the reward of the inheritance. It is the Lord Christ whom you serve (Colossians 3:23, 24).

Serving the Lord Christ

For all of us who identify Jesus Christ as our personal Savior, there must be a higher motivation for our work and our careers than that which is typical of most employees. The fact is, our job performance, or lack thereof, is a reflection on the Lord Jesus Christ. His presence in our lives, not the boss's presence, ought to be enough to push us toward being self-motivated. Is it?

When was the last time it even crossed your mind that you are serving Jesus Christ in your job? See how easily we forget?

For young adults the same principle applies to study, especially from the junior high level and up. Very often there is no great pressure to perform. If they study, if they complete the assignment, the reward is their grade point. If they don't, the reward is still their grade point. Depending on how the student's parents react to their grade point average, a healthy motivation to study may not exist.

Sooner or later, kids have to learn the discipline of study that comes with being self-motivated.

Self-discipline means many things, but its primary meaning is being able to motivate and manage yourself and your time. Self-discipline is pulling up and away from the laziness of doing too little. It is a universal value because its presence helps us and others. Its absence inevitably causes short- or long-term damage.

Any successful leader will tell you it is a lot easier to hire people who are already motivated. J. William Grimes, head of ESPN, the all-sports cable network says:

> I don't look for either youth or experience. I want intelligence and, primarily, motivation. I want people who are very eager to accomplish a task, who can't wait to get something done and will always look to do it in new ways.[11]

Let me say this: one of the ways you begin to instill self-motivation in a child is by expecting him or her to work around the house. Children can begin to learn responsibility and motivation at an early age. Younger kids can make their beds, clean up their rooms, set the table, and empty wastebaskets. Older kids can vacuum, mow lawns, wash cars.

As I write this, I realize that each of our kids is very different and will respond uniquely to the assignment of chores. You will need to understand their differences and approach them accordingly.

Recently, my youngest son wanted his shirt and slacks

ironed for Sunday. I normally don't volunteer for that assignment. I confess, ironing is not one of my spiritual gifts. Maybe I need therapy, I don't know. At any rate, on this particular weekend we had guests from out of state and Patricia was very busy.

So I said, "I'll handle it. I'll iron them."

Kent looked at me with that look that says, "Are you feeling all right?" and then the look that says, "You've gotta be kidding!" I wasn't. We went downstairs and I showed him how to get it done. He watched every move, and I could tell he was filing it away for his own personal use in the future. He's like that.

Earlier that week, our elder son, Jeremy, had made a similar request of his mother. She suggested that he watch her iron and learn how to do it himself. His response was light-years removed from Kent's. He said very seriously, "Mom, I don't need to learn that now. I'll learn it in college!"

To this day I am convinced he thinks there is a course in college called "Ironing 101." Different responses. But the assignments still must prevail.

Responsible parents and healthy expectations

A very young child should not be given many formal tasks independent of the parent. If you send a child of six out to weed the garden, an area six inches by six inches will seem like an acre. Whenever possible, work with your child and exude a little enthusiasm about what you're doing.

Responsible parents expect a healthy amount of household help from their children. They are motivated by the attitude that this house or apartment is not Mom's and Dad's, it is the family's. Living here is everyone's privilege, so it is also everyone's responsibility.

Another way to help instill self-discipline and motivation relates to schoolwork. Jerry Jenkins, in his fine book on parenting, *Twelve Things I Want My Kids to Remember Forever*, tells us what he has done as a father. Remember that he is speaking to his sons:

I know it's probably some vestige of a Protestant work ethic that always makes me require you guys to do your homework and your chores before we watch a game on TV or play in the yard or do anything fun. But it also pays off. I use such things myself as rewards for getting a chapter done, a book read, a project finished for Mom.

You complain and badger and wonder why we can't play now if you promise, promise, promise to do the other stuff later. Maybe when you're grown or almost grown you'll try it your way. You'll put off the tough stuff to enjoy the moment, but you'll discover what I've discovered:

A game of touch football is not as much fun when you keep recalling that you still have to rake those leaves or clean the garage or do the dishes. Doing chores, on the other hand, is not so bad when you can look forward to some fun. . . .

I know you feel put upon when I'm rigid on this and you can't watch the Bears or the Cubs or the Bulls until that homework is completely done. And no, I can't think of a reason it would be so bad if you watched now and worked later—except that it works better this way. Work before you play.[12]

I would add, "Don't forget to play afterwards." But when we're talking about kids, that is usually not where the problem lies.

Part of parenting, then, is instilling a spirit of self-motivation, along with a desire to work with energy and thoroughness.

Consider Solomon's perspective in chapter 10:4 and chapter 12:27.

Poor is he who works with a negligent hand, but the hand of the diligent makes rich.

A slothful man does not roast his prey, but the precious possession of a man is diligence.

The generalization presented in verse 4 is that the industrious, conscientious worker is eventually recognized by his superior and rewarded, while the person who constantly watches the clock and gives out as little effort as possible will stay in the same job slot forever (if he or she manages to keep the job).

Modeling your work ethic enthusiastically

Parents, you need to instill some enthusiasm into your kids through your own example. Knute Rockne was a great football coach. He had the ability to energize his players like no other coach. His biography tells of the day he revved up his troops so much at an away game that they went out the wrong door from the dressing room, and the first three fell into the swimming pool. They were hot. They were high. High on Rockne. He put heart and energy into them.[13]
You need to pass that on to your kids.
I love what John Powell writes about intensity. Listen please:

. . . Fully alive people are those who are using all of their
human faculties, powers and talents. They are using
them to the full. These individuals are fully functioning
in their external and internal sources. They are comfortable with/and open to the full experience and expression
of all human emotions. Such people are vibrantly alive
in mind, heart and will. There is an instinctive fear in
most of us, I think, to travel with our engines at full
throttle. We prefer, for the sake of safety, to take life in
small and dainty doses.[14]

I find it significant that the word translated "diligent" in the book of Proverbs comes from a word that means "to decide." Elsewhere in the Old Testament, the same word reads as "to act with decision, or to act promptly."

Teach your child how to be diligent

Give your kids room to make decisions. Help them with the process of thinking things through, but then let them make some decisions. If you make all the moves for them, it will sap their energy. It will drain them dry, and they will go through life unenergized, and unable to act with decision. When they come up with an idea, unless it is something you know will put them in danger or harm them, fan the flames of their energy. Don't throw water all over their enthusiasm.

But in the process, remind them that enthusiasm and energy needs to be linked to *thoroughness*. That's the idea behind Solomon's word picture in Proverbs 12:27: "A slothful man does not roast his prey."

In other words, he doesn't finish the job. He gets it partly finished, and no more. He catches the rabbit, but he doesn't skin it or cook it. He fills out the job application, but never sends it in. He says he thinks he can do the job, but he doesn't submit a bid.

"Sure, I'll make the sales quota," he brags. But he never makes any second calls. In fact, he has trouble making the first one. He swears that he will get the extra credit in math completed for a B, but somehow all of his swearing does not help him get it done—and he settles for a D.

The point is, it doesn't matter what the job is that we have to do. We need to be sure to finish it. Do a thorough job.

Does it need painting? Paint it, and do a thorough job.

Does it need cleaning? Clean it—thoroughly.

Does it need ironing? Iron it—wrinkle free, with gusto.

Does it need attention? Give it thorough, unrestrained attention.

Stop being satisfied with a half-hearted, incomplete job. Shock those around you with a completely finished product. And stop putting it off. The difference between something good and something great is attention to detail. That is true of a delicious meal, a musical production, a new automobile, a well-kept home, a church, a business, a lovely garden, a sermon, and a well-disciplined family.

" 'Did you do your best?' I started to say, 'Yes, sir,' but I remembered who this was . . . and I finally gulped and said, 'No, sir, I didn't always do my best.'

He looked at me for a long time and then turned his chair around to end the interview. He asked one final question, which I have never been able to forget, or to answer. He said, 'Why not?' I sat there for a while, shaken, and then slowly left the room."[15]

CHAPTER NINE

Lengthening the Short Fuse

Selected Proverbs

It was the first homicide in six months for Cheyenne, Wyoming, and one that area residents will long remember. When Richard C. Jahnke, 38, an IRS senior agent, stepped out of his blue Volkswagen to open the garage door of his red brick home on Cowpoke Road, he walked into an ambush of shotgun slugs. He died instantly, and the attacker swiftly fled with an accomplice through a bedroom window. But when, within twelve hours, police arrested the two alleged murderers, the reaction was shock more than relief. Charged with the crime were Jahnke's children, Richard, Jr., 16, and Deborah, 17.

According to the criminal complaint later filed by officials, Richard admitted to city police, "I shot my father for revenge." Indeed, the family had fought bitterly on the day of the slaying. That evening Richard, armed with a loaded 12-gauge shotgun, lay in wait behind the garage door. Taking a back-up position, Deborah allegedly cradled a .30-calibre automatic carbine in the living room, in case their father escaped the first line of fire. The planning was unnecessary: Richard, aiming through the plywood garage door, hit his father with four pump-action blasts while his mother sat in horror in the car.

But despite the coldly premeditated nature of the slaying, public sentiment in Cheyenne began to shift to the alleged killers as details about the Jahnke household emerged. Jahnke, Sr., was described by those who knew him as an ultra-strict disciplinarian with an explosive temper that boiled over into physical violence. He doled out severe beatings to his children for the most minor infractions so that a friend of the family said, after the killing: "What those children did . . . it made terrible sense."[1]

Days of rage

Perhaps it makes sense to some people, if we see this as an isolated result of anger. But our anger defies the category of "isolated." One man described our country this way:

Americans, very many of them, are obsessed with tensions. Nerves are drawn tense and twanging. Emotions boil up and spill over into violence largely in meaningless or unnatural directions. In the cities people scream with rage at one another, taking out their unease on the first observable target. The huge reservoir of the anger of frustration is full to bursting.[2]

Recently, *The New York Times* devoted front page coverage to the latest killings inside the post office. The article was entitled, "Anger in the Post Office," and the opening descriptions read like this:

As shaken Post Office officials gathered information on the latest shootings in Michigan and California, some psychologists described much of postal work today as a treadmill of angry monotony, with labor-management hostility making many post offices minefields. . . .

The article went on to indicate that the third-leading cause of work-related death is murder.[3]

And it's not just a problem in the post offices of America, or somewhere as far removed as Cheyenne, Wyoming. A 1992 survey of teenagers in Sunday schools and youth groups found that 50 percent of fourteen- to nineteen-year-olds are angry. Dr. Robert McKee, president of Rapha, the Christian psychiatric service that conducted the survey, suggests that this anger is different from that expressed by the sixties generation. Young people then were angry but thought they could change the world. Today's teens feel overwhelmed and hopeless.[4]

The battleground at home

And what is true for many young adults is true for families in general. For many families, home is a battleground, filled with constant bickering, shouting matches, and exhausting power struggles. Nancy Samalin, in her book on parents and anger, describes a parent's plight. Does this sound like your own experience?

Parents are amazed that they can go from relative calm to utter frustration in a few seconds. An uneaten egg or spilled juice at breakfast can turn a calm morning into a free-for-all. In spite of parents' best intentions, bedtime becomes a wartime, meals end with children in tears and food barely touched, and car rides deteriorate into stress-filled shouting matches. . . . Whatever its source, we often experience parental anger as a horrifying encounter with our worst selves. I never even knew I had a temper until I had children. It was very frightening that these children I loved so much, for whom I had sacrificed so much, could arouse such intense feelings of rage in me, their mother, whose primary responsibility was to nurture and protect them.[5]

It should not come as a surprise to us that the Old Testament book of Proverbs directs attention to the rising temperature of our anger. In a series of staccato bursts, we are introduced to the subject beginning in chapter 14:17, 29:

A quick-tempered man acts foolishly. . . . He who is slow to anger has great understanding, but he who is quick-tempered exalts folly.

Now before you dismiss these introductory words about anger too quickly, please understand that the most recent findings report to us that about 20 percent of the general population has levels of hostility high enough to be dangerous to their health. Another 20 percent has very low levels, and the rest of the population [60 percent] fall somewhere in between.[6]

Anger—hazardous to your health

So Solomon writes to most of us, but particularly to those of us who are prone to chronic anger. There is an edge to almost everything we do. A cutting, critical attitude seems to encircle our days. We find ourselves not momentarily upset or angered, not temporarily upset, but seeming to burn white-hot as we smolder our way through the week.

Now consider, from Solomon's perspective, what the smoke from those smoldering fires of anger looks like. In the verses we just read, the term "quick-tempered" appears twice. Although it looks the same in English, Solomon actually uses two different Hebrew expressions that help us understand the nature of our anger.

The first word is used often to mean being impatient with others—of being short with them. It is often the case that those of us who are terribly impatient with others tend also to have a quick fuse. For whatever reason, the two seem to go together. Whether it is a long red light, a slow cashier at the grocery store, an order that didn't come in on time, or a child that doesn't behave perfectly, our expectations have little room for flexibility or patience. We either do a slow burn or we give off a hot blast.

The second expression that Solomon so carefully chose for the words "quick-tempered" literally means "short of breath or spirit." He is describing what happens when we start to get angry. Our breathing becomes quicker, shallower. We then become agitated; our face and neck often begin to turn red— and then we blow up. And when that happens, we usually do and say ridiculous things that we may later deeply regret, but are unable to undo.

Solomon is reminding us that in the heat of anger we invariably act the fool. Our anger clouds our judgment and robs us of all sense of perspective. As a result, we react impulsively in ways that are out of proportion to the situation. That should not be news to most of us. But here is an insight that may be.

Look again at the end of 14:29: "But he who is quick-tempered exalts folly [or foolishness]."

The verb "exalts" has the idea of "bringing something into full view, of lifting up for show." What that tells me is that some people use their angry outbursts to steal attention from others. It helps them to exit the shadows of their dimly lit and frustrating life and, for a moment, burst into the spotlight of attention that comes their way when they explode in anger.

Countless adults have never grown out of the temper-tantrum stage of early childhood. They have never outgrown the same motivation that causes the two- or three-year-old to hold his breath or stomp his feet—the need for attention.

When you think about it, what are toddlers trying to accomplish by throwing a temper tantrum? They are trying to get from you what they could not get by "goo-ing" and "ahh-ing." Too many adults operate at the same level. They can't seem to get what they want through appropriate behavior, so they throw a fit.

But that kind of habitual behavior pays some rather negative dividends. Consider Proverbs 19:19.

A man of great anger shall bear the penalty, for if you rescue him, you will only have to do it again.

The point is that hot-tempered people will find themselves constantly in trouble. Children or adults who are quickly and chronically given to anger frequently land themselves in enough trouble to reveal their mistakes.

But they will not learn their lesson.

Recently, I attended one of our son's indoor soccer games. I enjoy them immensely because the pace is so quick. At this particular game however, it became apparent very early on that one of the players on the other team was a walking time-bomb. It wouldn't take too many goals scored against his team, or very many questionable calls by the referee, and he would be over the edge.

Well, he didn't disappoint us. Early in the second half, a call did not go his way and he went ballistic. So much so, that after receiving a two minute penalty, his language and actions earned him an ejection, not just from the game, but from the arena. But this kid wasn't going quietly. He chose the far side of the arena to exit the playing field. And then as he slowly walked around the perimeter of the field, he gestured obscenely while spewing forth a stream of profanity that would make the most seasoned linguist blanch.

Then, as he came to the exit, he did not stop but came strutting over to his buddies who were part of the crowd. They were on their feet applauding, high-fiving, and head-butting him to show their approval. As he finally turned to leave, the rest of his crowd cheered him wildly.

Guess what? At the next game, and the game after that, he will perform the same way—as long as he continues to be approved in the process.

The certainty of diminishing returns

Now if you as a parent, or a friend, make it a habit to bail people out of the trouble their angry outbursts create, your intervention is counterproductive, even though you mean well. It will only encourage them to think that they will always get away with their angry shots.

Part of the role of parents then, is to somehow communicate to our children the trauma that anger produces. It must be done without shutting down their emotions, and without excusing and bailing them out of negative consequences their emotions get them into.

Linda and Richard Eyre, in their best-selling book, *Teaching Your Children Values*, offer some very practical suggestions on how to do this with very young children and adolescents. Listen to their advice:

Give your [young] children the vocabulary they need to talk about anger and give them a way to conceptualize why anger is dangerous and harmful. Show children a pan of cool water. Have them touch it and put their finger in it. Then put it on the stove over heat. Explain that when we get mad and lose our tempers, we start getting hot. When the water is boiling, say, "This is like getting angry and losing our temper—we get all bubbly and upset and we can hurt people. Would you like to touch that water now?" [No!]

"So let's try not to boil—not to get mad, not to lose our temper."

[They suggest the following with adolescents:]
Help your teenagers conceptualize the benefits of trying to understand rather than trying to win. At dinner or some other natural conversation time make the statement that we have many situations in which there is a choice between two "A" words—arguing or analyzing.

In other words, when someone does something to us or says something with which we disagree, we can either fight back and argue or we can try to analyze why he did or said it. Point out the second choice is better because we learn something whenever we try to figure out why, and we keep our cool and keep our friends.[7]

I cannot emphasize enough the importance of parental involvement through teaching and modeling in the area of anger. Current research consistently points out that children who are raised by supportive, accepting parents with whom they can identify tend to develop into self-aware adults capable of formulating long-term goals. They often engage in constructive self-examination and cherish their relationships with others.

In contrast, children whose parents are overly critical, angry, and authoritarian often turn into self-absorbed adults whose impulsiveness can lead them to angry violence and substance abuse.[8]

M. Scott Peck, whose writings I enjoy (although I don't always agree with him), makes this insightful comment in his recent book, *A World Waiting to Be Born*:

Early in my psychiatric career I observed a strange pattern. Children who grew up in warm, loving, nurturing homes usually had relatively little difficulty in leaving those homes, whereas children raised in cold homes filled with hostility and (unkindness) had great difficulty leaving them. Logically, the opposite should have held true. It seemed to me that children growing up in warm, nurturing, loving homes would want to stay there, while those in cold and hostile homes would want to get . . . out.

But gradually it dawned on me that the experience of their home life tends to shape the children's visions of the world. If they grow up in a warm, nurturing home, they tend to envision the world as a warm, nurturing place and think, "Hey, I want to move out there; I want more of this." Children raised in cold and hostile homes, however, tend to see the world as a cold, hostile place and think, "I don't want to go out there. At least here I know what the rules are and how to keep myself safe." Parental [kindness and control of anger], then, provides the springboard from which children can leap into a separate, independent childhood.[9]

Now some of us respond to all of this by thinking, "Well, that's good stuff. And I'm glad that some people are getting to read this, because they really need it. But I'm not the angry-parent type."

Confronting your anger

If you are drifting that way, then find Proverbs chapter 14, and let's consider verse 30. It identifies a characteristic of anger, or a cause of it, that we might not normally connect to anger. In fact, what we find here often masks our anger—and that is why we don't see the connection.

A tranquil heart is life to the body, but passion is rottenness to the bones.

The word "passion" is our key. It is a word of deep emotion. In fact, it refers to the color produced in our faces by intense emotions such as envy, jealousy, and anger.

Solomon is saying that envy, jealousy, and anger are rottenness to the bones. It's a funny thing, but envy and anger seem to have an invisible attachment in our lives.

Why is that? Well, think of it this way. Envy and jealousy are corrosive human emotions. In a very real sense, people given to jealousy observe others through an immense magnifying glass, but look at themselves through the wrong end of a telescope. What that does is to magnify what other people have, what they do, what they accomplish. It all looks bigger than life. Meanwhile, the envious person's own accomplishments appear miniature in comparison.

The comparison trap

Because of that, many authorities on the subject believe jealousy is rooted in low self-esteem or insecurities about our self-worth. Jealousy or envy ferments inside of us because we see ourselves as having less, or having less to give to others, than those who seem to have it so all together.[10]

Feelings like that can breed anger—or mask it. We are jealous or envious of those we compare ourselves to. Because we can't be like they are or have what they have, our frustration increases and our anger begins to show. Current research indicates that men and women who score high in anger or hostility tend to be quite lonely, depressed, and have low self-esteem.[11]

Now here is where we parents need to be careful. If you find yourself regularly drooling over somebody else's accomplishments, education, job, home, and family, it will show up in your parenting style. Most often your jealous-angry link will push you to be very critical of others or yourself.

But more than that, you will treat your kids the same way. Often we will hear ourselves shouting to our kids: "Why can't you be like Sandra?" or, "I don't understand why you don't act like Jimmy; he is always so well-behaved."

If we constantly compare our Johnny or Susie to somebody else's children (and our comparisons usually make our kids look bad) we are cultivating a view of themselves that will tilt them toward jealousy and anger. And that is not healthy.

Anger kills

Solomon says in Proverbs 14:30 that envy, fueled by anger, produces "rottenness" in the bones. And although there is no magic formula, it is still true that a healthy mind often assists in producing a healthy body, while sickness in the mind, such as consistent jealousy and anger, actually can induce physical illness.

Husband and wife team, Doctors Redford and Virginia Williams have written widely on the subject of anger. Their books receive high praise from people such as Dr. James Dobson. In their most recent offering on the subject, called *Anger Kills*, they caution each of us with these words:

Anger kills. We're speaking here not about the anger that drives people to shoot, stab, or otherwise wreak havoc on their fellow humans. We mean instead of the everyday sort of anger, annoyance, and irritation that courses through the minds and bodies of many perfectly normal people.
- If your immediate impulse when faced with everyday delays or frustrations—elevators that don't immediately arrive at your floor, slow-moving supermarket lines, dawdling drivers, rude teenagers, broken vending machines—is to blame somebody;
- If this blaming quickly sparks your ire toward the offender;
- If your ire often manifests itself in aggressive action;

then, for you, getting angry is like taking a small dose of some slow-acting poison—aresenic, for example—every day of your life. And the result is often the same: Not tomorrow, perhaps, or even the day after, but sooner than most of us would wish, your hostility is more likely to harm your health than will be the case for your friend whose personality is not tinged by the tendencies to cynicism, anger, and aggression just described.

For your non-hostile friend, becoming angry when "mistreated" by others is relatively harmless—he or she becomes upset only when really mistreated and, even then, his or her blood pressure doesn't go through the roof. But for you, anger is a constant companion every day of your life, and each outburst is accompanied by a large rise in blood pressure . . . Anger is a toxin to your body.[12]

If you don't think you're an angry person, do a little inventory. What is your patience quotient? How do you do with jealousy? How often are you comparing yourself and your family with others and coming up short? Your answers, if they are honest, may help you to admit your anger.

There is another characteristic of anger. For those of us who insist that we are not angry parents, this trait is a dead giveaway, whether we acknowledge it or not. Look at the opening words of Proverbs 15:

A gentle answer turns away wrath, but a harsh word stirs up anger.

The word "harsh" in this verse refers to words that create pain—mentally or emotionally. To use a "harsh" word with someone is to cause pain for them and invite an angry response.

Obviously then, the way we parents answer our children

will have an effect on their response to us. The same goes for kids and young adults as they answer their parents.

Sometimes, though we swear we are not angry, our speech has a caustic, brittle, sarcastic edge to it that is not connected to immaturity (if we are younger), or to our verbal prowess (if we are older). Our caustic, cutting, slashing words are anchored to an anger that is submerged deep in our heart of hearts.

Frequently we shout at our kids, "You make me so angry!"

Although that might make us feel better, it's not very sound thinking. Anger is a choice, as well as a habit. It is a learned reaction to frustration, in which we behave in ways that we would rather not. But when we are angry, we are acting out our contempt for others, as well as our frustration with them.

Anger?—It's your choice, not your "right"

We parents must constantly remind ourselves that we always have the choice of getting angry.

Rights have nothing to do with it. How other people act is their responsibility. But how I think, feel and act is my responsibility. The question is, "Does anger help or hinder you?"

When our anger produces a steady stream of painful words, there is no way it can be helpful. That suggests the third characteristic of anger and angry people.

Proverbs 15:18 points it out to us: "A hot-tempered man stirs up strife."

Now add Proverbs 29:22: "An angry man stirs up strife, and a hot-tempered man abounds in transgression."

The expression "stirs up strife" literally means "to attack or be at war with someone." The person who stirs up divisions is often a person given to anger. You get the impression sometimes that they are eager to create conflict. The point is that angry disputes and quarrels depend more on people willing to fight than they do on subject matter.

We can all remember times when a sensible discussion

became a war of words because someone lost his or her temper. The sad fact is that people who have not learned to control their temper are always at odds with someone else. Somehow, they derive an inner satisfaction of being in control, even if that control divides people. Invariably, they leave in their wake the wreckage of relationships blown apart by their unrestrained anger and their need to be in control.

One authority put it this way:

Although anger may make you feel more powerful, it usually won't get you what you want in the long run. You can, at times, use anger to get what you want in the short run by intimidating others. However, anger is a failure force. Anger blurs your vision, misdirects your attention, depletes your . . . energy, breeds other painful emotions, and destroys cooperation. If you are chronically angry people will avoid you. No one wants to form a lasting collaboration with someone who is always angry. Problems with anger are a significant reason for inability to keep relationships going and a major reason many people are unsuccessful on their jobs and in their careers.[13]

Show me someone who has great problems with his neighbors; show me someone who cannot get along at school, work, or even at church, and I will show you someone who is being strangled by anger. Anger almost always creates distance.

Gary Smalley and John Trent say that "If your children are angry at you, they will not be comfortable in your presence. They won't want to do things with you. They won't want you in their rooms."[14]

I realize that no teenagers want a parent in their room very often. I think I'm allowed in about once a week to check the toxic fume level.

That's not what I'm talking about here. I'm talking about

never wanting you near.

Smalley and Trent warn us that "Distance, most often, is a destroyer. It causes parents and children to drift away from each other. Home becomes little more than a dormitory with hostile roommates."[15]

Now I also recognize that people who love each other can at times be cruel and vindictive. This happens throughout the course of our family relationships under a variety of circumstances. Sometimes we're angry at other people, like our boss, a friend, or a former spouse. But we can't, or won't, take it out on them. So those who are closest to us become the recipients of our rage.

Sometimes we respond in anger when our expectations of others' behavior is too high. Disappointment is bound to occur because they can't possibly live up to our expectations. Sometimes our fuse fizzles inappropriately because we are facing an inordinate amount of stress, or our pride has been hurt, or we are extremely tired, or embarrassed, or we have been confronted with an especially painful or frightening illness. I understand all of these things, but the fact remains—the damage done by our anger is significant. So the issue is how to deal with our anger.

The right way to deal with our anger

Let me suggest several principles that you may be familiar with, but which are worth reviewing.

The first principle is that of *self-control*. Proverbs 16:32 and 17:27 point us in this direction.

He who is slow to anger is better than the mighty, and he who rules his spirit, than he who captures a city. . . . He who has a cool spirit is a man of understanding.

It has been widely held in therapeutic circles that one of the best ways to deal with anger is to ventilate—that is, we need to express our anger. In doing so, we will feel less anger. The belief that to discharge one's feelings is beneficial is also prevalent among the general public. Friends of yours are encouraged to "get it off their chests"; they are helped to "blow off steam," or encouraged to "let it all hang out."

Even Christians are counseled to "speak the truth boldly in love—release your pain, get it all out in the open."

The high price of ventilation

Unfortunately, the medical and scientific data is now in on this theory, and the conclusion is that expressed anger is hazardous to your health. Men with high expressions of hostility, for example, have six times as much probability of having a heart attack.

Furthermore, those who are most prone to give vent to their rage tend to get angrier, not less angry. The weight of evidence indicates that expressing anger makes us angrier, solidifies an angry attitude, and establishes a hostile habit. But as a result of our venting, there are a lot more hurt feelings among those on the receiving end of our rage.[16]

As one authority has said:

This simpleminded and extraordinarily wrongheaded solution—to let it all hang out, as though the catharsis alone would solve the problem—has found particular favor at a time and in a subculture that have glorified the self and therefore self-expression. . . . [but] we have a responsibility not only to [others], . . . but also to our personal dignity to keep "it" in.[17]

The New Testament certainly extols the value of love. It even mentions it as a fruit of the Holy Spirit (Galatians 5:22). But we also need to realize that in the same context, another fruit of the Spirit is self-control. And self-control and love are not mutually exclusive. Whatever we do in the name of love must also have a measure of self-control attached to it. Solomon would agree.

When he speaks of a person who "rules his spirit" or who has "a cool spirit," he means that the person has his emotions under control. That kind of person, Solomon says, is more significant than a soldier who conquers a city. You see, the person who keeps a tight rein on his temper is able to think clearly and act rationally. He is able to take a long, cool look at the situation and weigh it carefully.

I am not suggesting that your home will be like this every moment of the day. When you put kids and parents together, that won't happen all the time. You need to recognize that self-control does not translate into perfect peace and calmness at all times. The most laid-back and passive parent can be pushed to lose it. And even the best parents find that to be true.

So allow yourself some room. Don't punish yourself because you don't always respond as you should. Concentrate on lengthening your fuse, not eliminating it.

You may ask, "How do I do that?"

Stretching your fuse

First, admit your anger. The most effective admission is verbal, but not in the sense of ranting and raving. Simply tell your spouse or your kids that you are angry at them. Don't pretend you are not.

Someone has said that when you're angry you should count to three. Others move it up to ten. I'd suggest taking a math course at a local college if it will help, but admit that you are angry. Most of us are not very good at that.

Our spouse will ask us if something is bothering us and our reply is typically, "There's nothing wrong with me. Don't bother me. I'm just fine!" And while we are shouting that lie, our fists are clenched, and the hair on the back of our neck is up— along with our blood pressure.

If you admit to your anger up front, you will be able to maintain your composure and self-control. When you allow your anger to build inside you to the exploding point, you cannot handle your anger properly.

Second, concentrate on resolving your anger, not nurturing it. Try to come to agreement with the person you are angry with. This may mean asking for his forgiveness, or forgiving him.

You also can resolve your anger by prayer. If the other person will not admit any wrong or be sympathetic to your point of view, you may have to go to God and deal with your angry feelings before Him.[18]

The bottom line is that we parents must behave the way we want our children to behave. Parents are the most important models that children have. Linda and Richard Eyre say:

Children need calmness. It gives them a kind of security. Peace and the control of temper is a powerful and important value that is largely a product of love and of the atmosphere created in a home! Understanding is the key. We seldom lose our temper when we are trying to understand. Children who are taught to try to understand why things happen and why people act the way they do will become calmer and more in control. . . . Peaceability [in the home] does not mean the elimination or ignoring of emotions. Rather, it means to control them and to prevent their causing hurt to other people.[19]

To help you get an even better handle on this issue of self-control, let me give you some "reverse" guidelines to guarantee increasing your anger.

Eight ways to guarantee failure

1. Be picky and finicky with your kids. Demand perfection.
2. Don't listen to the point of view of others, including your

family members. In family discussions be concerned only with getting your point of view across.

3. Pride yourself on never having fun or being crazy. That is, don't laugh and have a good time. Be deadly serious.

4. Overload your schedule. Avoid leisure time and relaxing activities.

5. Expect others to cater to your every desire. Rather than trying to serve others, maximize your selfishness and demand your rights.

6. Speak in a loud, booming voice when you have a point to make.

7. Don't look too carefully at your own strengths and weaknesses. Angry people very rarely change or improve themselves.

8. Learn to nag and criticize. Look for the worst in your kids and focus on it.

Practice these and you'll lose all control of your anger.

Solomon's common sense approach

Another principle may be helpful in dealing with anger: know when to fight and when to surrender.

Look at Proverbs chapter 17:14.

The beginning of strife is like letting out water, so abandon the quarrel before it breaks out.

This verse uses the image of a dam breaking under pressure to illustrate human relationships that rupture because of angry outbursts and arguments. A leak in a dam begins with only a damp spot. Eventually the spot starts to glisten with wetness, then a trickle of water escapes, until the pressure bursts a section of the dam, and that's all she wrote.

Angry quarrels that break out between family members are

like those damp spots in dams; if they continue to grow in intensity they will damage us for a long time. How often we allow that to happen.

And yet, when you get right down to it, certainly some areas in the behavior of our kids—blatant disobedience and sin—require punishment, and in some cases, outrage and righteous anger.

But for most of us, that is not where the real battles are.

They rage over little wet spots that we are too stubborn to back away from. There are two very simple rules to remember in parenting:

Don't sweat the small stuff. Most matters are small stuff.

Developing a balanced perspective

Much of our trouble stems from the fact that we make everything a matter of life and death—and it simply is not that way.

In Indonesia, there is a commonly used word that helps me understand this. *Belum* means "not quite yet." This lovely word suggests flexibility and possibility.

"Do you speak English?"

"Belum." Not quite yet.

"Do you have any children?"

"Belum." Not quite yet.

"Do you know the meaning of life?"

"Belum."

This leads to some funny moments, of course.

"Is the taxi on fire?"

"Belum." Not quite yet.[20]

The point is simply this: Is it worth fighting over?

"Belum." Not quite yet.

"Is it worth exploding in anger?"

"Belum."

Know what to fight for and what to back away from.

That kind of attitude is helped along by the final principle we will consider in dealing with anger. We must cultivate a forgiving heart for our family.

Proverbs 19:11 says it all for us: "A man's discretion makes him slow to anger, and it is his glory to overlook a transgression."

The word "overlook" literally means "to forgive." It is the same word used of God's forgiveness in the book of Micah. Listen to the description:

Who is a God like Thee, who pardons iniquity and passes over [or overlooks or forgives] the rebellious act of the remnant of His possession? He does not retain His anger forever, because He delights in unchanging love (Micah 7:18).

And that is what we, as parents, want to delight in—unchanging love. Love that is able to forgive, to overlook some of the stuff that makes our blood boil. When we hang on to that kind of stuff, we slide easily toward resentment and grudge-carrying, don't we?

And what holds for parents is also true for kids. Sometimes the only way through our anger is by accessing the door called "forgiveness." Sometimes that must happen even when the offending person does not ask us for our forgiveness. Still, we must give it, for our own soul's sake.

Sometimes the forgiveness is granted formally upon request. Either our kids ask for our forgiveness or we go to them and ask for theirs, especially when we have blown it with our angry words and responses. I love what Zig Ziglar says in his book on parenting:

Forgiveness! Surely the most important, difficult and dangerous act in life is that of forgiveness. . . .

Forgiveness gives you a clear path to the love and power of your heavenly Father, and it clears the air and opens the communications door to the person who has abused or offended you. If there is hatred, resentment, or bitterness between you and a relative . . . you can completely free yourself only through forgiveness . . . If I were to single out one thing from this entire book that I believe will enable you to do more with and for your children and your career while giving you peace of mind and helping you enjoy life more, it would be this: Seek out the people in life you feel have wronged you. Ask each individual to forgive you for what you might have done to them. Then assure each one that you certainly have forgiven him. . . . If you have a real or an imagined difficulty with a . . . loved one, regardless of the harm or damage inflicted upon you, I urge you to forgive that person and ask him or her to forgive you for anything you might possibly have done. It's the best possible thing you can do for both parties.[21]

A Little Humble Pie

Proverbs—Selected Verses

Fairview, Pennsylvania, is not a well-known town—it has a population of 7,500. Yet it is the first town in American history to cancel a high school graduation because of a suspected suicide pact. One hundred and fifty high school graduates are all primed, ready with gowns. The day they have looked forward to for at least three years, maybe longer, is just a few days away. Certainly it would be considered one of the highlights in the life of any young adult.

Yet, it was canceled, because during Christmas of 1987 one of the students picked up a .44 Magnum and took his own life. The rumors were that there was a suicide pact among others in the class, who would seize the graduation occasion to take their own lives and create a moment of terror the community would never forget.

School officials also received threatening letters. And so with great misgivings on the part of the students, faculty, and community, the graduation—an event designed to signal that you have your whole life in front of you—was canceled.

I do not remember a single suicide when I was in high school, or even very much talk about it. But it is so common among young people today that counseling about suicide begins as early as the sixth grade.

Still the question remains: why would anyone take his life, or even threaten to, in his senior year of high school when he has his whole life in front of him?

Maybe he feels his whole life is *behind* him. That is, whatever good was going to happen must have already happened, and the rest is downhill. That may be part of it. At the other end of the scale, it may be that since nothing good happened in high school, nothing good will ever come his way.

The desperation of despair

Several years ago, the leading song on the hit parade was about the agonies of a dateless teenage girl. The lyrics of the song, *At Seventeen*, describe that suffering eloquently. A few phrases from the song express the pain of the girl who waits for what never comes to her: "Ravaged faces," "inventing lovers," "dubious integrity," "ugly duckling girls," and "ugly girls like me."

The song became popular because teenage girls across America identified with its message. They bought more than two million copies of the record because it spoke of miseries that were too deep for them to express or perhaps even admit to anyone but themselves.[1]

Today's teenagers are apathetic and despairing about life because they know just enough about the world to think that they don't matter.

You say, "I wouldn't have thought that about my kids." Really? In many ways they are simply a reflection of us, their parents. Only we have done something about it; we have moved from putting ourselves down to glorifying ourselves.

The generation of the late seventies and the entire eighties has been aptly dubbed "the culture of narcissism." Christopher Lasch, who wrote the book by that title, describes those of us who lived through the eighties this way:

The contemporary climate is therapeutic, not religious. People today hunger not for personal salvation, let alone for the restoration of an earlier golden age, but for the feeling, the momentary illusion, of personal well-being, health and [psychological] security.[2]

That psychological security has generally meant that we must begin to feel good about ourselves. We must take pride in who we are, even to the extent of *saying* we feel good about ourselves, and *acting* as if we feel good about ourselves, when we know we *don't* feel good about ourselves at all.

We have done that in any number of ways, but one method that is increasingly popular is cosmetic surgery. A nip here, a tuck there, and the face you have at forty is no longer the face you deserve, but the face you can afford. In the last decade cosmetic surgery has soared in popularity.

Los Angeles plastic surgeon, Dr. Richard Grossman, describes the phenomenon as "another transition" for the restless "Me" generation. He says, "They protested against the wars, and now they're protesting against the mirrors." Between the years 1985 and 1987, the number of men seeking cosmetic correction has increased 35 percent.[3]

Dr. Melvyn Dinner, director of the Center for Plastic Surgery in Cleveland explains why: "The 40-year-old who has lost his job is competing with a young hotshot. It's the competitive demand to look youthful."[4]

With that constant push to look better and to feel better, we have manufactured an artificial image for ourselves that invariably translates into arrogance and pride.

Let's stop kidding ourselves

If you can't identify with cosmetic surgery, then think in terms of diets, exercising fads and machines, or jogging. Much of this is fueled by an adult population of parents who keep telling themselves everything is great. They are being told over and over to believe in themselves, to feel good about themselves, to create a positive image of themselves. They try, but deep down in the combat zone of their minds, they believe exactly the opposite.

Nonetheless, they fight off admitting that, and as a result, it either drives them to an increased manufacturing of self-pride and arrogance, or to the edge of despair. It's the same edge their own high school seniors have come to much earlier—at age seventeen—when they have their whole lives in front of them.

Now don't get me wrong. Professionals are certainly correct in desiring to implant a sense of true worth and self-appreciation in children and adults. But what a quick step it is from those well-known feelings of inadequacy and inferiority to a colossal egotism that feeds on arrogance and snobbishness, and takes a deadly toll on our relationships.

So we walk a very narrow tightrope. We want our kids and ourselves to be able to look in the mirror and smile genuinely about who we are and where we are going. At the same time, we don't want to become smug and arrogant.

At the other end of the tightrope, we want to be able to view ourselves honestly without becoming punishing or negative about everything we do and everything we are. It's a hard tightrope to stay balanced on. We have a tendency to be easily swayed and to fall to one extreme or the other.

Solomon understood that. Consider his over-arching observation about that tightrope in Proverbs 11:2:

When pride comes, then comes dishonor, but with the humble is wisdom.

In Proverbs, there are basically three words that describe pride. The first word is the one we find in this verse. It refers to "an arrogant person who makes exaggerated claims about himself." In the original language, this word translated as "pride" literally meant "to boil over, to seethe inside."

It is a strong word, and it was often linked to anger and malice that lay hidden behind the veneer of pride. Sometimes people attempt to look good, to become larger than life. They do so because they are angry about who they are, or perhaps more likely, who they are not, and what they have not accomplished. Or, they are angry at others who seem to do better than they.

Any way you slice it, compared to so-and-so, they don't seem to measure up. Sometimes that makes them mad and, to cover their anger, they may slap on the mask of pride.

The two other words in Proverbs that are linked to pride come from roots whose basic meaning is "to be high, or raised up."

The self-deception of pride

That presents the odious element of pride in a nutshell. Proud people figure they are a cut above others. Invariably, they look disdainfully at those they consider beneath them. Their self-esteem is totally out of proportion to what they actually have accomplished, or can accomplish. As a result, they have an inflated sense of their own value and importance, and expect others to view them that way as well.

Solomon declares that a consistent pattern of life that leans toward pride will ultimately produce dishonor.

Sooner or later, the inflated ego bubble will be burst. What happens is that people given to pride are blind to their weaknesses, and therefore never grow through them. After all, if they have to keep smelling like a rose, the last thing they want to do is deal with the ultimate rose killer—their weaknesses. That would cause their newly created image and ego to wilt beyond recognition. So, they ignore, deny, or turn a blind eye to those weaknesses.

But those denied weaknesses will finally trip them up.

Here is the ironic thing. Many experts agree that one common manifestation of low self-worth is an inflated self-worth.

Gary Smalley and John Trent, two fine Christian authors, say, "Pride can certainly cloud the issue of self-identity. It can mask a deep sense of low self-worth as an imperfect person fights to 'claim' an exalted identity he really doesn't feel inside."[5]

Hiding behind pride

If that describes you, then you may have taken a beating for much of your life. Maybe you, like your own high school senior, figured that upon graduation, the best of your life was already behind you. Like one of the "ugly duckling girls," perhaps you seem to be pretty much on your own. And ever since that graduation day, nothing seems to have gotten better, at least not in your eyes—eyes that continually scan the cultural horizon for those who are doing better than you.

It's not hard to find people like that, and as you do, your view of yourself sinks well below the horizon and you don't like that for a second. So, you do what you can. You compensate for how you feel about yourself by pulling out the old ego-inflating pump and you begin to rigorously work that until you feel worthwhile.

Dr. Theodore Isaac Rubin understands what we're talking about, and has written a wonderful book called *Real Love*. In it, he talks a little about pride or arrogance, and the consequences of it, along with one of its causes:

Arrogance makes us truly unlovable and very difficult to get along with in just about any circumstance. This corrosive makes people attribute qualities to themselves,

such as prestige, power, knowledge, assets, and exalted
standing in all areas of life, often beyond human proportion and that they simply don't have. Unfortunately, they
demand to be treated as if they do own all the properties
they have [attributed] to themselves. . . .

The real truth is that arrogance is used to cover up
fear of great vulnerability born of low self-esteem and
feelings of inadequacy. But the real truth remains . . .
buried by the cover-up of arrogance. Relationships and
love suffer the consequence unless the individual can
face the truth about himself.

Of course, the ultimate cure is humility.[6]

Solomon would agree. Remember what he said in Proverbs
11:2?

When pride comes, then comes dishonor, but with the
humble is wisdom.

Humility is the counterweight

Humility, properly understood, is the perfect balance to the
extremes of arrogance and self-persecution.

That's the first thing we parents must understand. Then, we
need to communicate and model that understanding to our kids.

I recognize that humility is not rated very highly in our
competitive and narcissistic society. It is often seen as a sign of
weakness, as opposed to a mark of character. In some circles,
humility is considered an invitation to be stepped on by those
with ambition to get on in life and get to the top. But Solomon
saw humility as a mark of wisdom because he understood what
true humility is. Let me summarize the key ingredients of genuine humility.

A person of humility neither oversells nor undersells his
value as a person. A humble person knows his or her place and

is marked by the attribute of being teachable. People of humility understand their strengths and seek to use them in the best possible way. But they also are aware of their weaknesses and are willing to work on them. That is so important to understand.

I meet a lot of people who know what their weaknesses are. After all, from the day they could put two words together their parents were pointing them out to them. A lot of people can pinpoint their weaknesses when they are honest. In moments of transparency, they can draw things from the hat you might think they are blind to.

The difference between "most people" and humble people is that the latter know what their weaknesses are, and are prepared to work on improving themselves.

Moving from weakness to strength

Parents, it doesn't do a lot of good to continue pointing out your children's deficiencies, unless in doing so, you offer help; a way they can work toward strengths. That is the way to build this quality of humility into their lives.

But this willingness to work on weakness is part of the humble person's resume. Inherent in the word "humble" in the Old Testament, is the idea of being dependent upon God. Those of us who are depending on God are not as fearful of facing weaknesses. That's because we understand that God is in the business of transforming us—of changing us to better represent the character of His Son, Jesus Christ.

When you depend only on yourself and the manufactured image you create of yourself, your natural tendency is not to face your weaknesses. We can't seem to change them anyway, so there is no point messing up the picture.

But dependence, or trust in God, moves us toward the healthy prospect of personal growth. In fact, that is precisely what God asks of us. Listen to His own words starting in Micah 6:6:

With what shall I come to the Lord and bow myself before the God on high? . . . He has told you, O man, what is good; And what does the Lord require of you but to do justice, to love loyalty, and to walk humbly with your God? (Micah 6:6a, 8)

The writers of the Old Testament highly valued the humble person, who went about his business, who was aware of his strengths and limitations, but who was also leaning heavily upon His God for help and growth.

That will never begin to happen in our lives, or in the lives of our children, unless we recognize that a healthy self-image involves being committed to the truth regarding God's estimation of us.[7]

Think about this for a moment. As I understand it, a healthy and proper self-image has three essential components.

The first is a *sense of belonging, of being loved.* This is simply the awareness of being wanted, accepted, and cared for.

The second component is a *sense of worth and value.* This is the inner belief that "I count; I have something to offer, to contribute to others."

And the third component is a *sense of being competent.* It is the feeling that I can do this task; I can cope with that situation.[8]

For us as Christians, the beginning of a healthy and balanced view of ourselves starts when we recognize that those three components are found in our relationship to God through Jesus Christ.

As we enter into a personal relationship with Christ through faith, we realize that we have been adopted by God into His family. Our sense of belonging to someone begins to be met.

Additionally, as we recognize that Jesus Christ died for our sins on the cross and has provided us forgiveness and eternal life, our sense of worth and value begins to take shape. And then, as we enter into a relationship with Jesus Christ, we realize that God personally gives us gifts through the Holy Spirit, and promises to always be with us.

With those understandings, our sense of being competent, of being able to do a task, of being able to cope with life, begins to enlarge. Unless we parents resolve this fundamental issue of self-worth, we will be crippled in our relationships with one another and with our children. The only sure and effective solution is found in our understanding of our relationship to God through Jesus Christ.

Could it be possible then, that we parents have not communicated effectively to our kids the value of our faith and spiritual relationship to God?

Do you ever talk about that?

Do you make it a point to communicate to your kids the incredible sense of worth that you have because of Jesus Christ, and the positive difference He makes in the way you view your life and circumstances?

A model of humility

Ben Haden talks about one man's keen sense of balance regarding the importance of God's work in us:

> It was Billy Graham's sixtieth birthday. A lot of successful American people who played a part in his ministry showed up. These people spoke of all the wonderful accomplishments of the Billy Graham Crusade; all the registered decisions; all the people who think better of the Lord because Billy has lived and preached. They told how Billy had kept his life clean and how much he meant to them personally. Then Billy got up to respond. "I don't want to be impolite," Billy said, "but I would remind you—the Lord will not share His glory with anyone . . . not with me, not with the Billy Graham team . . . with no one on the face of the earth."[9]

But you may be thinking, "I don't struggle with pride. Really, I don't."

Before you carefully insulate yourself from this subject, consider two patterns of pride, two tendencies of behavior, that seem to be attached to those of us who secretly worship at the shrine of ourselves.

Pride goes before destruction, and a haughty spirit before stumbling (Proverbs 16:18).

Now where might we stumble if we struggle with pride? One of the places is in our evaluation and resulting associations with people. Look at the next verse and you will see that:

It is better to be of a humble spirit with the lowly, than to divide the spoil with the proud.

Earlier in this chapter, I suggested that we have a tendency to view ourselves as larger than life, and to look down at others who we don't think measure up to us. The flip side of that is that we also attempt to hang out with only a certain kind of person—usually the kind of person we think has arrived at our level.

Our mistake, however, is that our "read" on people is restricted to an external, surface impression. That usually tells us nothing about the character of an individual. And that is where Solomon makes his point.

He suggests that pride causes us to stumble badly because we make surface judgments about people based on what we can see on the outside. We are attracted to those who have the right "stuff," or "the spoil," as Solomon describes it. We are magnetized by that kind of person, even though their dominant personality is poisoned with pride. At the same time, we shy away from others who don't have as much, even though their character is molded by humility.

It is true of elections, as much as it is true of relationships; people tend to vote for money and not for character. And it is not simply greed that motivates us in this direction. Frankly, it is pride.

We have a tendency to put good judgment on the shelf because we are impressed with the way people look. And if money and things are what we are proud of, that is what we will look for in others. We won't mind surrendering our values and ethics, just as long as we can run with those kinds of people.

William Glasser put it this way:

It is as if we have two stockpiles of labels—one good, the other bad—stored in the back of our cameras. As soon as we see anything that significantly differs from what we want, without any awareness we attach a label from the "bad" stockpile and see it as bad. If what we see coincides with what we want, a good label is instantly added to the picture in the same way . . . . [Now here is where our pride enters in—the pride of the way we see things. Listen carefully.]

Many people have a money filter in their camera and view all they see in terms of what it costs. If they are economical, cheap is good, expensive is bad. If they are status-conscious, or anxious to impress with wealth, expensive is good, cheap is bad . . . The people with whom they associate are clever or attractive in proportion to their wealth: They filter their lives through their bank accounts. Fashion and money are good examples of the many personal values systems that color our lives.[10]

What colors your relationships?

Now it doesn't have to be money that colors our relationships and prejudices our view of others. That is the point of contact that Solomon makes with us, but it could be anything: education, or the lack of it; the type of work we do, or wish we did—blue collar versus white collar; even the location and size of our home.

Solomon's emphasis is this: Don't let the *externals* in someone's life—those things that impress you because they are what you want—don't let those externals prejudice you toward that person and against someone else. Concentrate on the *character* of the person, which Solomon labels with the words "a humble spirit," or you will stumble badly in relationships.

Now as parents, we have a colossal assignment in helping our kids see relationships with their peers clearly. Arrogance regarding our economic life style hurts our kids as they attempt to develop relationships. Sometimes parents discourage the building of friendships if the other kids don't check out economically.

And that works both ways with pride. If we are positioned near the lower end of the economic scale, we may keep our kids away from the "rich" kids. We do it because we are proud of where we are, or maybe we're just jealous of where they are.

At the other end, those of us who are on the higher income brackets may discourage our kids from linking up with those who don't quite match our wardrobe standards.

But that kind of approach is taught; it is not latent within your child. It has been my experience that young children, as they meet new friends, don't begin the relationship with questions like: "So, tell me, where does your father work, and at what level of income has he arrived?"

I don't hear any of them saying, "You'd like me to come over to play at your house? Tell me first, what is the square footage of your home, and when did you last redecorate?"

Kids never say, "I know you're only four years old, but tell me, are you planning to go to a four-year college, a two-year college, or a trade school after high school? I need to know if our relationship is to proceed."

Children don't naturally think that way. But they may be pushed in that direction by their parents. That attitude of pride is taught through parental statements and attitudes. We must get beyond an approach to relationships that values externals above character.

If we don't, we instill into our children an arrogance that will show up in another way.

Look at Proverbs 21:24.

"Proud," "Haughty," "Scoffer," are his names, who acts with insolent pride.

The person is described in this verse as a "scoffer" because of his attitude. If there is an important dimension to our parenting, it lies not only our own attitudes, but in helping our kids with theirs.

When your son or daughter speaks about one of their friends, or somebody at school, and says "They have an attitude," they are talking about the "scoffer" of Solomon's era. Let me explain.

Solomon considers the scoffer one of the worst kinds of fools. He pulsates with pride and arrogance. At his best, he will never try to see, far less respect, someone else's point of view. He is always right, and the other guy is always wrong. At his worst, he walks around with a patronizing grin on his face that speaks volumes of contempt toward other people.

The scoffer's arrogance is made the measure of all things, and it is fed by putting others down. He never has a positive or a good word to say about anybody or anything, but is always quick to let drop a sharp and caustic comment.

Dealing with arrogance

Quality parents will not tolerate that kind of conversation from themselves, let alone their kids. When the arrogant attitude pushes our children to become disrespectful of others and constantly caustic in conversation, it needs to be dealt with.

In his book, *Back to the Family*, Dr. Ray Guarendi includes a chapter called, "Rules of the House." In it, he talks about guidelines that must be followed in order to direct your children well. Significantly, the very first category of regulations comes under the heading, "Rules of Respect." And the first one of those is "No back talk." Listen to what he says at this point:

> If any rule can be considered universal among these families, it is this one. No parents condoned back talk, and most took an unbudging stand against it. Back talk here is not defined as respectful disagreement or questioning. Neither is it a whiney, complaining commmentary [such as] "When I'm a parent, I'm going to let my kids wear their socks as long as they want"; "I'm nothing but a slave around here"; "How'd you run the house before I was born?"
>
> Such comebacks are best described as grumble talk, which parents typically ignored or acknowledged with a silent stare. On the other hand, back talk is distinctly unpleasant. It is nasty, or abusive, or disrespectful in tone. It prompts a fast and firm reaction [of discipline]."[10]

Let me suggest one of the ways I see this begin to leak into parent-child relationships. It shows up when children/ adolescents in the home decide that it is time to address their parents by their first name. Now for you parents who figure that's harmless and really a term of friendship, let me be quick to point out that all my experience shouts that this is not a term of friendship, but in fact a term of disrespect.

If either of my sons determined, in a moment of weakness, to call me at the office and say, "Hey Dave, ole buddy, why don't we hit the links, play eighteen?"

I'd reply: "Sure, after you land back on this planet, then maybe we'll talk. And it won't be about golf, it will be about attitudes."

The price of unrestrained arrogance

Good parents know that if that kind of attitude is not dealt with, their child will run the risk of living a very isolated and lonely life. Or, at the very least, they'll experience a life pot-holed with strained relationships. And that is exactly what Solomon predicts in Proverbs 13:10:

> Through presumption [that is the same word translated as "insolent pride" in 21:24] comes nothing but strife.

The scoffer's arrogance and unteachable attitude are exceeded only by his or her desire to stir up arguments and fights. Arrogant, "I-am-always-right" kinds of people—whether children or adults—thrive on family quarrels. They never miss a chance to fan any dispute into full flame. As a result, they will leave a trail of strained, and often destroyed, relationships behind them.

Antidotes to arrogance

Into those dynamics must come a parental model that encourages, among other things, honest apologies. Apologies are absolutely a treasure in both breaking pride deadlocks and in generating humility.

Unfortunately, some severely pride-ridden people view an apology as humiliation rather than humility.

"I was wrong," or "I need advice" are difficult phrases to utter for some of us because they require humility.

How completely mixed up we have become! Remember what Solomon said in 11:2? Listen again—and allow me to add some other verses from the book.

When pride comes, then comes dishonor, but with the humble is wisdom.

Before destruction the heart of man is haughty, but humility goes before honor (18:12).

A man's pride will bring him low, but a humble spirit will obtain honor (29:23).

Solomon is convinced that the character trait of humility marks a person's life with wisdom. And that is the direction we want to go. We want our kids to make wise choices—to live wisely, not capriciously. Remember, wisdom in the Old Testament represents a manner of thinking and an attitude regarding the experiences of life. Wisdom, according to the ancients, was the skill of living life.

In their definition, wisdom is not something you accomplish overnight; it involves a process of learning over time. This kind of wisdom includes a proper discernment of who you are and what you've done. And a key ingredient in landing on your feet as you look at yourself involves cultivating an attitude of humility.

Humility teaches people—children, teenagers, or adults—the limits of their strengths and knowledge. But it also opens them up to being teachable, to learning all they can from others. Furthermore, proper humility pushes people to value and see the grace of God, and His role, in their life.

Now, let me add one other key dimension to developing this trait of humility in our kids and ourselves. Proverbs speaks to it in a number of places, but perhaps verse 27:2 is the clearest example.

Let another praise you, and not your own mouth . . .

Why do some kids chronically brag about themselves and

their accomplishments? Why do some kids insist that they got straight As when in fact, they are barely holding down Cs? Why do some kids make you think they are the star hitter on their little league team, when in fact, they haven't hit all season? Why do they seemingly always need to draw attention to themselves and make others notice them?

Part of the reason may be that Mom and Dad aren't bragging about them—or their parents aren't paying attention to who they are and what they have accomplished. Maybe their parents never verbally tell their children how proud they are of them.

But every one of your children is good at something.

Do you know what it is? Have you told your kids that you are grateful for that part of their character? Or do you have a tendency to push your kids to be good at something they are not gifted at?

The power of affirmation

I see parents on a regular basis trying to make their son an American League baseball star, when the boy would much rather be practicing his trombone or reading a book. Still they drive their kids to do well—not in the areas of the kids' strengths—but in the area of the parents' fantasies. In the process, instead of verbally praising their kids for what they are good in, they hammer them for what they may not at all be gifted for. How sad!

How is *your* level of verbal encouragement and praise for your kids? I'm not talking about an artificially created praise, in which you brag about your kid in areas that are make-believe, or aren't true, areas you've created just to feel better about your kids. I'm talking about genuine praise for the good points in your kids. Praise they deserve, and need.

Praise, by definition, has to come from others or it easily slides us down the slippery slope of pride. Parents, if healthy self-esteem involves a sense of belonging, a sense of orth and value, and a sense of being competent, then next to your children's relationship to Jesus Christ, your relationship to them will be the key to developing those three senses in their life.

And each of the three senses has something to do with your genuine, heartfelt praise and encouragement.

Author and counselor Larry Crabb speaks for many of us, including our seventeen-year-olds, as he tells of his childhood experience with stuttering:

In the ninth grade I was elected president of our junior high student body. During an assembly of the entire student body, I was beckoned by the principal to join him on stage for the induction ceremony.

Standing nervously in front of the squirming, bored crowd, I was told to repeat after the principal the words, "I, Larry Crabb, of Plymouth-Whitemarsh Junior High School, do hereby promise. . . ." That's how the principal said it. My version was a bit different: "I, L-L-L-Larry Crabb of P-P-P-Plymouth-Whitemarsh Junior High School, do hereby p-p-p-promise. . . ."

The principal was sympathetically perplexed, my favorite English teacher wanted to cry, a few students laughed out loud, most were awkwardly amused, some felt bad for me, and I died a thousand deaths. I decided right then that public speaking was not for me.

A short time later, our church celebrated the Lord's supper in a Sunday morning worship service. It was customary in our congregation to encourage young men to enter into the privilege of worship by standing and praying aloud. That particular Sunday I sensed the pressure of the saints (not, I fear, the leading of the Spirit), and I responded by unsteadily leaving my chair, for the first time, with the intention of praying.

Filled less with worship than with nervousness, I found my theology becoming confused to the point of heresy. I remember thanking the Father for hanging on the cross and praising Christ for trimphantly bringing the spirit from the grave. Stuttering throughout, I finally thought of the word Amen (perhaps the first evidence of the Spirit's leading), said it, and sat down. I recall staring at the floor, too embarrassed to look around, and thinking solemnly never again to pray or speak aloud in front of a group. Two strikes were enough. When the service was over, I darted toward the door, not wishing to encounter an elder who might feel obliged to correct my twisted theology. But I was not quick enough. And older Christian man named Jim Dunbar intercepted me, put his arm on my shoulder, and cleared his throat to speak.

I remember thinking to myself, "Here it comes. Oh well, just endure it and then get to the car." I then listened to this godly gentleman speak words that I can speak verbatim today, more than twenty years later.

"Larry," he said, "there's one thing I want you to know. Whatever you do for the Lord, I'm behind you one thousand pecent." Then he walked away.

Even as I write these words, my eyes fill with tears. I have yet to tell that story to an audience without at least mildly choking. Those words were life words. They had power. They reached deep into my being. My resolve never again to speak publicly weakened instantly.

Since the day those words were spoken, God has led me into a ministry in which I regularly address and pray before crowds of all sizes. I do it without stuttering. I love it. Not only death, but also life lies in the power of the tongue.[11]

I would ask you to seriously consider this aspect of your parenting style, and consider it quickly, before it's your turn to face graduation with a seventeen-year-old high school senior who thinks his best days have already passed.

Substance Abuse

Proverbs 23:29–35

It appeared in *TIME* magazine several years ago under the title, "Out in the Open." A man who spent twenty-eight days in a treatment center in the northeastern United States offered his reflections on alcohol:

Dying of alcoholism normally takes years. But before a final, prolonged bout of uncontrolled drinking caused my physical collapse and led to treatment, there was no doubt I was well on my way. My appearance was shocking. I was about twenty pounds underweight and malnourished, the result of giving up almost all forms of food except coffee, sugar and, of course, alcohol. I was in the early stages of delirium tremens, the DTs.

I sometimes heard faint ringing noises in my ears and suffered unexpected waves of [dizziness]. I felt near constant pressure in my lower back and sides from the punishment my liver and kidneys were taking. My personality was also seriously diseased. I was nervous, reclusive, by turns extravagantly arrogant and cringingly apologetic. I tried to cover my extremes of mood with brittle cheerfulness, even though I was desperately afraid. . . .

None of the growing physical pangs of alcoholism—the retching, nervous spasms, sweaty and sleepless nights, dehydration—matched the moments of hammering panic I felt every morning for months on end, as I tried to remember exactly what I had done the night before. At one point, terrified that I might kill someone with my car, I gave up driving, but never alcohol. Along with the fear came sudden rages—at my wife, at my friends, at anyone who tried to stop me from drinking. My home life became a nightmare.[1]

The pain of substance abuse

Compare his experience to a different story, but the same subject. It's a look backward by a parent who remembers growing up. It might even be your story:

The example my father showed me in his life-style—alcoholism, affairs—left me with little respect for him, and I pretty much did as I pleased. We had no family traditions. The holiday season was an unhappy time for my family. . . . When I was younger, because my mother was so frustrated with my dad, she was pretty abusive. [But] from my junior high through high school years, my parents were both alcoholics and spent most of these years in the bars. From that period on, we [kids] were basically left on our own. . . . My parents never came home, and when they did, they were always fighting. I remember the terrible fights and waiting in bed at night for Mom and Dad to come home. I always had mixed emotions because I was relieved they made it home, but I hated to have to listen to the fighting. It seemed as though we suddenly ceased to be a family, and I was bitter and angry at my parents for making that choice. The impact on me now is a decision to abstain from alcohol. I am no longer bitter toward my parents for the choices they made at that time. However, my priorities are now being the wife and mother that I know the Lord wants me to be. . . .[2]

There are many more stories. One counselor shares this one:

Tom and Linda always seemed the "perfect family" in our church. They were leaders in Bible study, gifted musicians, and had two beautiful teenage daughters who were also Christians. They were the last family I would suspect to have a drug-abusing child. Now they were sitting in my office saying, "We never dreamed it could happen to us."

The night before, their 17-year-old daughter, Terri, had been picked up for driving under the influence. In addition to open cans of beer, the police had found marijuana and a bag of cocaine. The previous Sunday at our youth group, Terri helped lead singing and had led one of the small groups.[3]

As current as our culture's struggle with alcohol and drug abuse is, the book of Proverbs tackles the subject of alcohol abuse with loud warnings.

I believe that, by application, Proverbs also speaks to other substance abuse. Solomon's thoughts are relevant on this issue, for substance abuse, of whatever form, is no longer a hidden subject.

Substance abuse is no longer limited to the sleazy back

alley. It's now in the high-rise owned by the high roller, in nice homes where small children play, in efficient offices where business is transacted, in military barracks where boredom is high, and on professional sports teams where competition is fierce and where money is plentiful. It's even in prisons where men and women serve time.[4]

The stories are endless and the evidence is staggering—even worse than Solomon could have imagined. Yet his initial words, although often relegated to the files of ancient and irrelevant literature, have a hauntingly accurate timeliness to them. Notice carefully his introductory comments in Proverbs 20:1.

Wine is a mocker, strong drink [or literally "beer" as the New International Version of the Bible translates it] a brawler, and whoever is intoxicated by it is not wise.

Solomon is obviously concerned about the behavior of the person who uses alcohol. Often, even small amounts of alcohol push a person into a different stratosphere of behavior.

Alcohol's unpredictible effect

An individual might be a quiet, unassuming person when he is sober, but under the influence of a few beers, he creates an angry, quarrelsome atmosphere. Others add to that atmosphere their loud, aggressive, and belligerent attitudes, to the point that many are out of control.

Solomon's point is simply that the person who drinks is "unwise," because wisdom involves the skill of living life, of putting into practice the knowledge that we accumulate on our journey to maturity. When we are out of control, or under the control of a substance, it works against wisdom; it short-circuits maturity. It is patently unwise.

Now you may be thinking, "Let's not overstate the case. Solomon really wasn't in touch with the technology and lifestyles of our era. I'm sure his point of view would be different if he could hang around our enlightened airspace."

Or perhaps your line of reasoning is more influenced by the fact that you are a church-going, Christian family, and so you really don't have a problem with this, and certainly your kids or grand-kids don't struggle with substance abuse.

Wherever you find yourself on the "opinion Richter scale," let me take some time to survey the situation as it exists today. You will want to read slowly and carefully, and think precisely. If you do that, Solomon's warning in this verse will howl with reality—and from there, we will zero in even more specifically on the nature of the problem.

How big is the problem?

A number of years ago, a Gallup poll showed one in three families were troubled by alcohol—the highest incidence of problem drinking in thirty-seven years. Our government estimates that a record number of adults, some 10.6 million, are alcoholics. Seven million more are problem drinkers.[5]

Alcoholism is the third-largest health problem in the United States, following heart disease and cancer. Dr. David Musto, professor of psychiatry and the history of medicine at the Yale School of Medicine says: "Americans are coming to see alcohol as a toxin or poison that has no minimum safe limit."[6]

The poisoning by alcohol costs sixty billion dollars annually in terms of medical costs. Nearly two hundred fifty thousand people die every year from alcohol, and its related illnesses and crimes.[7]

One American life is lost every twenty minutes in an alcohol-related accident. Half of all Americans will be involved in an alcohol-related accident during their lifetimes. Alcohol-related crashes are the leading cause of death among Americans between the ages of sixteen and twenty-four years. Two thousand persons are injured each day in alcohol-related accidents. Two million drunk-driving collisions occur each year. Eighty percent of Americans drive after drinking and yet only about one in one thousand drunk drivers on the road is arrested.[8]

Alcohol is involved in 50 percent of automobile-related deaths and 67 percent of all murders. Nearly one-half of the arrests made each year are alcohol related, while 90 percent of all assaults and 60 percent of all rapes are committed by persons under the influence of alcohol.[9]

But that is only part of the complete picture.

More bad news

Nearly 25 percent of those people seeking employment in retail occupations in 1988 tested positive for drug use.[10]

Furthermore, in the U.S. there are at least two million women who abuse alcohol or who are alcoholics. As a result, more than fifty-thousand babies a year are born with fetal alcohol syndrome or other related birth defects. More than 20 percent of mental retardation is attributed to fetal alcohol syndrome. Any drug, alcohol or otherwise, taken even in moderation constitutes a medical risk to an unborn child.[11]

In spite of that, each year some three hundred seventy-five thousand babies (approximately 10 percent of all newborns in the United States) are exposed before birth to illegal drugs, most commonly cocaine. Some hospitals in major cities such as New York and Los Angeles report that 20 percent or more of their newborn patients suffer from prenatal exposure to narcotics.[12]

Now almost everything I have reported to you so far has been related to the *adult* use of drugs or alcohol. So perhaps the question some would ask is, "What has this got to do with parenting? With the family?"

At the risk of overkill, I'd like you to consider some further data, refined to address the context of teenagers and elementary school children. All of these statistics, I assure you, are documented and are readily available to anyone who will look carefully.

Substance abuse and our children

According to the June 30, 1993 issue of *USA Today*, alcohol remains the most serious problem facing U.S. high schools. That conclusion comes from student government leaders who recently attended the National Association of Student Councils conference in Newark, Delaware. Student leaders there said:

- Fifty-eight percent of their schoolmates drink beer at least once a week.
- Forty-seven percent drink liquor at least once a week and 25 percent of their school's students use marijuana at least once a week.

According to the Office of the Surgeon General of the United States, of the 20.7 million seventh-through-twelfth-grade students nationwide, 10.6 million say they have drunk an alcoholic beverage, and in fact, eight million drink weekly.[13]

Other surveys indicate that 87 percent of all high-school seniors admit to taking at least one alcoholic drink during their school years. Further, 5 percent of seventh grade boys and 4.4 percent of seventh grade girls are already problem drinkers. The greatest increases in drinking come between the seventh and eighth grade for boys, and the eighth and ninth grade for girls.[14]

Yet another study revealed that 32 percent of all high school students had ingested five or more drinks in a row [binge drinking] within two weeks of the survey, and 33 percent said they didn't think it was bad. On college campuses, 41 percent said they had been on a binge within two weeks of the survey, and the same percentage didn't think it was harmful.[15]

Listen to Dr. Antonia Novello, former U.S. Surgeon General:

It is time we all wake up to the fact that alcohol is a drug—one of the most powerful and abused drugs in our country today. Our kids are hooked on alcohol, while parents are hooked on the '60s mentality—"I drank when I was young, and now I'm okay," or, "Thank God, Jimmy only drinks beer; he doesn't do drugs."

But binge drinking [taking five drinks in a row] is a way of life for a half-million U.S. teenagers in the seventh to twelfth grades. The average binge drinker, contrary to popular belief, is white, male, 16 years old and in the 10th grade. Surveys show that nearly 14 percent of the nation's eighth-graders already binge, and 26 percent of eighth-graders are already drinkers.

The truth is that beer is the preferred beverage of youth. Minors illegally consume more than 1 billion beers each year. . . .They don't realize that one can of beer, five ounces of wine or one wine cooler has roughly the alcohol equivalent of one shot of vodka. So deep is their misunderstanding that 80 percent of students surveyed did not know that a 12-ounce can of beer has the same amount of alcohol as one shot of whiskey.[16]

The problem of multiple addictions

Having surveyed the battlefield of alcohol abuse, let me turn briefly to the arena of other drugs. Unfortunately, the picture is not any brighter. Many young drinkers are groping with multiple addictions—cocaine, heroin, even eating disorders.

"The days of the garden-variety alcoholic are over," said one authority in the USA Today. "Most are poly [or multiple] drug users."[17] In April, 1993, a USA Today cover story reported that drug use is on the rise among kids as young as eighth graders—usually thirteen—and they are using more LSD and inhalants, such as glue and air freshener. The annual National High School Senior Survey on Drug Abuse finds "statistically significant increases" in eighth-graders' use of many drugs, including marijuana, cocaine, crack, LSD, and inhalants.[18]

Seven million young people are addicted to sniffing inhalants, such as glue, paint thinner, and typewriter correction fluid.[19]

William Kilpatrick, who is Professor of Education at Boston College, reports in his book, *Why Johnny Can't Tell Right from Wrong*, that:

> While educators have been busy helping youth to explore values and decide for themselves, the drug problem has continued unabated.
> • Nearly six out of ten high school seniors say they have used illegal drugs (not including alcohol)
> • The percentage of children using drugs by the sixth grade has tripled since 1975.
> • One in fifteen high school senior boys has used steroids.
> • One in twelve high school students admits to using LSD.[20]

Christian kids are not immune

If you are under the delusion that none of this could touch *your* family because your kids are Christians, consider that by the time Christian young people turn eighteen:

• Eighty-five percent will have experimented with alcohol.
• Fifty-seven percent will have tried an illicit drug.
• Thirty-three percent will smoke marijuana on occasion.
• Twenty-five percent will smoke marijuana regularly, and
• Seventeen percent have tried cocaine or crack.[21]

Having been barraged with such a litany of numbers, statistics and surveys, you might now want to: stop and take a deep breath; stop, take a deep breath—and run; or stop, take a deep breath—and then stop listening.

Let's choose the first option: simply take a deep breath, and then let's continue to examine this all-encompassing problem. As you are catching your breath, turn to Proverbs 23:29–35. These verses contain the most comprehensive description of the side-effects of alcohol in the Bible. They present the longest and most articulate warning in the book of Proverbs against alcohol or substance abuse:

> Who has woe? Who has sorrow? Who has contentions? Who has complaining? Who has wounds without cause? Who has redness of eyes? Those who linger long over wine, Those who go to taste mixed wine. Do not look on the wine when it is red, when it sparkles in the cup, when it goes down smoothly [This sounds vaguely like a beer commercial; "the smooth, rich taste of. . ."]. At the last it bites like a serpent, and stings like a viper. Your eyes will see strange things, and your mind will utter perverse things and you will be like one who lies down in the middle of the sea, or like one who lies down on the top of a mast. They struck me, but I did not become ill; they beat me, but I did not know it. When shall I awake? I will seek another drink.

In these verses, six questions call attention to four specific consequences associated with alcohol abuse. Those consequences include:

1. *Emotional problems*, identified in verse 29 with the words "woe and sorrow." In fact, the word "woe" refers to an impassioned expression of grief and despair. In addition to emotional problems, there are:

2. *Social problems*, which are pinpointed in verse 29 with the words "contentions and complaining."

3. *Physical problems* linked to alcohol that both verses 29 and 34 address.

4. *Mental problems* that center on hallucinations, according to verse 33.

Emotional problems

Even the most distant observer of the culture of alcohol and drug abuse understands the tremendous emotional problems associated with them. Dr. Lawrence Wallack of the School of Public Health at the University of California, Berkeley puts it this way:

Drinking. . . . contributes to a wide range of social and health problems for the society, and lowers materially the quality of life for communities across the country.[22]

The reduced quality of life he speaks of includes immeasurable emotional and psychological costs; the damage done to family life, for example, by a mother drinking secretly but chronically, by long-term marital quarrels over a husband's drinking habits, or by the devastating effects of a teenager's death in an alcohol-related car crash.[23]

And consider the emotional impact of this fact: There are an estimated twenty-two million adult children of alcoholics in the United States, making up 13 percent of the adult population.

Many of them carry the emotional scars of their childhood into their adult lives. Many also describe themselves as having "a gaping hole inside" them. Worse than that, some seven million children in this country, under the age of eighteen, are living with an alcoholic parent. These children live in an atmosphere of anxiety, tension, confusion and denial, often having no idea of what a normal family life is like. These children have terrible images of themselves and are emotionally insecure about their parents' love. They say to themselves, "If he really loved me, he wouldn't drink."[24]

Long-term teenage use of drugs and alcohol, although perhaps not considered at the outset, impact these teenagers down the road in tremendous ways. Young drug abusers divorce more quickly, suffer from greater job instability, commit more serious crimes, and are generally more unhappy in their personal lives and relationships than those who are not involved in those habits.[25]

Solomon's well-chosen words in verse 29—"Who has woe? Who has sorrow?"—are current reminders of the emotional trauma of substance abuse.

Social problems

Related and somewhat parallel to that are the social problems that accompany substance abuse. Solomon labels this consequence with the words "contentions and complaining." Both terms revolve around arguments and quarrels, which are nurtured by the anger and belligerence that alcohol so easily draws out of a person's temperament.

Into that kind of environment, relationships of any quality with others are almost impossible, because the person's behavior is unpredictable. The same thing, interestingly, occurs with adult children of alcoholics.

They also invariably have problems with relationships and are unable to get close to anyone. They often marry unstable mates or alcoholics in an attempt to "fix" them—trying to succeed with their spouses where they failed with their parents.

In addition to the myriad of terrible consequences from substance abuse we considered earlier, we have added the specific difficulties of emotional and social problems. The list expands further when we consider the physical or medical consequences of addictive behavior.

Glance once more at Proverbs 23:29, and then at verses 34 and 35.

> Who has wounds without cause, who has redness of eyes? . . . And you will be like one who lies down in the middle of the sea, or like one who lies down on the top of a mast. They struck me, but I did not become ill; they beat me, but I did not know it.

Physical problems

Verses 29 and 35 are all too familiar to those who are imprisoned by substance abuse. Everything hurts. Their eyes are bloodshot and they end up nursing wounds that are often the results of fights or beatings. Frequently, however, people who are drunk or high are incapable of feeling pain. They are, in a sense, anesthetized and beyond feeling, because they have poisoned their system. There is a deadening effect on the body. The same problem is seen with the misuse of barbiturates, tranquilizers, and sedatives. They have a numbing effect.

Verse 34 describes the giddy head, heaving stomach, and unsteady legs, so that even when a person is clinging to a toilet bowl or lying sprawled out on his bed, he feels like he is on a boat that is tossing at sea during a storm. In many ways, this is an accurate description of what we call the "hangover"—that debilitating combination of dry mouth, sour stomach, headaches, and exhaustion for which no remedy has ever been found. It is all part of the abuse system.

But let me go beyond the descriptive text of Proverbs and explain the horrendous—even life-threatening— personal medical consequences associated with substance abuse.

Chronic use of alcohol can seriously damage nearly every function and organ of the body. In the gastrointestinal tract, alcohol is a stomach irritant. It adversely affects the way the small intestine transports and absorbs nutrients, especially vitamins and minerals. Added to the poor diet of heavy drinkers, this often results in severe malnutrition. Alcohol causes fatty deposits to accumulate in the liver. Cirrhosis of the liver, an incurable and often fatal disease, can be the final result.

Its effects on the cardiovascular system are no less horrifying. Heavy drinkers are more likely to have high blood pressure than teetotalers. Additionally, heavy alcohol consumption damages healthy heart muscle and puts extra strain on an already damaged muscle. And it can damage other muscles besides the heart.[26]

The bottom line is that the average life span of a heavy drinker is generally shortened by eleven years.[27]

Studies at the Harvard Medical School and the National Cancer Institute report that even women who drink moderately have a 30 to 50 percent greater chance than nondrinkers of developing breast cancer.

I won't take the time to detail the physical/medical consequences of other drug usage, except to comment briefly on the impact of drugs on babies. We know of the fetal-alcohol syndrome, but let me bring you up to date on the impact of cocaine. It is immense.

Twenty-five percent of women who enter a city hospital, or even a private hospital, have a positive urine test showing the presence of drugs.

Dr. Brazelton, who is chief of the Child Development Unit at Boston Children's Hospital, and a professor of pediatrics at Harvard University, describes the problem:

Cocaine is a bad actor. It causes big holes in the baby's brain, and at least one kidney is always damaged at birth. Some of them are born with amputations of their fingers and toes—things like that. So we know cocaine is really terrible for fetuses, because every time the mother has enough for a rush, her baby gets that rush through the placenta, and he can't excrete the same cocaine back to her. It gets caught in his system, and he may get twenty rushes out of every hit she gets. What goes with a rush is that your blood pressure goes up, and there's a spasm that can cut off circulation to the brain, to the kidneys, and to the limbs. These babies are born with defective systems.[28]

Now about this point, you might respond by saying, "Look, I understand what you're driving at, but the Bible doesn't say, 'Thou shall not drink.' So why are you pushing so hard?"

Are there biblical rules on substance abuse?

The Bible does not say we should not drink. I cannot point you to a verse like that any more than I can put a finger on a verse that says anything directly about illicit drugs. But the Bible doesn't need to lay it out like that. Not in light of the emotional, social, and medical consequences we have already considered.

Those alone are enough to say, "Don't!"

If a biblical command is the only thing that would motivate people to consider seriously the information we've just covered, than I wonder about their internal conscience. It is probably also safe to say that a "Thou shall not," in the Bible probably wouldn't stop them. Any more than biblical commands such as, "Thou shall not commit adultery," would stop Christians from behaving immorally.

The evidence is compelling enough on the basis of common sense alone to push us to abstinence. Let's not raise the strawman argument of the lack of a biblical mandate.

Proverbs 23:33 and 35 have one more thing to say about substance abuse: "And your eyes will see strange things, and your mind will utter perverse things. . . . When shall I awake? I will seek another drink."

Many people do not understand that once an ounce of alcohol is absorbed into the bloodstream, it takes the body about an hour to burn it. Thus, because alcohol is removed slowly from the blood, more than one drink per hour produces a steady increase in blood alcohol levels.

Once the alcohol is in the bloodstream, nothing can be done to hurry the process of removing it. You cannot run or swim alcohol away, or get rid of it by eating a meal, taking a cold shower, or drinking coffee. As blood alcohol concentration increases, a person's judgment, memory, and perception are all progressively impaired. Thoughts begin to get jumbled, and concentration and insight are dulled.[29]

Similar effects are registered for other drugs. Cocaine and crack often cause the user to speak in incomplete, meaningless sentences. Heavy users are often chronically depressed or paranoid, or show psychotic symptoms—like the delusion that insects are crawling under their skin, for example.[30]

In the words of verse 33, "they see strange things."

Back in the hazy world of alcohol abuse, these verses describe the mental turmoil experienced during any period of withdrawal. That's when the user may experience delirium tremens, or "the DTs." Dr. Anderson Spickard is Professor of Medicine and Director of the Division of General Internal Medicine at Vanderbilt Medical Center. He is also Medical Director of the Vanderbilt Institute for Treatment of Alcoholism, so he knows what he is talking about when he describes the DTs:

> The DTs include some of the most acute mental and physical suffering known to man. The alcoholic's escalating confusion, anxiety, and terrifying hallucinations result in a racing pulse, fever, high blood pressure, uncontrollable shaking, profuse sweating, and a high rate of respiratory and infection problems. Fifteen to 20 percent of alcoholics who have DTs die.[31]

But here is the most incredible part of all. Despite the evidence, despite the information overload, most abusers blow it all off. Look at the end of verse 35.

The abuser says to himself: "When shall I awake? I will seek another drink."

Not only are they unable to stop using drugs on their own, most won't acknowledge that they have a problem. After all these horrible after-effects, abusers can only say, "When will I wake up so I can find another drink?" They have descended to the ultimate abyss—denial of a problem.

Denying a problem exists

You may never have touched a drop of alcohol in your life. You may never have entertained the use of other drugs—yet you, too, may suffer from denial. You may deny that your kids are involved or could be tempted; you may deny that your school or your youth group could be tainted by the malady. You may try to whistle dixie through the entire decade of the nineties, and wake up at the other end completely dumbfounded as to why the problem struck your family.

At least part of the problem—and solution—involves facing the reality of where we live. Putting our heads in the sand and convincing ourselves that our world is not like this world, leaves our family easy prey.

What I have attempted to do, if you have stayed with me, is to give a wake-up call to Christians, who are most prone to denial.

Having done that, I'd like now to suggest some principles that move beyond identifying the problem, and may help in preventing it from sinking its teeth into your family.

Let me say this, however. It is not by accident that I have left this subject to nearly the end of this book. Many of the principles we have considered thus far, if consistently modeled, will have a tremendously positive impact on directing your kids away from involvement with alcohol and drugs.

Remember the things we have looked at, such as consistent discipline, the setting of standards and boundaries, teaching responsibility, encouraging through verbal praise, monitoring of friendships and dating patterns, communication, and talking about spiritual truths and values. All of those areas, experts agree, begin to turn the tide in your favor.

But there are some additional guidelines and principles to keep in mind.

Six principles to help protect or rescue your kids

Principle 1—*Examine your own behavior as parents.* The best predictor of drinking and drug habits is parental attitude and behavior. Children are more prone to abuse drugs and alcohol if their parents smoke cigarettes, abuse alcohol, take illicit drugs, or even impart an ambivalent or positive attitude toward drinking or drugs.

Throughout these chapters, parental modeling has been held very high. There is perhaps no area where consistent vigilance is needed more than here. If you are currently using alcohol or other substances, discontinue that usage—or you have no leg to stand on as you try to point your children toward abstinence.

Principle 2—*Know your children's friends.* Don't underestimate the power of peer pressure. Children often become like the friends with whom they spend time. So it makes sense that you spend time with your children, and especially your teenagers. All the knowledge of the facts will not change their need for your positive physical presence.

Principle 3—*Encourage, even mandate, your child's involvement in the youth group of the church.* So many times we give that involvement very little push. We'd rather have them involved in sports or other activities. Our own inconsistent worship behavior patterns and constant complaining about church only drive our kids away from involvement. You cannot fight the battle alone, and other positive role models are essential for your kids. One of the best places for that kind of positive input is a youth program.

To see how anemic we are in this area, most of us don't blink about sending our kids off to a sports camp for a week or perhaps even two. But when was the last time we encouraged them to spend a week at youth camp, or to be a counselor at a children's camp?

Principle 4—*Take advantage of every teachable moment to reinforce the values and rules you teach in a positive atmosphere.* Encourage discussion, but do not be afraid to set limits and to discipline when those limits are crossed. Moral choices should never be left up to the child. Those choices must be guided by parental standards that are higher than street level.

Principle 5—*Pray for your kids and have others pray for them*—specifically on this issue. We have friends who meet three lunch hours a week just to pray for their kids while they are at school. And when they meet, they target their prayers to the issues of peer pressure and the temptations they know their kids face every hour of the day.

Principle 6—*If you discover that alcohol or other substance abuse is part of your family system, fight off the tendency to deny its presence, and seek help.* Locate a group, or a professional hands-on person, or find a reliable clinic that specializes in helping people deal with their addiction. Don't wait until next week. Seek that help today. It's available if you ask.

At the beginning of this chapter, I shared with you the story of a man who spent twenty-eight days in a treatment center. It was called "Diary of a Drunk." At the end of his reflections, the author wrote:

> I still consider the fact that I did not die to be a miracle, meaning that some kind of providence intervened. . . . I finally broke down and admitted that I needed help. That simple admission, so long in coming, brought an enor-

mous release. Suddenly, alcoholism was no longer something I had to endure in private. . . .

Years later, after hundreds of Alcoholics Anonymous meetings and many hours of intensive counseling, I am happy to acknowledge that I have a serious, progressive ailment, with no cure. Alcohol is no longer a terrifying, destructive force in my life. It is just another chemical. . . .[but] I avoid it . . . Friends say I am a completely different person now. Only, sometimes, I remember the feelings of hopelessness and shame from those terrible years, and I still have to struggle to hold back the tears.[32]

CHAPTER TWELVE

Are There Any Guarantees?

Proverbs 22:6; 24:3–4

THE ARTICLE SCREAMED FOR ATTENTION. In bold letters across the top of the page in *Newsweek* magazine, the title "Somebody Else's Kids" begged me to investigate. This is what I read:

> There are more than a million of them on the streets of our major cities, and most of us would like to believe that they are all other people's kids. They are America's lost tribe of teenage runaways, hustling boldly in doorways or retreating into distant drugged [fantasies]. They are prostitutes, male and female, thieves petty and grand. Most act like hard cases, posing as predators so they will appear less like prey.
> But today, for every annual wave of new runaways, the game becomes increasingly deadly. Selling sex was always a wrenching act of forfeiting self-esteem. In the age of AIDS, prostitution is synonymous with slow sui-

cide. And because almost all street drug users share needles, the [peddlers] in the doorways and alleys are also peddling wholesale death. [Furthermore], whatever sexual, physical or psychological abuse may have driven them away from home, the runaways—who are really throwaways—are often perceived as simply "bad kids."

Passersby wonder why they don't go home. "What they don't know," says executive director Jed Emerson of San Francisco's Larkin Street Youth Center, "is that in 68 percent of our calls to parents of children who would consider going home, the response [from the parents] is, 'You keep the kid.'"[1]

The tragedy cuts both ways. A Christian father writes:

My wife died earlier this year. We have a son who lives halfway around the world. Our son wrote recently to say that he had adopted a religion that we know nothing about—and specifically in his letter, he renounced Christ. He also added that he wanted nothing to do with his family—and then a postscript: "I have AIDS . . . and one year to live."[2]

The pain of parenting

You may not have faced the debilitating trauma of a runaway teenager. You may not have been derailed by a son or daughter who has denounced his or her connection to Jesus Christ, while shouting at the same time their link to an HIV-positive diagnosis.

Nevertheless, you may be hurting as a parent.

Countless hurting parents feel that they have failed at their God-given assignment of Christian parenting. They have tried to build family unity on a firm foundation of Christian faith, but somehow their kid has zigged horribly when he or she should have zagged wonderfully.

These parents are crushed when their kids throw aside the moorings of their family. The pain may enter uninvited, and knifelike, when a son leaves home without any explanation, or when a sobbing fifteen-year-old daughter admits her pregnancy. The throbbing may start with a child's involvement in a non-Christian lifestyle—drugs, a strange religious cult, or living together before marriage. The pain will surface when a high schooler resists going to church because he says it is so boring. Then again, it may show up when the freshman in college, recently exposed to a new intellectual atmosphere, concludes that he has outgrown his parents' provincial beliefs.

The crisis point will vary, but the results are invariably the same—parents hurt with the frustration of what they see as their own failure. And they judge themselves guilty with the nagging question: What did I do wrong?

I recently received a letter from Christian parents who understand this pain. It is with their permission that I share with you some of their thoughts:

> . . . As we look back or forward, we feel "good" and "bad" about the results of our parenting. Although not always ecstatic, but always hopeful, we generally feel a satisfying sense of accomplishment as we continue to watch our young adults attaining their own sense of independence. There are times, too, when we feel an overwhelming sense of failure as we watch them make mistakes or unwise choices. . . .
>
> We've had this parenting privilege for twenty plus years. Our experience in reality of American society and its values and mores is showing us our job isn't over. . . .
>
> Our son . . . is the bright, shiny side of the coin as he struggles with many choices and decisions. Although he's made some he has later come to regret (us too), he owns and takes responsibility for them. He consults us

often and solicits pros and cons from others. He's not where we'd like him to be, but then he's not where he always wants to be either. . . . Spiritually, although he has made a profession of faith, he, in our estimation, often walks a tightrope but sees what he needs to do and is generally open to hearing our inquiry—"How's your spiritual temperature?" He doesn't seem to turn off our comments about how God might want him to respond. Did we succeed or fail? Are we successful parents or total failures? Can we classify and/or identify what we did right and wrong?

Our daughter is the dark, cloudy side of the coin. . . . She, too, has made a profession of faith but has been hurt by Christians, and walks a bitter road. She struggles intensely. Her strong will has gone out of control and rules her all too often. She's slammed doors of relationships, both family and friends, and blames others for the results. . . . She struggles in what would be classified a "bad" marriage relationship. Did we succeed or fail? How do we feel OK about her failures? Can we identify where, when and if we need to look back and ask forgiveness? We've done that but is there more of which we are not yet aware? Can we classify or identify what we did right or wrong? . . . Where/when do we draw the line in aiding her and loving her back to a coping existence when she's feeling so downtrodden? How do we impact her and our granddaughter for the Lord? How do we go through all of this without feeling as if we are either total failures or self-sacrificing martyrs?

When I read things like that I feel very much like the parents of a college sophomore who had spent most of the school year in one kind of trouble or another. In the midst of that, he received the following card from his parents who were vacationing in Greece:

Dear Son. We are now standing high on a cliff from which the ancient Greek women once hurled their defective children to the rocks below. Wish you were here.

The question of guarantees

As we come to the end of our study of the family, I would like to, at least in part, answer the question all parents ask at one time or another: "Are there any guarantees?"

To give a fair answer, let's consider again briefly the most frequent recurring theme in Proverbs related to the family. It's found in 24:3–4.

By wisdom a house is built, and by understanding it is established; and by knowledge the rooms are filled with all precious and pleasant riches.

The writer is using symbolic language to describe our families. As he does, he offers some encouragement, even some hope. At the end of verse 4 he tells us that our homes can be filled with "all precious and pleasant riches."

He's not talking about expensive artwork, designer decorating, or hand-crafted furniture. He is describing the things that really last, like happy memories, positive and wholesome attitudes, feelings of affirmation, acceptance and esteem, good relationships, and depth of character.

You may be thinking, "But my family is not like that. We're falling apart even as I speak. Nothing seems to work!" Well, there is some hope even for you. Look at how Solomon expresses it. Regarding our families, he chooses the verbs "built and established."

Both words assume that some difficulty exists in the family system. In fact, the Hebrew term for "built" suggests restoring something, rebuilding it so that it is healthy again. The same idea is buried within the meaning of the verb "established." It has the idea of putting something back into a standing position—something that was once leaning badly, falling regularly, or twisting painfully.

All of us parents long for that if we are in pain. Some of us want it so bad we can taste it. So how do we begin the renewing process? By sticking with some basics we have already covered, but that bear repeating. You will have observed that Solomon speaks of wisdom in these verses with three closely related words: wisdom, understanding, and knowledge.

The first two words, wisdom and understanding, are twins in their meaning. They refer to a manner of thinking, and an attitude about life's experiences, that includes a basic morality. You see, an integral part of Old Testament wisdom is the understanding of a personal God who is holy and righteous, and who expects those who claim to believe in Him to demonstrate His character in the many practical details of living.

This kind of wisdom and understanding involves discernment. The original Hebrew word emphasizes accuracy, the ability to sense what lies beneath the surface. Wisdom refuses to skate across the surface and ignore what is deep within. It looks carefully at life and senses the difference between good and evil, virtues and vices, between responsibility and self-indulgence. As a result, a person of wisdom and understanding begins to learn how to make careful choices related to life.

The parental role in modeling and instructing is imperative when it comes to encouraging children and young adults to embrace wisdom and understanding. We often stumble here because we, perhaps more than any generation, are almost afraid to set boundaries or to expect certain behaviors, especially related to morality and ethics. We think that if we do, we'll lose our kids. As a result, we become over-permissive. One authority puts that mythical thinking to rest when he writes:

Over-permissiveness comes from an inability to take authority, uncertainty of one's abilities and judgment, and of being irresponsible and of being uncaring. The child suffers accordingly—feeling uncared for, unloved, and confused for lack of know-how and direction.[3]

On the other hand, maybe we don't model and instruct in areas of morality and ethics because we're afraid that our own hypocritical cracks will begin to show. Each of us hides a certain amount of darkness from others that we fear may one day be exposed.

But wisdom is not *perfection.*

Modeling wisdom does not mean you will never fail or never make a mistake in judgment. In fact, part of modeling wisdom is acknowledging and confessing your mistakes.

You may be thinking, "What? Confess my *mistakes*? Not to *my kids*?"

Yes, to your kids.

Demonstrating wisdom

What do you need to confess in order to demonstrate wisdom?

- You've been preoccupied, and ignored your family when they needed attention.
- You haven't always faced them with their sins (confrontations are hard for you); you didn't always punish them when they needed you to, and their bad habits remain as a testimony against you.
- You've been tired at times, and you've yelled at them; you've been too harsh, and injured them as a result.
- You have unthinkingly withheld the support of verbal praise and encouragement.
- You've simply blown it.

Wisdom would have you tell them. Tell them how sorry you are, and ask their forgiveness.[4]

Now that's the parental part of the equation that Solomon is driving at in these verses. But there is also a part that our children, our young adults, need to play.

Proverbs 23:4 describes their role with the word *knowledge*: "And by knowledge the rooms are filled."

Knowledge is learning with perception. It includes things like a teachable spirit, a willingness to listen to advice and counsel, a desire to discover the truth—and not to be satisfied with anything less than that.

Over and over, we are reminded that even the best training, the best modeling by parents cannot instill wisdom. It can only encourage a child's desire to pursue it. The key to wanting to make that pursuit a lifetime quest is "teachability." Early on, we parents must demonstrate that characteristic, and try to help our kids see the absolute necessity for it.

But some kids are too opinionated to learn from anyone. They may make it their life's calling to despise, laugh at, and curse their parents. And while there are parents who have only themselves to thank for that kind of behavior, it is ultimately the young adults themselves who must bear the blame, for it is their attitude toward wisdom, their willingness to listen and be teachable, which will set the course of their lives.

What about "the promise"?

Now I'd like us to think for a moment about one final verse in the book of Proverbs. It is probably the most widely recognized verse of the book. It is one that you as a parent have clung to for years, and it is one that our kids have heard enough times to be able to quote it themselves. You'll find it in Proverbs 22:6.

Train up a child in the way he should go, and when he is old he will not depart from it.

In many ways, this verse is a summary of everything we have considered throughout this book. At the same time, it offers a few new wrinkles that we need to file away for future reference.

The first thing that strikes me is the verb "train." This word includes the idea of "setting aside, narrowing, or even, hedging in." Solomon suggests that the training of our children, whatever their ages, involves narrowing their conduct, focusing their behavior away from that which would prove harmful and toward that which would be beneficial.

It runs parallel to "wisdom" in that it emphasizes the establishing of guidelines, boundaries, and standards. Any parenting style that avoids this is not to be considered training in the biblical sense of the word.

You probably realize that this training is constant. It's not something you do only three days a week, or up to the age of ten. The word "child" in this verse was used to describe Moses when he was just three months old. And it was used to describe Joseph when he was seventeen. It also described someone who was old enough to get married. So we are talking really about a process of "narrowing" that begins at the birth of your kids and continues until they are married or living on their own.

That doesn't mean that your advice and counsel is not valid after that point. But it is crucial to realize that once your kids move out and establish a home life of their own, either as married or single persons, your formal responsibility of training is minimal.

The choices your kids make from that juncture on are not your responsibility, nor should you persecute yourself with guilt if they disappoint you.

There is something else about this "training" that we must always keep in our sights. Inherent in the meaning of the word, beyond the idea of narrowing or setting boundaries, is the idea of *dedicating someone for the service of God*. In fact, the word "training" is the Hebrew word *Hanukkah*. The *Hanukkah* celebration revisits, in the mind of the Jewish person, the dedication ceremonies of the temple during Solomon's time.

As part of this eight-day celebration even today, hymns are sung from the Psalms, and Hanukkah lamps are lit in the windows of private homes. In other words, parental training of children must have a spiritual dimension to it.

The importance of training

In fact, the training of our kids must be viewed as an act of dedication or commitment to the Lord.

But it is this spiritual dimension of training that often gets the dregs of parental effort. We often leave it up to our kids, and are then surprised when their spiritual heartbeat is next to nothing.

In her book, *Confessions of a Totalled Woman*, Karen Wise says:

> We love to quote [this] verse: "Train up a child in the way he should go, and when he is old, he will not depart from it." The word is TRAIN—not "Let it happen." The word is TRAIN—not "suggest." Training is hard work. WE DON'T TRAIN ANYMORE. We car pool and sign our kids up for twelve different activities instead. Consequently, we have kids who play an instrument, kick a good ball, know how to use a calculator—and tell their folks where to get off.
>
> I will never forget a statement a child psychologist made one day while speaking to a group of mothers. She said, "How can you expect your kids to respect God, whom they cannot see, when they don't respect you? How can you expect them to be obedient to God's Word when you have never taught them obedience or expected it from them?"
>
> These words stuck with me. As a Christian parent, I

want my children to know who is head of our house: God is first and, whether they like it or not, parents are next in line.[5]

That is all part of the training process. But notice something else about the first part of Proverbs 22:6. It talks about training "in the way he should go," or as some translations put it, "according to his way." What does that mean?

I think there are a couple of ideas that grow out of that expression.

First, it reminds us that our training must be tailored to fit the needs and aptitudes of each individual child in our family. In other words, each of our kids is different and our training styles should therefore vary with each one, even as we try to point them all in the same direction.

It is very natural to want to bring up all our children alike, or train them the same way. But this verse indicates that parents should discern the individuality and special strengths that God has given each of our kids. While we should not excuse or condone self-will, each child has natural inclinations that we should develop, whether or not those inclinations fit into our preconceived plan as to what our child should do.

Please, always remember that no two children are alike—physically, intellectually, or temperamentally. This is a truth that every parent must learn. Because of his nature, or inborn "wiring," each child will react uniquely to life and to his parents' effort to teach him about life.

Popular author and lecturer Leo Buscaglia explains it this way:

Each of us possesses gifts that make us distinct. These qualities only await recognition and development. The problem is they may not always be what others expect. For instance, Eddie is sitting on the end of the bench waiting to get into the game. He can't hit a ball, but he has marvelous musical talent. And there, buried in the third row of dancers, is Beth, stomping her way through her tenth ballet recital. She'd rather be learning about animals, a subject that has interested her for a long time.

Eric is a stargazer. Like Einstein, who hated formal schooling, he dreams of distant corners of the universe and faraway planets. His teachers say he is inattentive and a daydreamer. His parents don't understand why his grades are poor. One day he is given a telescope and a new world opens up to him. Now the universe is limitless. Perhaps his future is better focused.[6]

That is the first thing we should note about the expression "in the way he should go." It includes the way God has equipped him for living. But there is a second emphasis here. To illustrate it, let me translate this verse literally for you:

Train up a child on the mouth of his way. . .

What is the "mouth of his way?" And how do you train with that in mind, whatever it is?

When a Hebrew midwife delivered a baby in the early days of Israel, she would get sweet oil from the common date we eat around Christmas time. She would place that sweet oil on the roof of the infant's mouth, then instantly hand the baby to her mother to nurse, giving the baby a thirst for the mother's milk.

That is the second idea behind the word "train" and the expression "in the way he should go"—to develop a thirst for God's way.

Finding "God's way"

Of course you don't develop that thirst in every child the same way, with the same style, with the same words, with the same kind of training. It has to be individually tailored according to each child's personality and needs.

Think about how many kids have Bibles, have heard prayers and spiritual things said in their home—yet not once has anyone given attention to developing in them a thirst for the way they should go—God's way.

But that thirst can only begin when and if those children, those junior high or high school students, embrace Jesus Christ personally as Savior. At some point, every child or young adult must acknowledge his or her own personal sin, and his or her need for a Savior.

In other words, they are not depending on your faith, or their attendance at church, or even being enrolled in a Christian school. Rather, their personal thirst for God begins when they commit their lives to Christ.

Many parents wonder why their kids are bored with church, with youth activities, with anything connected to God. Often the answer is because those young people have never been connected by faith to Jesus Christ. Are yours?

Really, do you know? You know their grade point average, what college they are applying to. You know what sports they are good at, what colors and styles of clothes they like. But do you know whether or not they have embraced Jesus Christ sincerely as their personal Savior? That's where their thirst will start.

And that's when the last part of this verse will begin to offer a degree of comfort. Look at it with me:

Train up a child in the way he should go; even when he is old he will not depart from it.

When is a promise not a promise?

One of the finest Old Testament scholars and preachers today, Dr. Walter C. Kaiser, in his book, *Hard Sayings of the Old Testament*, offers these enlightening words:

Readers often assume this verse is a promise without any exception given to all godly parents: Raise your children as moral, God-fearing believers, and God promises that they will turn out all right in the end. But what about children raised in just such a Christian home who appear to abandon their faith or lapse into immorality? . . . This verse is no more an ironclad guarantee than is any other proverb in this same literary category. As in many other . . . proverbs, it tells us only what generally takes place without implying there are no exceptions to the rule. The statement is called a proverb, not a promise. Many godly parents have raised their children in ways that were genuinely considerate of the children's own individuality and the high calling of God, yet the children have become rebellious and wicked despite their parents' attempts to bring about different results.

There is, however, the general principle which sets the standard for the majority . . . give special and detailed care as to the awesome task of rearing children so that the children may continue in that path long after the lessons have ceased.[7]

Being godly parents is no guarantee that you will have godly kids. Doing a good job of training children and teens provides no airtight promise that they are going to turn out exactly right.

You and your spouse may walk very close to God today. You may have had the highest hopes for your children, but one or more of them has rubbed your nose in the dirt. That is an ache that cannot be described.

But at some point, if before God you have done the very best you knew how, you must realize that the problem is now your child's, not yours.

Furthermore, as John White says:

. . . You cannot solve his problem for him, so quit trying.

Until he wants with all his heart to deal with it, until he himself cries out for help—to Christ, to you,—nothing will ever take place. Until that time all you can do is pray and adjust your life to the problem, making what changes you can to protect yourself, your child and the rest of the family from his untrustworthiness.[8]

Tony Campolo is helpful and encouraging when he offers this insight:

When a mother has done and said all she can, and has provided the best possible example for her children, she must learn to resign herself to the fact that her children are individuals with free wills. They are quite capable of rebelling against everything that she is and advocates. . . . Mothers must not condemn themselves too harshly when their children fail. They need to remember that even Mary, the mother of Jesus, had sons who were not believers in the Christ.[9]

No guarantees—but with God, hope remains

Solomon would have you take courage, and be encouraged. Although there are no guarantees, still the evidence is strong: Many children who have a consistently Christian upbringing will return, by one road or another, to the faith of their parents.

Ruth Bell Graham, the wife of Billy Graham, who knows some of the pain of difficult kids, put it into a prayer-poem:

She waited for the call that never came; searched every mail for a letter, or a note, or card, that bore his name; and on her knees at night, and on her feet all day, she stormed Heaven's Gate in his behalf.

She pled for him in Heaven's high court. "Be still, and wait," the word He gave; and so she knew He would do in, and for, and with him, that which she never could.

Doubts ignored, she went about her chores with joy; knowing, though spurned, His word was true. The prodigal had not returned but God was God, and there was work to do.[10]

Believe me, I realize it sometimes seems an impossible task. You may find comfort knowing that others have been there before you—and survived.

This is 1963. . . .

. . . A young father, his three-year-old son, an upturned shopping cart, and a good part of the pickles shelf—[lie] in a heap on the [supermarket] floor.

The child . . . is experiencing . . . "significant fluid loss." Tears . . . [mix with] mucous from a runny nose . . . blood . . . saliva. . . . The kid has also wet his pants and will likely throw up. . . .

The father is [amazingly] calm because he is thinking about . . . driving away somewhere . . . changing his name. . . .

. . . He is sorry he had children . . . and . . . sorry that this particular son cannot be traded in for a model that works. . . .

Later, the father . . . [holds] the sobbing child in his arms until the child sleeps. He drives home and carries the child up to his crib and tucks him in. . . .

This is 1976.

Same man paces my living room. . . cursing and weeping by turns. In his hand is what's left of a letter . . . from his sixteen-year-old son (same son). . . .

The son says he hates him and never wants to see him again. . . . The son thinks the father is a failure as a parent. . . .

This is 1988.

Same man and same son. The son is twenty-eight now, married, with his own three-year-old son, home, career, . . . The father is fifty.

Three mornings a week I see them out jogging. . . . laughing as they run on up the hill. . . . And when they sprint toward home, the son . . . runs alongside his father at his pace.

They love each other a lot. . . .

This is now.

And this story is always. . . . The sons leave, kick away and burn all bridges, never to be seen again. But sometimes . . . they come back . . . in their own time and take their own fathers in their arms. That ending is an old one, too.

The father of the Prodigal Son could tell you.[11]

Notes

CHAPTER ONE

1. Charles Swindoll, *Home Where Life Makes Up Its Mind*, (Portland: Multnomah Press, 1979), 100–101.

2. *Moody Monthly*, January 1987, 10.

3. James R. Schiffman, "Children's Wards," *The Wall Street Journal*, February 3, 1989.

4. Harold O.J. Brown, "Will the Family Still Exist in 2020?", *Religion & Society Report*, August 1990, 7–8.

5. Elizabeth Stark, "Mom and Dad: The Great American Heroes," *Psychology Today*, May 1986, 12.

6. Wenda Goodhart Singer, Stephen Shechtman, Mark Singer, *Real Men Enjoy Their Kids* (Nashville: Abingdon Press, 1983), 16.

7. Ben Haden, "Bonding Crisis," *Changed Lives* (Chattanooga: 1988), 10–11.

8. Bill Moyers, *A World of Ideas* (New York: Doubleday, 1989), 141.

9. George Barna, *What Americans Believe: An Annual Survey of Values and Religious Views in the United States* (Ventura: Regal Books, 1991) 83.

10. "Few Believe in Moral Absolutes, But Most Want to Follow God's Teachings," *PRRC Emerging Trends*, February 1992, 3.

11. Richard C. Halverson, *The Timelessness of Jesus Christ*, (Ventura: Regal Books, 1982), 2–26.

283

12. An Interview with Howard Hendricks, "Prescription for a Healthy Family," *Moody Monthly*, January 1987, 67–69.

13. Dr. Ray Guarendi, *Back to the Family*, (New York: Villard Books, 1990), 104.

14. Erma Bombeck, *Stoke the Home Hearth* (Universal Press Syndicate).

CHAPTER TWO

1. Robert Fulghum, *Uh-Oh* (New York: Villard Books, 1991), 153–157.

2. Myron Magnet, "The Money Society," in *Fortune Magazine*, (New York: The Time Inc., Magazine Company, 6 July 1987), 30–31.

3. "Mall Mania," from *University of California, Berkeley Wellness Letter*, February 1988, Vol. 4, Issue 5, 1–2.

4. Myron Magnet, "Money Society," 26. (See also *Leadership Journal,* Winter 1989, vol. X, Number 1, 81.)

5. Ron and Judy Blue, *Money Matters for Parents and Their Kids* (Nashville: Oliver Nelson, 1988), 14–15.

6. Ray Guarendi, *Back to the Family*, 89.

7. *The Wall Street Journal*, September 1987.

8. Leo Buscaglia, *Bus 9 to Paradise* (New York: William Morrow & Company, Inc., 1986), 116.

9. *Current Christian Abstracts*, June 1990, Ab. 6447.

10. Dr. Dan Kiley, *The Peter Pan Syndrome* (New York: Avon Books, 1983), 29.

11. David Elkind, *The Hurried Child* (Reading: Addison-Wesley Publishing Co., 1981), 19.

12. From Ray Stedman, *Preaching Today*, Tape No. 25.

13. Charles Swindoll, *Living Beyond the Daily Grind* (Dallas: Word Publishing, 1988), Book 1, 224.

14. Ron and Judy Blue, *Money Matters*, 50–51.

CHAPTER THREE

1. Irving Kristol, "AIDS and False Innocence," *The Wall Street Journal*, 6 August 1992.

2. Karen S. Peterson, "A Million Dollar Question," *USA Today*, 7 April 1993.

3. Barbara Dafoe Whitehead, *Atlantic Monthly*, April 1993.

4. George Grant, "Sex, Lies & Planned Parenthood," *Current Thoughts and Trends*, October 1990, #6657, 2.

5. William Bennett, *The Index of Leading Cultural Indicators*, Volume 1 (New York: Simon and Schuster, 1994) 73–77.

6. *Psychology Today*, December 1985, 70.

7. Bennett, *Cultural Indicators*, 69.

8. *Current Thoughts and Trends*, September 1992, Vol. 8, Number 9, Summaries 8060-8115, 25 (fast fact).

9. Bennett, *Cultural Indicators*, i, ii.

10. Ben Haden, *Changed Lives*, 1988, 4.

11. A.W. Tozer, *Born After Midnight* (Harrisburg: Christian Publications, Inc., 1959).

12. Bennett, *Cultural Indicators*, iii.

13. David A. Hubbard, "Proverbs," *The Communicator's Commentary*, (Dallas: Word Books, 1989), 88.

14. *Atlantic Monthly*, April 1993.

15. Jeff Meade, "The Moral Life of America's Schoolchildren" *Teacher Magazine*, March 1990, 39.

16. Ibid, 40.

17. *Psychology Today*, October 1988, 8.

18. William D. Gairdner, *The War Against the Family* (Toronto: Stoddart Publishing Company, Ltd., 1992), 240–242.

19. Charles Colson with Ellen Santilli, *The Body: Being Light in Darkness* (Dallas: Word Publishing, 1992), 45.

20. Michael Quintanilla, "Affection-Starved Girls Becoming Sexually Aggressive," *The Cleveland Plain Dealer*, 14 July 1991, 5–6.

21. Peterson, *Million Dollar Question*.

22. Max Lucado, *On the Anvil* (Wheaton: Tyndale Publishers, Inc., 1985), 91–93.

CHAPTER FOUR

1. Max Lucado, *No Wonder They Call Him The Savior* (Portland: Multnomah Press, 1986), 31–32.

2. Allan Bloom, *The Closing of the American Mind*, (New York: Simon and Schuster, 1987), 141.

3. Ben Haden, "Out of Control?/Is Your God Jealous?", *Changed Lives*, (Chattanoooga: 1992), 5–6.

4. "Sex is Up," *Pyschology Today*, December 1988, 8.

5. Bloom, *American Mind,* 106.

6. "Sexually Active Teens," *Christianity Today*, 6 February 1987, 42.

7. Lence Williams, "Teen Sex: They alone call shots," *The Arizona Republic*, 27 February 1989.

8. Cal Thomas, *Occupied Territory*, (Brentwood, Tenn.: Wolgemuth & Hyatt, 1987), 156–157.

9. "Born-again makes little difference in behavior," *National & International Religion Report*, 8 October 1990, 8.

10. Daniel Yankelovich, *New Rules* (New York: Bantam New Age Books, 1982), 74.

11. Max Lucado, *God Came Near* (Portland: Multnomah Press, 1987), 95–96.

12. "Moral Issues—Teen Pregnancy Rises," *Preaching*, January-February, 1987, 53.

13. *Current Thoughts and Trends*, Vol. 7, Number 10, Summaries 7454–7512, October 1991, 16–17.

14. Frank Minirth, Paul Meier, Frank Wichern, Bill Brewer, States Skipper, *The Workaholic and His Family* (Grand Rapids: Baker Book House, 1981), 112.

15. John Elson, "America's New Fad: Fidelity," *TIME*, 19 February 1990, 91.

16. "Marriage: Practice Makes Imperfect?," *Psychology Today*, July/ August 1988, 15.

17. Frank Pittmann, III, M.D., "Beyond Betrayal: Life after Infidelity," *Psychology Today*, May/June 1993, 35.

18. Ibid., 35, 82.

19. William L. Yarber, "Sexually Transmitted Diseases and Young Adults," *Teen Health*, Vol. 65, Number 3, Spring 1987.

20. Dave Davis & John F. Hagan, "1,500 deaths in three years tied to AIDS," *The Plain Dealer*, Lorain County Edition (Cleveland: Friday, April 2, 1993), 1.

21. *Science Impact Letter*, July 1988, Vol. 2, No. 2, 7–8.

22. Vincent Bozzi, "Teens and Condoms: An Uncomfortable Fit," *Psychology Today*, October 1988, 14.

23. "The Big Chill: Fear of AIDS," *TIME*, 16 February 1987, 51.

24. M. Scott Peck, *People of the Lie*, (New York: Simon & Schuster, 1983), 65.

25. *Current Christian Abstracts*, Volume 6, Number 5, May 1990.

26. "Abstinence Contract," provided by the Responsible School Values Program.

27. Lewis B. Smedes, *Caring and Commitment* (San Francisco: Harper & Row, 1988), 64.

28. Jerry B. Jenkins, "Of Scandals and Hedges," *Moody Monthly*, July/August 1987, Vol. 87, Number 11 (Chicago: Moody Bible Institute), 6.

CHAPTER FIVE

1. Leo Buscaglia, *Bus 9 to Paradise*, (New York: William Morrow & Co., Inc., 1986), 119–120.

2. John Koten, "A Once Tightly Knit Middle Class Finds Itself Divided and Uncertain," *The Wall Street Journal*, 9 March 1987.

3. Lou Holtz, "A Letter to the Next Generation" *TIME*, 10 April 1989.

4. Ray Guarendi, *Back to the Family*, 71.

5. Rodney Clapp, "Vanishing Children," *Christianity Today*, 15 June 1984, 21.

6. *U.S. News & World Report*, 10 March 1986, 62.

7. *Parables, Etc.*, January 1989, 5.

8. C.H. Toy, *International Critical Commentary Book of Proverbs*, (Edinburgh: T & T Clark, Ltd., 1988), 59–60.

9. Karen Mains, "Warriors of Light," *Christian Parenting Today* (September/October 1990), 30.

10. Ibid., 30.

11. Lloyd John Ogilvie, *Discovering God's Will in Your Life* (Harvest House Publishers, 1982), 41.

12. Dennis & Barbara Rainey, *Building Your Mate's Self Esteem* (San Bernardino: Here's Life Publishers, 1986), 62.

13. Leo Buscaglia, *Loving Each Other* (Thorofare, N.J.: Slack, Inc., 1984), 181.

14. Bob Laird, *USA Today*, 24 April 1990.

15. Charles R. Swindoll, *The Grace Awakening* (Dallas: Word Publishing, 1990), 269.

16. *Current Thoughts and Trends*, Vol. 7, No. 7, Summaries 7270–7329, July 1991, 18.

17. Ruth Harms Calkin, *Lord, Don't You Love Me Anymore?*, (Wheaton, Ill: Tyndale House Publishers, Inc., 1988), 124.

CHAPTER SIX

1. Ben Haden, *Changed Lives.*

2. Robert Fulghum, *All I Really Need to Know I Learned in Kindergarten*, (New York: Villard Books, 1988), 19–20.

3. John E. Miller, "The Continuing Search for Community in Higher Education," *Vital Speeches of the Day*, March 15, 1993, Volume LIX, No. 11.

4. Max Lucado, *No Wonder They Call Him the Savior* (Portland: Multnomah Press, 1986), 24–25.

5. Janet Carson, "Hate-filled Speech," *U.S. News & World Report*, June 25, 1990.

6. Robert W. Wilson, 1980

7. *Chronicle Telegram*, 29 April 1991, A-8.

8. Leo Buscaglia, *Loving Each Other* (Thorofare, N.J.: Slack, Inc., 1984), 76.

9. *Webster's New World Dictionary*, Second College Edition (New York: New World Dictionary/Division of Simon & Schuster, 1984), 1337.

10. *International Thesaurus of Quotations*, Section 898, # 13, (New York: Harper & Row, 1970), 595.

11. Carole Mayhall, *Words That Hurt—Words That Heal* (Colorado Springs: NavPress, 1986), 53–54.

12. Theodore Isaac Rubin, *The Angry Book* (New York: MacMillan Publishing Co., 1969), 130–131.

13. Linda and Richard Eyre, *Teaching Your Children Values* (New York: Simon & Schuster, 1993), 42.

14. Alan Redpath in "A Passion for Preaching" cited in *Christianity Today*, 20 August 1990.

15. Lewis B. Smedes, *Shame & Grace* (San Francisco: Harper San Francisco, 1993), 75–76.

16. Gary Smalley and John Trent, *The Blessing* (Nashville: Thomas Nelson Publishers, 1986), 58–59.

17. Leo Buscaglia, *Born For Love* (Random House, 1992), 82.

18. *Christianity Today*, September 1991, 42.

CHAPTER SEVEN

1. Charles R. Swindoll, *You and Your Child*, (Nashville: Nelson Publishers, 1977), 69–71.

2. Ray Guarendi, *Back to the Family*, 26, 179–183.

3. Wes Willis, "The Difference Between Punishment & Discipline," *Parents and Children* (Wheaton, Ill.: Victor Books, 1986), 453.

4. W. Glasser, *Reality Therapy* (New York: Perennial Library, Harper & Row Publishers, 1975), 19–20.

5. Paul Chance, "Kids Without Friends," *Psychology Today*, January/February 1989.

6. Guarendi, *Back to the Family*, 191–192.

7. Ben Haden, *Changed Lives*.

8. H. Norman Wright, *Premarital Counseling* (Chicago: Moody Press, 1977), 10.

9. Glasser, *Reality Therapy*, 22.

10. "Spare the Rod and Save the Child," *The Harvard Medical School Mental Health Letter*, January 1989.

11. Linda and Richard Eyre, *Teaching Your Children Values*, 171.

12. Allan Petersen, ed., *The Marriage Affair* (Wheaton, Ill.: Tyndale House Publishers, 1971), 274.

13. L. and R. Eyre, *Teaching Your Child Values*, 231.

14. Michael K. Meyerhoff and Burton L. White, "Making the Grade as Parents," *Psychology Today*, September 1986.

15. Charles Swindoll, *Growing in Family Life* (Portland: Multnomah Press, 1988), 119.

16. Dr. James Dobson, *Hide or Seek*, (Old Tappan, N.J.: Fleming H. Revell, 1974), Chapter 4.

CHAPTER EIGHT

1. Norman Polmar and Thomas B. Allen, *Rickover: Controversy and Genius* (New York: Simon and Schuster, 1982), 267.
2. Erma Bombeck, *Family Ties That Bind...And Gag!* (New York: McGraw-Hill Book Co., 1987), 108–109.
3. Ray Guarendi, *Back to the Family*, 161.
4. John Naisbitt and Patricia Aburdene, *Re-inventing the Corporation* (New York: Warner Books, Inc., 1985), 85.
5. R.C. Sproul, *The Hunger for Significance* (California: Regal Books, 1983), 21–22.
6. Jay Kessler, Ron Beers and LaVonne Neff, eds., *Parents and Children* (Wheaton, Ill.: Victor Books, 1986), 572–573.
7. Gary Inrig, *A Call to Excellence* (Wheaton, Ill.: Victor Books, 1985), 85.
8. James W. Michaels, "Ph.D. in Hypocrisy," *Forbes*, March 29, 1993.
9. Zig Ziglar, *Top Performance* (Old Tappan, N.J.: Fleming H. Revell, 1986), 207–208.
10. Warren Bennis and Burt Nanus, *Leaders—The Strategies For Taking Charge* (New York: Harper & Row Publishers, 1985), 7–8.
11. John Naisbitt and Patricia Aburdene, *Megatrends 2000* (New York: William Morrow & Co., 1990), 229.
12. Jerry Jenkins, *Twelve Things I Want My Kids to Remember Forever* (Chicago: Moody Press, 1991), 93.
13. Knute Larson, *The Great Human Race* (Wheaton, Ill.: Scripture Press, 1987), 137.
14. John Powell, *Fully Human, Fully Alive* (Allen, Tex.: Tabor Publishing, 1989), 19–20.

CHAPTER NINE

1. "It Made Terrible Sense," *TIME*, 13 December 1982, 29.
2. John Steinbeck, *America and Americans* (New York: Viking Press, 1966), 139.
3. Felicity Barringer, "Anger in the Post Office: Killings Raise Questions," *The New York Times*, Saturday, 8 May 1993, Vol. CXLII, No. 49325, p. 1, column 3, p. 6, column 1.
4. *Current Thoughts and Trends*, October 1992, Vol. 7, No. 10, Summaries 8116—868, 15.
5. Nancy Samalin, *Love and Anger: The Parental Dilemma* (New York: Viking Penguin, 1991), 5.
6. Redford Williams and Virginia Williams, *Anger Kills* (New York: Times Books, Random House, 1993), 3.
7. Linda and Richard Eyre, *Teaching Your Children Values*, 82-83, 87.
8. Eric F. DuBow, "We Reap What We Sow," *Psychology Today*, December 1987, 12.

9. M. Scott Peck, *A World Waiting to be Born* (New York: Bantam Books, 1993), 170.

10. Peter Salovey and Judith Rodin, "The Heart of Jealousy," *Psychology Today*, September 1985, 22.

11. James V.P. Check, Neil M. Malamuth, Barbara Elias and Susan A. Barton, "On Hostile Ground," *Psychology Today*, April 1985, 60–61.

12. R. and V. Williams, *Anger Kills*, xiii-xiv.

13. Gary Emery and James Campbell, *Rapid Relief from Emotional Distress* (New York: Rawson Associates, 1986), 118–119.

14. Gary Smalley and John Trent, "Untying the Knots of Anger," *Moody Monthly*, December 1991, 57.

15. Ibid.

16. See for extended discussions on this research, Willard Gaylin, *The Rage Within—Anger in Modern Life* (New York: Simon & Schuster, 1984), 92–102; also Carol Tavris, *Anger, the Misunderstood Emotion* (New York: Simon & Schuster, 1982), Chapter 5.

17. Willard Gaylin, *The Rage Within*, 102.

18. Ross Campbell, "A Parent's Anger," in *Parents and Children*, 627.

19. Linda and Richard Eyre, *Teaching Your Children Values*, 77.

20. Adapted from Robert Fulghum, *It Was on Fire When I Lay Down on It* (New York: Villard Books, 1989), 189–190.

21. Zig Ziglar, *Raising Positive Kids in a Negative World* (Nashville: Oliver Nelson Books, 1985), 199, 200, 204.

CHAPTER TEN

1. Anthony Campolo, Jr., *The Success Fantasy* (Wheaton, Ill.: Scripture Press Publishers, 1980), 67.

2. Christopher Lasch, *The Culture of Narcissism, American Life in an Age of Diminishing Expectations* (New York: Warner Books Edition, W.W. Norton & Company, Inc., 1979), 33.

3. Martha Smilgis, "Snip, Suction, Stress and Truss," *TIME*, 14 September 1978, p. 70.

4. Ibid.

5. Gary Smalley and John Trent, Ph.D., *The Gift of Honor* (Nashville: Thomas Nelson Publishers, 1987), 141.

6. Theodore Isaac Rubin, *Real Love* (New York: The Continuum Publishing Co., 1990), 72.

7. Josh McDowell, *His Image, My Image* (San Bernardino: Here's Life Publishers, Inc., 1984), 98.

8. Maurice E. Wagner, *The Sensation of Being Somebody* (Grand Rapids:

Zondervan Publishing House, 1971), 32–37.

9. Ben Haden, "Why Do Christians Suffer?/Looking for Love?, *Changed Lives*, (Chattanooga: 1992), 17–18.

10. William Glasser, M.D., *Take Effective Control of Your Life* (New York: Harper & Row, 1984), 82, 83.

11. Guarendi, *Back to the Family*, 235.

12. Gary Vandernet, "The Skill of Controlling the Tongue," *Discovery Papers*, 1 June 1986.

CHAPTER ELEVEN

1. Edward W. Desmond, "Out in the Open," *TIME*, 30 November 1987, 84–85.

2. Guarendi, *Back to the Family*, 41–42.

3. Jim Burns, "Help Your Teens 'Say No,'" *Moody Monthly*, September 1991, 51.

4. Charles R. Swindoll, *Living Beyond the Daily Grind: Reflections on the Songs and Sayings of Scripture* (Book II), (Waco: Word Books, 1988), 431.

5. "Coming to Grips with Alcoholism," *U.S. News & World Report*, 30 November 1987, 57.

6. Howard A. Snyder, "Demon Rum on the Run," *Christianity Today*, 18 June 1990, 25.

7. Jay Strack, *Shake off the Dust* (Nashville: Thomas Nelson Publishers, 1988), 49–50.

8. Bruce B. Dan and Roxanne K. Young, *A Piece of My Mind* (Los Angeles: Feeling Fine Programs, Inc., 1988), 225–227.

9. Strack, *Shake off the Dust,* 49–50.

10. *Current Thoughts and Trends*, September 1990, 20, #6637.

11. *Current Christian Abstracts*, July 1990 (Patricia Mutch, "Infant Addicts: A Preventable Rage," *Vibrant Life*, May/June, 1990), 16–17.

12. *Current Thoughts and Trends*, Vol. 7 No. 6, Summaries 7205-7269, June 1991, 23. (Anastasia Toufexis, "Innocent Victims," *TIME*, 13 May 1991, 56–60.)

13. Michelle Healy," Drinking is high schoolers' number one problem," *USA Today*, 30 June 1993, 1, 11a.

14. J. Strack, *Shake Off the Dust*, 51–52.

15. S.L. Englebardt, *Kids and Alcohol: The Deadliest Drug* (New York: Lorthrop, Lee & Shepher, 1975), 9–15.

16. *USA Today*, June 30, 1, 11a.

17. *U.S. News & World Report*, 30 November 1987, 57.

18. "Drug Use Up at Younger Age," *USA Today*, Wednesday, 14 April, 1993, 1.

19. Jolene Roehlkepartain, "Cheap Highs, Costly Consequences," *Jr. High Ministry*, November/December 1990, 4–5.

20. William Kilpatrick, *Why Johnny Can't Tell Right From Wrong*, (New York: Simon & Schuster, 1992), 46.

21. Burns, "Help Your Teens," 51.

22. "Alcohol & American Life," *Wellness Letter*, University of California, Berkeley, Vol. 2, Issue 6, March 1986, 4.

23. Elizabeth Stark, "Forgotten Victims: Children of Alcoholics," *Psychology Today*, January 1987, 59, 62; cf. Charles Sell, "Sins of the Fathers (and Mothers)," *Christianity Today*, 10 September 1990, 20.

24. Ibid.

25. Ibid, 2.

26. "Alcohol and the Body," *Wellness Letter*, University of California, Berkeley, February 1986, 5; cf. *Science Impact Letter*, Vol. 3, No. 4, April 1989, 2.

27. *1984 Statistical Analysis* (Washington, D.C.: United States Department of Commerce, 1984).

28. Bill Moyers, *A World of Ideas* (New York: Doubleday, 1989), 145.

29. "Alcohol and the Body," 4.

30. *Executive Strategies*, 20 August 1990, 2.

31. Anderson Spickard and Barbara Thompson, *Dying for a Drink* (Waco: Word Books, 1985), 132.

32. "Out in the Open."

CHAPTER TWELVE

1. Pete Axthelm, "Somebody Else's Kids," *Newsweek*, 25 April 1988, 64.

2. Ben Haden, "Is It Bad News?" *Changed Lives* (Chattanooga: Ben Haden Evangelical Association, Inc., 1990), 4.

3. Theodore Isaac Rubin, *Real Love*, (The Continuum Publishing Co., New York 1990), 131.

4. Adapted from Anne Ortland, *Children are Wet Cement* (Old Tappan, N.J.: Fleming H. Revell Company, 1981), 182.

5. Karen Wise, *Confessions of a Totalled Woman* (Nashville: Thomas Nelson Publishers, 1980) 65–66.

6. Leo Buscaglia, *Bus 9 to Paradise*, 148–149.

7. Walter C. Kaiser, *Hard Sayings of the Old Testament* (Downers Grove, Ill: InterVarsity Press, 1988), 179, 181.

8. John White, *Parents in Pain* (Downer's Grove, Ill.: InterVarsity Press, 1979), 70.

9. Anthony Campolo, Jr., *The Success Fantasy* (Wheaton, Ill.: Scripture Press Publishers, 1980), 106.

10. Ruth Bell Graham, *Sitting by My Laughing Fire* (Waco: Word Books, 1977).

11. Robert Fulghum, *It Was on Fire,* 93–97.